MARK BEECH

The Unknown Village

The crossroads at Mark Beech, 1999.

MARK BEECH

The Unknown Village

Timothy Boyle

Phillimore

1999

Published by
PHILLIMORE & CO. LTD.
Shopwyke Manor Barn, Chichester, West Sussex

ISBN 1 86077 091 3

Printed and bound in Great Britain by
BOOKCRAFT
Midsomer Norton

For Mary,
Uxor delicatissima

Contents

List of Illustrations

Sponsors

The author, the Mark Beech Millennium Committee and the publisher are extremely grateful to the following organisations and individuals who sponsored this history and without whom it could not have been published:

The Community of St Andrew, Eaton-Williams Group Ltd., Goldsmiths' College, London, Hever Castle, The Independent Insurance Co., Kent Archaeological Society, The Landmark Trust, Sevenoaks District Council.

Mrs. L. Adams, Mr. John Adkins, the late Mrs. Eric Asprey, Mr. Stephen C. Bagnold, Mr. and Mrs. A.F. Barnett, Mr. and Mrs. David Beaty, Mr. and Mrs. Peter Bellamy, Mr. A.J. Bowden, Mr. and Mrs. R.H.D. Boyd, Viscount Bridgeman, Mr. and Mrs. R. Brookes-Smith, Mrs. Anthea Brown, Dr. Ken Brown, Mr. James Calvocoressi, Mr. and Mrs. Carroll, Rev. Derek Chapman, Mr. and Mrs. Dennis Clark, Mr. John Coldman, Mrs. Joan Cole, Mr. L.E.W. Cole, Mr. Richard Coomber, Mr. Charles Cornell, Mrs. J.V. Cust, Mr. Christopher Dane, Mr. Alan Dell, Hon. Robin C. Denison-Pender, Mr. and Mrs. Alan Dickins, Mr. Peter Draper, Mrs. Sybil Eadie, Mr. Barry Eyre, Mr. Terry Farrington, Mr. Valentine Fleming, Mr. and Mrs. V.C. Frank, Mr. and Mrs. Stefano Furno, Mr. D.J. Garman, Mr. J.R. Gee, Mr. Chris Gillett, Mr. and Mrs. John Gladstone, Mr. and Mrs. Peter Goodliffe, Miss Doreen Graves, Mr. Denis Greig, Mr. John Green, Miss Barbara Hale, Mrs. and the late Mr. Eric Finden Hall, Mr. V.L. Harnett, Mr. Donald Hepworth, Mr. Douglas Higgs, Mrs. Rosemary Hill, Mr. Michael Holland, Mrs. Barbara Horton, Paul Houlton and Charlotte Desorgher, Mr. Peter Jamieson, Mrs. Barbara Jiskoot, Mr. and Mrs. T. Johnson, Mr. David and Mrs. Rosemary Jones, Sir Christopher and Lady Kaberry, Mr. Ian King, Mr. J. Kirby, Mrs. Walter Leppard, Mr. Ian and Mrs. Susan Lewis, Mr. and Mrs. Leonard Linden, Mr. Andro Linklater, Hon. J. McDonnell, Mr. and Mrs. John Martin, Mr. and Mrs. W.J. Martin, Mr. and Mrs. Meekings, Mr. Peter Mendelssohn, Mrs. Felicity Miller, Dr. and Mrs. Brian Milner, Mrs. Daphne Montgomery, Mr. Clive and Mrs. Sally Mortimer, Mrs. Gwen Mott, Mr. and Mrs. J.R. Nelson-Roberts, Mr. and Mrs. B.J. Oldfield, Maria O'Hara and John Evanson, Mrs. Geraldine Oliver, Mrs. Betsy Overton, Mr. Cecil Paynter, Mrs. Barbara Penman, Mrs. Marjory Peters, Lady Jean Philipps, Mr. Graham Phillips, Mr. and Mrs. Ronald Philpott, Mrs. Rachel Pittman, Dr. R.C. Porcherot, Mr. John and Dr. Pat Porter, Mr. Victor Pugh, Mr. and Mrs. Simon Radcliffe, Mr. and Mrs. Peter Rayner, Mr. Mark Roberts, Mr. and Mrs. Michael Roberts, Mr. Timothy Roberts, Mr. Robin Rouse, Dr. Andrew Russell, Mr. Laurence D. Rutman, Mr. Nick Scott, Dr. John Shaw, Mrs. Constance Shoppee, Mr. and Mrs. David Skinner, Mr. and Mrs. John Skinner, Mrs. Joan Smith, Mr. and Mrs. Alan Smith, Mrs. Anne Sorby, Mr. and Mrs. Jeremy

Speakman, Rt. Hon. Sir John Stanley, M.P., Mrs. Margaret Steer, Mr. A. William Stephenson, the late Sir John Stephenson, Miss Rose Streatfield, Mrs. E.M. Strudwick, Mr. and Mrs. Kenneth Sweeting, Mr. Charles J. Talbot, Mr. Bob. Theobald, Mrs. D. Thomas, Mr. J. Thompson, Mr. and Mrs. David Turner, Mr. Don Tyler, Mr. J.F. Villiers, Mr. H.H. Villiers, Mr. Roger L. Wadsworth, Mrs. Margaret Watts, Mr. David Weston, Mrs. Mary Wigan, Mr. David Woollett, Mr. Peter Woollett, Mrs. Margaret Wright.

Foreword

I have lived in the Kent village of Mark Beech (or Markbeech) since spring 1966, whilst teaching History at Goldsmiths' College, University of London and, with my wife, brought up our children here (although our eldest son was two-and-a-half years old when we arrived). The area was unknown to me, coming as I did from East Anglia via Cambridge and London. From time to time I discussed the village's past with some of the older inhabitants, such as Billy White, Jack Seymour and Bert Everest, none of whom, unfortunately, is with us any longer. Billy White's memories went back before the First World War as he had migrated to Mark Beech from Buckinghamshire in 1906 to take up the tenancy of the Falconhurst home farm. In 1978 I published an article on the Mark Beech Riots of 1866, the village's only claim to fame, and I have long considered the possibility of writing a history of Mark Beech as a retirement project. The start of this enterprise was accelerated by an invitation in the autumn of 1996 to write an historical pamphlet on the village church, which I completed in about four months, and the formation in the village early in 1997 of a Millennium Committee which proposed, *inter alia*, that a history of Mark Beech should be produced, for which I volunteered.

My expertise, such as it is, lies entirely in Modern History. For more than thirty years I have taught undergraduates the History of Britain since about the middle of the 18th century and a few other matters. For several years I ran an inter-collegiate Special Subject within the University of London entitled 'Britain and the Diplomatic Revolution, 1892-1907', and my post-graduate teaching, research and publication have been within the field of diplomacy, defence and colonial policies and their relation to British domestic politics, especially for the Liberal Party, in roughly the period 1890-1914. It is, therefore, with some trepidation that I present this study, for it has forced me to read and think about matters which I have neglected since I was an undergraduate 40 years ago, or which I have never adequately considered at all. It has been a humbling experience as it has revealed to me vast areas of ignorance, and my colleagues will be astonished that I have anything sensible to say (if I have) on, for example, the Jutish settlements or medieval land tenure. I expect that in what follows there are many omissions and errors, for which, of course, I alone am responsible.

I have always called the place where I live Mark Beech because that was the form I encountered on arrival. Nevertheless, in the course of this study I have concluded that the correct style is Markbeech, which is that used by many other villagers. It conforms with the original Old English name of this place, even if variations are to be found on signposts, maps, etc. Markbeech is the spelling employed by the Ordnance Survey and now, I believe, by the emergency services.

Perversely, however, I am leaving it as Mark Beech both in the title and the text because it is what I am accustomed to and what I started with. Perhaps from now on I will adopt the 'correct' spelling—at least, when my present stock of writing paper is exhausted.

In the course of the research for and the writing of this book I have incurred many debts and it is impossible to repay them adequately. First, I would like to thank all my former colleagues at Goldsmiths' and in the History School of the University of London, who over many years have provided intellectual stimulation, professional support of high quality, and friendship. In particular, I wish to thank Dr. Jennifer C. Ward, who joined the Department at exactly the same time I did, who has given more than thirty years of friendship and professional co-operation, and Dr. Paul Fouracre, both of whom very kindly read drafts of chapters and provided useful and constructive comment, although, of course, they are not responsible for any mistakes that remain. Not to be omitted either are Mr. Derek Jarrett, a fine 18th century expert, and Dr. Liam Smith, scholar of the Second Empire, who always provided us with an inexhaustible stock of amusing anecdotes and trenchant observations on his native Ireland, France, History, the College or on the world in general. I remember with great affection the late Professor John Dinwiddy, who tragically died so young, and with whom I frequently shared a meal, a bottle of wine and stimulating chat when he was Chairman and I was Academic Secretary to the University of London Board of Studies in History. My mid-Friday meetings with this gentle, caring, courteous, intelligent man, prior to meetings of the Board, were always delightful and memorable and certainly not confined to 'official' business. Also there are, of course, my students: I estimate that I may have taught nearly a thousand over the years and they too have given much stimulation. Then I would like to thank all the Archivists and Librarians, who have consistently made work as congenial as possible, at the various places at which I have done my research. These include Goldsmiths' College, the University of London Library, the Institute of Historical Research, the Kent County Libraries at Edenbridge and Sevenoaks, the Local Studies Centre at Sevenoaks, the Centre for Kent Studies at Maidstone, the British Library and the Manuscripts Department at the British Museum, the Local History Centre at Lewisham, Queen Mary and Westfield College, University of London, the Museum and the Reference Library at Tunbridge Wells, the Public Record Office at Kew, the Historical Manuscripts Commission and the City Archives at Sheffield. I would especially like to thank Mr. Andrew Lister, the Archivist at Sevenoaks, Dr. Mark Ballard at the Centre for Kent Studies, Mr. Jonathan Oates, the Assistant Archivist at Lewisham, and Dr. Malcolm Mercer of the Public Record Office. I thank Sister Teresa for discussing the history of her Order with me and for showing me many documents from the Archive at St. Andrew's. Next I must thank very much Mrs. Ann Bellamy and Mrs. Gladys Smoult, the Clerks to Hever and Cowden Parish Councils, respectively, for making the records in their custody available to me and Mrs. Sybil Eadie, Secretary to Mark Beech W.I., for access to their records. Mrs. Jill Linden of Saxbys, Churchwarden, kindly made all Holy Trinity's Records available to me and lent me her copy of Ewing's *History of Cowden*, which is long out of print. Mrs. Barbara Penman of How Green, who is working on the history of Four Elms, found many old photographs and copies of *The Church Magazine* back to 1919 for me. I am grateful to *Sussex Past* for kindly allowing me to re-use material, which first appeared in the *Sussex Archaeological Collections* in 1978 and to the Archivist at Sheffield City Archives for permission to cite extracts from the Wharncliffe Muniments. I thank the Registrars of both the Rochester and Canterbury dioceses, particularly the former for allowing me to reproduce the 1852 parish map, Willy Buntinx of the Rijksarchief te Gent, the Archivist at Queen Mary and Westfield College for access to the Neville Lyttelton Correspondence and many, many others. I would like to thank Mr. L.E.W. Cole of Hawkhurst, who for several years has been doing research on his family in the Edenbridge area, for the map on page 23. Mrs. Mary-Lou Linklater, who is a professional photographer, provided modern photos both for this book and the little pamphlet on the church which I concocted as a preliminary to this larger piece, and my neighbour, Mr. Paul Houlton, took photos and gave the time and skill of his computer knowledge and a great deal of truly neighbourly friendship and encouragement. So I am exceptionally grateful to him. As far as the illustrations are concerned, I regret that I collected at least twice the number that space and cost would allow, and therefore I apologise to all those expecting to find a particular picture who do not do so. I would have liked there to have been more pictures of people, rather than buildings, but one can only choose from what is available and appropriate. I am very sad that my friend of 30 years, one of the first people I met in Mark Beech, Mr. Robert (Bob) H. King has not lived to see the completion of this history; his mother was married from Pilegate Farm and he had lived in the area all his life, except during the Second World War and for a year or two afterwards. He died in Mark Beech in 1996 aged 76 and was a fount of information. My publishers, Phillimore of Chichester, have been so very helpful throughout, especially Mr. Noel Osborne, Mrs. Carolyn Oliver, Miss Nicola Willmot and Mr. Simon Thraves. I must thank my black labrador, Sophie, for faithfully keeping me company in my computer room late at night, although I knew she would have preferred me to go to bed so that she could get her head down too.

I would like to thank all the members of this community and others from a wider area, many of whom appear as interviewees at the end of the book, who have encouraged me to write it, have lent me books, pamphlets, maps, deeds and other documents, have written me letters, have shown much interest and support, and have in many cases been generous sponsors. Mr. Alan Smith of Edells and the Topham Picture Library encouraged me to write this book several years ago, although he was not to know that he was preaching to the already converted, and he most generously offered financial assistance which, in the event, was not necessary. Those who lent me original documents are acknowledged in the bibliography and/or the footnotes, but I would like to thank those who lent me books, etc. in their possession, including Mr. James Calvocorresi, Mrs. John Gladstone, Mr. Donald Hepworth, Mr. Michael Holland, Mr. Peter Jamieson, Mrs. John Leppard, Mrs. Walter Leppard, Mr. Peter Rayner, Mr. Jeremy Speakman and Mrs. Eileen Vicary. I gratefully remember Mr. and Mrs. Henry Bluff, who gave me some vital leads at an early stage, and Mrs. Ann Roberts, neighbour, parish councillor (of Hever) and Chairman of the Mark Beech Millennium Committee.

I hope that everybody derives pleasure from their history, as well as, possibly, a little enlightenment: perhaps one or two myths will be confirmed or shown to be nonsense. I trust that they do not find this study too 'academic' for their taste and concerned too much with events prior to our own and recent times, as I realise it is probably the immediate past in which most people are interested and about which they will be most critical. I can only plead that I decided quite early on that, if possible, it would be more fruitful to try to analyse the whole of Mark Beech's past, if it was worth doing at all. A history from only, say, 1850 was not worthwhile without the village's antecedents and roots. Above all I would thank Paul Houlton, again, and Mr. Charles Talbot. As the great-great-grandson of John Chetwynd Talbot, who started modern Mark Beech, and the occupant of Mark Beech's manor house, as it were, as the organiser of our marvellous biennial mini-Glyndebourne and as the owner of much of the land in the village, Charles has given me information, support and encouragement and shown me many interesting documents and photographs, some of which I have used.

Finally, I cannot express sufficient thanks to the local person who met the difference between what we were given by our generous sponsors and the total sum required and without whom publication would have been impossible. I would very much like the benefactor's name to be in the public domain, but there is a wish for anonymity, which I respect.

When I started this book I assumed, falsely, that there would not be very much material on Mark Beech before the mid–19th century. This is untrue and there is documentary evidence even for the Jutish and medieval periods. Nevertheless, it has proved a disappointment to find that what might have been expected is missing. It has proved impossible, for example, to find any Log Books for Mark Beech School, which existed for nearly a hundred years. Holy Trinity's Vestry Minute Books for 1852-1915 have vanished into thin air as have the older Baptismal and Marriage Registers. Not even the Rural Dean can find copies of the informative *Church Magazine* for the years before 1919 (we know that it was started in 1897). Many of the early records of Falconhurst Cricket Club are unavailable. Shamefully, the Poor Law Records of the Sevenoaks Union were 'weeded' 50 years ago. Yet there remains quite a bit to give us some idea of our past, although I am conscious that I may be criticised for not making more use than I have of local newspapers; I can only plead that I made a preliminary sortie into them, although rather inaccessible, but found references to Mark Beech so infrequent and insubstantial, except in a few predictable instances such as the 1866 riots, that I concluded further research would take endless time with little to show at the end of it. It was a risk, and I hope I haven't, thereby, missed some vital bit of the village's history. Also, I have not used the Land Survey Records of 1910-15 because I only tracked them down after I had gone to press, but I hope to publish any findings at a future date, and I hope to do the same for the origins of Agnes de Montacute and the 1866 Cholera outbreak.

My dear wife, Mary, has, as always, been a tower of strength over the last eighteen months or so while I have been doing the research for and writing this book. Inevitably, she has suffered the usual privations of an author's family, whilst the book was being written, not least the obsessions which overcome writers in the process of research and composition. As the Clerk of Hever Parish Council for many years she knows as much about the recent history of this place as anyone. I dedicate *Mark Beech: the Unknown Village* to her with love and gratitude.

Tim Boyle,
Mark Beech, Kent.
February 1999.

◆ I ◆

The Setting

MARK BEECH (or Markbeech and variants such as Markbeach or Mark Beach, which are etymologically quite wrong) is a small village at the western end of the High Weald of Kent. It has more the character of a hamlet surrounded by homesteads, typical of Kent ever since it was settled by the Jutes, than a consolidated village which is more usual in other parts of England. Three miles to the west is the county boundary with Surrey, two miles to the south that with Sussex, and there is a point in the neighbouring parish of Cowden, the last in Kent and part of which Mark Beech once was, at which the three counties meet.

The Weald of Kent stretches from the edge of Romney Marsh to Surrey. There has long been dispute whether the Weald includes the Chart or Red Hills to the north or whether the true boundary runs along their southern fringe. Modern authorities favour the latter interpretation.[1] The Weald is, therefore, the flat fertile territory from Tenterden and Ashford westwards along the valleys of the Beult, the Teise, the central Medway and the Eden. To the south to the border with Sussex is the more elevated land of the High Weald, which extends from Newenden to the Surrey border, punctuated only by the north flowing rivers Teise, a tributary of the Medway, between Lamberhurst and Horsmonden, and Medway itself, between Ashurst and Penshurst. The Medway's deep valley at this point, the river flowing between Smarts Hill and Fordcombe, is only three and a half miles to the east of Mark Beech.[2]

The centre of Mark Beech is a crossroads, on which lie the church, Holy Trinity, and the pub, the *Kentish Horse*, which is the sole one of that name not only in Kent, but in the whole of England. This crossroads is on the northern escarpment of the High Weald, at a height of 425 feet above sea level, facing northwards across the Eden Valley to the Chart Hills, about eight miles away, and the North Downs beyond. North of the Downs is London, whose lights, depending on the weather conditions, can usually be seen glowing in the night sky. Immediately behind the village on the south-east quadrant lies a hill; at its northern end is a spinney and a large pond known as Marl Pit Shaw, *shaw* being an Old English term for a strip of woodland, and the southern part is called Hopper's Bank. On the top of Mark Beech Hill is a plateau of 26 acres which is at 482 feet above sea level. By contrast the Chart Hills rise to 771 feet at Brasted Chart and the North Downs go to 876 feet at Botley Hill above Titsey. The skyline to the south is dominated by Ashdown Forest in Sussex at 673 feet. Thus Mark Beech is at the highest point between the Chart Hills and Ashdown Forest, although as the High Weald extends westwards into Surrey, an area which was once part of

1   High Buckhurst, from the south, 1998. The line of the Chart Hills and of the North Downs can just be seen in the background. (Paul Houlton)

Kent, it reaches 564 feet at Dry Hill Camp, about three miles west of Mark Beech. Kent Water, another tributary of the Medway, forms a further valley along the boundary between Kent and Sussex just to the south of Mark Beech.[3]

Mark Beech is three miles from Edenbridge, until recently not much more than a large village but which since the late 1950s has grown into a small town with London overspill estates and other development so that it now has a population approaching eight thousand.[4] Edenbridge stands on the river Eden, a tributary of the Medway, at about 135 feet above sea level, so in about one and a half miles there is a descent of nearly three hundred feet from Mark Beech into the valley of the Eden. The village is six miles from East Grinstead in Sussex, eight from Sevenoaks, Tonbridge and Tunbridge Wells, and 20 miles from Maidstone, the county town. It is 23 miles from Rochester, the diocesan centre, but only 13 from Gatwick airport. London at Charing Cross is about 26 miles away and the sea at Newhaven 27 miles (see figure 2). Yet even in the late 20th century it remains an enclave of rural tranquillity within a crowded south-east of England, with a population of just under three hundred.

There are 16 different soil types in the High Weald, but around Mark Beech the predominant kind is clay on a base of Tunbridge Wells sandstone, popularly known as Kentish Ragstone.[5] There are no outcrops of rock in Mark Beech itself, although there is a spectacular example just outside the village on the road to Chiddingstone Hoath, originally Rendsley Hoath or Raneleigh's Hoath. There are pockets of lighter, sandy soils which carry scrub and heath, but overall there is the clay, which tends to go like concrete in summer and becomes a sticky bog in winter. It is probable that until at least the mid-19th century movement was difficult, especially in the winter, and during the autumn and winter, especially wet ones, hamlets and farms could be isolated for weeks at a time.[6] As early as 1625 George Markham wrote, 'This Weald was for many years held to be a wild desert, or most unfruitful wilderness'.[7] Writing in the late 17th century Daniel Defoe said of the area that 'I saw an ancient lady and a lady of very good quality, I assure you, drawn to church in her coach with six oxen, nor was it done but out of necessity, the way being so stiff and deep that no horse could go in it',[8] and in 1799 William Marshall wrote that 'the roads of the Weald are such as may be readily apprehended from the description of its lands. The common country roads, in summer and wet seasons, are such as no man, who has not stept out of his cradle into them, can travel without disgust'.[9] Some years later Dearn wrote that 'from the badness of the roads in this neighbourhood, Cowden is a place but little known ... The soil is a deep clay and from its retentive property the lands are for the greater part of the year extremely wet and miry.'[10] 'Miry' is a word that occurs again and again in the many descriptions from the past of the area around Mark Beech, although the name of Mark Beech itself is never mentioned. In the mid-19th century George Buckland reported that in winter some of the roads in the Weald could become 150 feet wide as travellers sought to avoid the worst of the gluey clay, which, he also said, was 'very wet and miry'.[11]

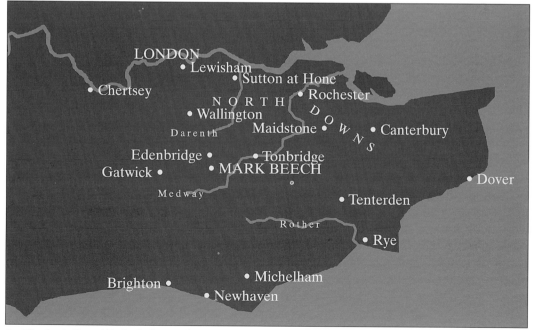

2   *The South East of England, showing the position of Mark Beech in relation to other features in the area. (Paul Houlton)*

The Weald and the High Weald were, of course, part of a larger entity. For hundreds of years they were part of the great, thick, primeval forest which was known to the Romano-British as Silva Anderida, to the Jutes as Andredesleah and later as Andredesweald or Andreasweald or Andreaswald. Surrounded by the sea and the chalk hills, it stretched from east Kent right across south-east England through Kent, Sussex, Surrey and Hampshire, being at least 30 miles from north to south and some 120 from east to west.[12] The very word 'weald' is derived from the German 'wald', meaning forest. Paradoxically, in A.D. 43 lowland Britain as a whole was possibly the least wooded part of Europe north of the Alps on account of man's removal of forest cover for up to 2,000 years before the arrival of the Romans.[13] In the first century B.C. the Roman writer Strabo described Andreasweald as being, *inter alia*, full of deer and large fierce wild boar;[14] and about eight centuries later Bede wrote that the Weald was a region 'thick and inaccessible, the abode of deer, swine and wolves',[15] and these wolves were certainly still present in the early 13th century.[16] Wild boar and cats survived until the 16th century and the pine-marten until the late nineteenth.[17] The area still abounds with deer, badgers, foxes, squirrels, rabbits and many types of bird and is still full of trees, copses, spinneys and woods. Within the Weald there are more than 200 names which include the word 'hurst', meaning a wood, and synonyms such as frith, shaw, copse, grove, snode and carvett are also very common. Bit by bit the area was cleared over hundreds of years but the extreme south-west of Kent was always the least densely populated part of the kingdom/county and was the last to be thoroughly cleared.[18] The area was probably heavily forested until at least the end of the 14th century or, maybe, later, and today Sussex, Kent and Hampshire remain the most densely wooded counties in England.[19] It is impossible to over-emphasise the extent to which Mark Beech was positioned in a heavily wooded region throughout centuries of its early history. The species of tree to be found in the forest were multifarious and most of them survive today, although, of course, in much smaller quantities. They include alder, ash, birch, elder, crab apple, elm, field-maple, hazel, holly, hornbeam, pear, plum, Scots pine, whitebeam, wild cherry, willow and yew. Other types have been introduced since the 17th century and the 'forest' as we observe it today is the result of human management rather than a primeval survivor. The most abundant trees, however, were the chestnut and, above all, the beech and the oak.[20] This is very important because it is probable that there was a prominent beech tree amongst the oaks near the present site of Mark Beech church from which the name of the village is derived.[21]

This brings us to the proposition that Mark Beech may be called 'the unknown village'. There are several reasons why we might justify such a claim. In the first place we have to ask where exactly Mark Beech was geographically and historically and of what did it consist? We will consider below the notion that it was—from pre-Conquest times—an identifiable location in the landscape, to which the early settlers gave a name, although there was no obvious focal point other than the famous beech tree: no settlement, as far as we know, no church, no man-made structure. There are very few houses from earlier than the 19th century, although there are some, and several rest on medieval sites, even from early in that period. The oldest extant houses, though not sites, are Old Buckhurst, which is a late medieval hall house, Hole Cottage, which was part of a 15th-century hall house, and Horseshoe Green Farm, the central core of which is also a late medieval hall house. Though just, by a matter of feet, the wrong side of the border with Cowden and, therefore, technically not in Mark Beech, Wickens is from the 15th century or earlier and was probably constructed as two halls. There are in the village at least a further eight structures, seven houses and a barn, which have been dated to the 16th or 17th centuries.

However, because there was no church until 1852 there was no historic parish and no ancient collection of parish documents, so modern historians have been unable or unwilling to study the village. Moreover, although families such as the Meade-Waldos or the Streatfields may have been influential as minor gentry at various times, the area has never been dominated or controlled by a powerful land-owning family. Even if the Talbots might be said to fit into that category, they did not arrive until the mid-19th century. Thus Mark Beech has not been of interest to historians of the landed classes whether in medieval or other times. Mark Beech was always divided between the parishes of Cowden and Hever and for non-ecclesiastical purposes still is. The Old English origins of its name, Mearcbeoc or Mearcbece, indicate that it was the border area between these two places, as we shall see.[22]

3 Hole Cottage, 1998. (Paul Houlton)

Mark Beech has not been much described then, or even noted, by historians or other writers. The earliest manuscript to record Mark Beech seems to be from 1461 and there are a few others from the 16th and 17th centuries. Between 1570 and 1838 at least a dozen monographs were published on the history and topography of Kent or of the Weald, but not a single one explicitly mentions, let alone describes, Mark Beech.[23] Several manuals of agricultural husbandry were written, mainly in the late 18th and early 19th centuries, culminating in Buckland's famous prize essay of 1845, which contains a 20-page section on the Weald; they all pass over Mark Beech in silence.[24] Travellers such as Celia Fiennes, 'the four Cambridge gentlemen' (Messrs Dodd, Riste, Shepheard and Whaley), Defoe, Arthur Young and William Cobbett toured Kent and kept diaries, but never mentioned Mark Beech even when they came near it.[25] The same is true of more modern publications: of the 11 volumes on Kent churches which have been produced since 1877 only the two that are essentially reference works, by Buckland and Homan, refer to Mark Beech[26] and this includes the famous and supposedly comprehensive works by Sir Stephen Glynne, Duncan, Fielding and Grayling.[27] Glynne is particularly surprising as he had family connections with the village. Of the 14 publications during this century on English or Kentish place-names only two mention Mark Beech,[28] and even Wallenberg's two well-known books omit any explanation of the origins of the place or first record of the name.[29] Furley's three-volume work on the Weald has nothing on the village, even though he was writing 25 years after the church had been built and the parish established.[30] All this can equally be said of books about Kentish country houses

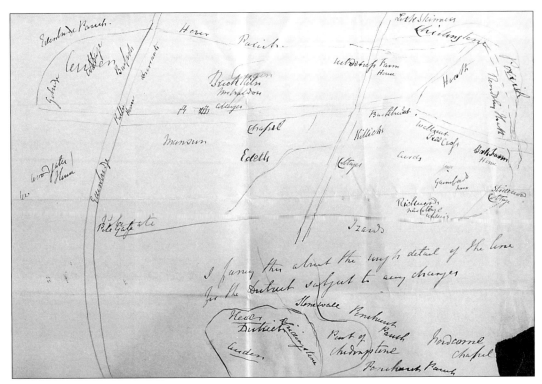

4 *Sketch map by John Chetwynd Talbot for the proposed parish of Mark Beech (by kind permission of the Centre for Kent Studies, Maidstone, and Charles J. Talbot).*

or pubs, and most 20th-century histories and tourist guides have often little, if anything, to say.[31] It is difficult to decide when the first description of Mark Beech mainly for reasons of definition occurs. The name is found as part of the address of at least one elector in the mid-19th-century poll-books. Gazetteers or directories such as Bagshaw's of 1848 and Kelly's of 1855 include it, although in the latter it appears only as part of the Cowden entry, not being given a separate entry until the 1878 edition; and there is a reference to the church in an article by Blencoe in the first volume of *Archaeologia Cantiana* in 1858.[32] Similarly there are mentions of the church in Eastman's *Historic Hever* of 1905, in Buckland's *Parish Registers and Records of the Diocese of Rochester* of 1912, and in Ewing's *History of Cowden* of 1926, but the first monograph to describe the village as a whole, and it is a very slight entry, seems to be the second edition of Cox's *Kent* published in 1915.[33] In reality, however, no extensive and adequate description or analysis of Mark Beech has ever been produced.[34]

When it comes to printed maps the story is similar. The first Ordnance Survey was made in the late 18th century and the first one-inch maps issued after the Napoleonic Wars. Mark Beech is not to be found on this map, although Horseshoe Green is. The earliest printed map of Mark Beech seems to be one included in a complete set of large-scale maps of Kent by Andrews, Dury and Hubert of 1769, where it is noted as Mark Beech Cross, and this map is clearly the basis for Hasted's similar map published in his history about thirty years later.[35] The village is shown on the Tithe Map of 1841[36] and in the first large-scale Ordnance Survey map of 1869, but the former was never published and the latter is very late in the day. It may also be noted at this point that the two fat volumes of bibliography of Kent of 1977 omit Mark Beech; its supplement of 1981 has only one entry for Mark Beech.[37]

Mark Beech has been an ecclesiastical parish only since 1852 and has never been a civil parish. Consequently no boundaries of the place are printed, for example, on any Ordnance Survey map of any scale, and most people, therefore, do not know where its precise borders are. In the Talbot Papers at the Centre for Kent Studies, Maidstone, there is a hand-drawn map (see figure 4) by John Chetwynd Talbot (1806-52), who was the effective founder of the parish, showing the boundaries as he wanted them to be.[38] Talbot's larger ambitions were not achieved, however: his scheme would have incorporated the area to Truggers Lane and beyond, and have taken in Walnut Tree Cross and Hill Hoath House, then still known as Batts (Farm House), before going across the fields to Stridewood. The official map of Mark Beech, as it was established in 1852, is to be found in the Rochester Diocesan Registry (in London). It shows a parish encompassing a smaller area than Talbot envisaged and was carved out of the existing parishes of Cowden and Hever with no part of Chiddingstone as he had wanted (see figure 5). Starting at Wilderness Farm the boundary goes down the centre of Wilderness Lane, leaving the farm in Hever (Talbot had wanted to include it), and follows the (old) boundary between Cowden and Chiddingstone, passing just east of Old Buckhurst, crossing the fields to Stridewood then down to Wickens Lane.

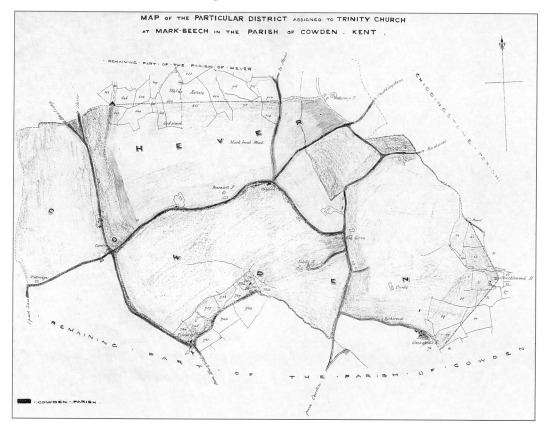

5 *Official map of the ecclesiastical parish of Mark Beech, 1852 (by kind permission of the Registrar of the Diocese of Rochester).*

It goes up the middle of this road, leaving Wickens in Cowden (Talbot had wanted it in Mark Beech), to Blowers Hill and then to Cowden Station, which is included. Thence it uses the stream to the west of the railway and goes up the unmade road to Pyle Gate (Pile Gate). It goes down the middle of the road to the Pound, turns to Gilridge, and from there follows the former Cowden-Edenbridge boundary, first northwards and then eastwards to the top of Stick Hill, so as to incorporate Mapletreuse/Eden Hall, Heathen Street and Bowlinglands. It then continues on a straight line across the fields until it reaches Uckfield Lane, and reaches the starting point by traversing the little slip road between Uckfield Lane and Wilderness Lane, which is known as Waldo's Cut.[39] Throughout this book there are references to two kinds of places: those strictly in Mark Beech proper and those, mainly within Cowden and Hever but also elsewhere, which need to be discussed in any analysis of Mark Beech.

We need also to consider the general awareness of the place among the contemporary population. There are many villages in England whose names, at least, are familiar. This is hardly so with Mark Beech. The statement that one lives near Tunbridge Wells or near Hever is usually greeted with a glimmer of recognition: Hever, of course, is known to many through its castle, its associations with Anne Boleyn (or Bullen), Henry VIII and the tourist industry in general; and other nearby places like Penshurst or Chiddingstone are also known, but the notion that one lives in Mark Beech is received with blankness, except by those who live in the vicinity. Even the emergency services were known to have had difficulty finding the place until computerisation was introduced, and first-time visitors, even those equipped with good maps, often arrive late or call for help from distant telephones or mobiles.

So we are entering new territory. This is exciting and presents opportunities and advantages, but we had better be honest and frank in facing openly the difficulties. In the course of this study it has been discovered that there is more primary material about Mark Beech than was initially expected, but the basic tools of the historian such as documentary and archaeological evidence are relatively scarce for Mark Beech prior to the middle of the 19th century, although there are a number of Anglo-Saxon and medieval charters which have a bearing, and there are relevant survivals of documents concerning the manor of Cowden Lewisham, which included Mark Beech.[40] The memories of the inhabitants do not now go back before the First World War, if that far; 1930, indeed, or at least the late 1920s now seems roughly to be the *terminus a quo* for the memories of even the oldest inhabitants. Thus we must to some extent extrapolate from what we know about the Weald and High Weald in general to Mark Beech in particular, while never forgetting that this is what we are doing. All the time we must cling to the little gems of real evidence that we do possess. In the process there are further things to note: the period during which Kent was part of a province of the Roman Empire lasted about 400 years; the time from the Jutish settlements to the Conquest was another six hundred; the era we choose to call medieval was a further four and a half centuries; and the time from Henry VIII to the start of continuous records of Mark Beech was yet another four. We must be aware that societies are constantly evolving and changing and that a generalisation about one part of an era may not be true of another.

Finally, writing as late as 1845, George Buckland said that the High Weald was a densely wooded district. Let us remind ourselves again that for a large part of its history Mark Beech was deep in the forest.[41]

◆ **II** ◆

Celts and Romans[1]

OUR STORY may be said to start in about 100 B.C. Just outside Mark Beech, down Oakenden Lane, Chiddingstone Hoath and near Lockskinners Farm, Chiddingstone, there are caves in the sandstone in which ancient peoples undoubtedly lived. At these sites and in Stonewall Park there have been found flints from the Mesolithic Age (between 10,000 and 2,500 years B.C.) and from the Neolithic Age (between 2,500 and 1,800 B.C.). Arrow heads from the Bronze Age (1,800-500 B.C.) have also been discovered, and all these items can be seen in the museum at Tunbridge Wells.[2] So there can be little doubt that men lived and hunted in the vicinity of Mark Beech from a very early date. Nevertheless, apart from the road, which passes east-west through the village, it is not until the beginning of the first century B.C. that we find major evidence of a civilised human presence in the area.

About three miles west of Mark Beech lies the Iron-Age fort known as Dry Hill, or sometimes, Lingfield Mark Camp or Fort.[3] It is a sizeable structure and its essentials can still be seen. It is on a well-chosen site with extensive views around most points of the compass and is at the highest place in the area. The fort covers an area of about 24 acres and has a circumference of about three-quarters of a mile. The outer defences consisted of three ramparts and two ditches, although on the south side there is a stretch of two banks and one ditch, and on the north part of the fortifications have been destroyed by ploughing. A section of the defences is 100 feet wide and the bottom of the inner ditch was 12 feet below the top of the inner bank. The outer ditch was about nine feet below the top of the somewhat lower middle and outer banks. The ramparts probably had wooden palisades on top and the fortifications surround a large, flat central area, which was reported in the 19th century to be divided by hedges into three fields and which was partly disturbed by the construction of a reservoir in 1905.[4]

Hill-forts of this kind are to be found all over southern England and into Wales. The oldest go back to the seventh century B.C. and in the Weald of Surrey and Kent to the mid-fourth century B.C., but Dry Hill probably dates from about 100-75 B.C.[5] Several digs have been undertaken here, a particularly important one in the 1930s, but no artefacts have been found, which leads to the conclusion that this site was not permanently occupied, but a fortress of last resort.[6] Iron workings have been found on the outer fortifications, but little else.[7] These are of either the Iron Age or the Romano-British period, more likely the former. Unfortunately, no thorough investigation has ever been made of the central area using modern archaeological techniques, from which more accurate dating might be made.

Nevertheless it would appear pretty certain that the fort dates from the beginning of the first century B.C. From time immemorial England had experienced a sequence of migrations of Celtic peoples from the continent. Until the land bridge was broken down by the sea in about 5,000 B.C.—or maybe a little earlier[8]—such movement was easy, but thereafter even the narrow English Channel provided no real barrier. The inhabitants of what is now west Kent and east Surrey, themselves the descendants of earlier migrants, began to feel threatened in about 100 B.C. by the arrival of another batch of people on the move, the Belgae.[9]

The Belgae do not seem to have penetrated much west of the Medway before the Romans arrived and altered the whole situation, but their arrival was perceived as a threat by the existing population.[10] So there began to be built a system of defences against the newcomers, which consisted of a series of hill-top forts in west Kent. Dry Hill was one of the most westerly of these fortifications and was linked by roads to others at High Rocks, Tunbridge Wells, Castle Hill, Tonbridge, Squerryes Park, Westerham, Oldbury, near Ightham, which covered 123 acres, Hulberry at Lullingstone, Caesar's Camp, Keston, and possibly others.[11] The main gateway at Dry Hill was in the south-west corner. There is another at the north-west corner and it has been suggested that the fort lay athwart an ancient trackway which ran between the North and South Downs, along a route at least 28 miles long.[12] However, a major access to the fort, probably the principal one, was from the east along the High Weald ridge, although there was no gate on the east. Ancient peoples naturally moved, where possible, along hill-tops and ridges, partly because these routes were drier—this would have been particularly pertinent in the 'miry' Weald, and partly because, despite dense forest, they provide opportunity for observation and a lessened chance of ambush. A line from the eastern ramparts of Dry Hill Fort, now the modern boundary between Surrey and Kent, follows a track which goes past Crippenden Manor to Gilridge and continues on public, metalled roads to Cowden Pound, Mark Beech and Newtye Hurst. Thence it progresses as a wide public footpath and east of the woods divides: one way continues down into the Eden/Medway valley via Chiddingstone and goes on to Oldbury Fort; the other goes to High Rocks and then almost on to the Rother as far as Newenden, almost certainly at that time on a navigable part of the river. This road is quite probably much older than the construction of Dry Hill and, thus, we can assert confidently that humans have been tramping, riding horses, pulling sledges and, later, carts through Mark Beech since at least 100 B.C. and probably for very much longer. The alignment may not always have been precisely as we see it today: an 18th-century map, for example, shows a piece of greensward on the opposite side of the road to Buckhurst Farm and Buckhurst Cottage, which un- doubtedly explains the sharpest bend on the modern road, as it skirts this old feature.[13] The road probably follows the route it always has for most of its length.

One problem remains regarding Dry Hill. All the indications are that the population of the area in the first century B.C. must have been very small and remained so for a very long time thereafter. As contemporaries believed that the Belgae represented a real threat it would have been no good taking several years to build a fortress; the job would have to be done very quickly, in months rather than years. And yet Mr. Peter Gray has estimated that the construc- tion of Dry Hill required the removal of about 35,000 cubic feet of earth, the equivalent of 100 men digging for a year. At the same time, the normal life of the community within a subsistence economy, especially the provision of food by hunting and farming, would have had

6   Old Buckhurst, 1998, was formerly known as Buckhurst Farm or Low Buckhurst. (Paul Houlton)

to continue, and once completed the defences would have to be manned by 300-400 able-bodied men. Even if, in the event, it was not used there must have been the assumption of such an eventuality. Mr. Gray has, therefore, suggested a local population of at least 2,000-plus, although we may assume that people would have marched up from the valley bottom through Mark Beech to augment the workers on site at Dry Hill.[14]

It would be an error to exercise any late 20th-century condescension and regard the people who lived around Mark Beech at this time as primitive. They could smelt iron and make iron tools and weapons. They wove cloth, produced pottery, and lived in wooden shelters. Although primarily hunter-gatherers, particularly of the deer and wild boar that flourished in the forest, they were agriculturalists and, even if there could not have been any very extensive clearing of the forest, it is possible that there was a clearance around Dry Hill where not only was iron produced but grain crops were grown. In some areas, though not in Kent, a few were urban-dwelling, and when the Romans arrived there were significant settlements at, for example, Colchester in Essex, which was to become the capital of the Roman province. The Celts had a highly developed cosmology complete with a priesthood, the identification of sacred places and, interestingly, among other things, the worship of trees. The Britons enjoyed a subsistence economy based principally on hunting, but with some agriculture and trade with the outside world. Although probably illiterate and without any written code of laws, they possessed developed social and political structures, which focused on the tribe and the tribal chief. To the west were what the Romans were to call the Regni and to the north the Trinovantes, but in Kent, on account of the recent incursions of the Belgae, there seems to have been no single or well-established ethnic group or tribe.[15]

It was into this milieu that, after two preliminary sorties by Julius Caesar in 55 and 54 B.C., the Romans under the Emperor Claudius's general, Aulus Plautius, invaded Kent in A.D. 43 and altered the history of England for ever. The geography of Kent at this time and for many centuries afterwards was not like that of today. As well as the extensive and deep forest the coastline was quite different: the Isle of Thanet was an island, the north coast westwards was different, and in the south neither Dungeness nor Romney Marsh as we now know them existed. Here instead was the great delta of the Rother, with ports at Appledore and Rye and a navigable waterway stretching westward to Newenden and Bodiam, about 23 miles from Mark Beech.[16]

Kent is the oldest county in England in the sense that its name has been in continuous use for the longest period of time. The name Cantium may have been in use as early as *c*.320 B.C. by Pytheas. Both Diodorus Siculus, writing around 36-30 B.C., and Strabo, whose geography was published between 58 B.C. and A.D. 21, were clearly aware of it, although in all three cases these authors were writing about a geographical feature, not a specific area.[17] The first to do so was Julius Caesar, who, writing before 44 B.C., referred to 'ei qui Cantium incolunt', but also said that the area was divided into four regions, ruled by kings whose names were known to him.[18]

The Roman was an assimilative culture, so that not only were England and Wales incorporated into the Empire as the province of Britannia, but the people were absorbed into an imperial civilisation. All freemen within the Empire were Roman citizens and the élites of pre-Roman Britain became, by and large, the élites of the province, forming a Romano-British ruling class, although, of course, people from other parts of the Empire lived, traded, soldiered and settled here, and helped to rule the province. The population was introduced to the customs, the laws and the language of the Empire. Within the province of Britannia, Kent became one of its administrative sub-divisions or *civitas* and its inhabitants were moulded by the Romans into the people we call the Cantiaci.[19]

The boundary of the *civitas* was further to the west than the present county border, that is, further away from Mark Beech. The border was possibly somewhere along the line of the present A22, although east of East Grinstead, but possibly further west still.[20] Moreover, the *civitas* of the Cantiaci was divided into two administrative districts. Roman civilisation tended to be an urban-based one and Canterbury and Rochester were developed as two important Roman cities.[21] This division, which reflected the one found by the Romans between the Belgic and non-Belgic Celts, was to be perpetuated down to the present day by, for example, the creation of two dioceses when Christianity came to Kent, by the existence of two distinct judicial areas in the Middle Ages based on Canterbury and Maidstone, by the division of the county into two parliamentary constituencies between 1832 and 1868, by the creation of an East and a West Kent Regiment in 1870, and by the well-known distinction between Kentish Men and Men of Kent.

The incorporation of Britannia into the Roman world lasted 400 years so that over time evolutionary change altered the character of Roman influence. The main areas of settlement in Roman Kent were in the east and along the North Downs and the Thames littoral, with penetration southwards down rivers such as the Medway and the Darent, as exemplified by such well-known Roman sites as Lullingstone and Farningham, the former about 14 miles north of Mark Beech.[22] The Darent was navigable as far as Riverhead, which is nine miles from Mark Beech, although there is the formidable barrier of the Chart Hills between them.[23]

Once the province was established south-west Kent was of no military importance and was, of course, still covered with dense forest. Thus the Weald and the High Weald remained largely unsettled in Roman times, as they had in the period of the Celts. It is probable that the population remained more or less the same as previously and the economy largely a subsistence one. The Weald was, however, exploited by the Romans both for its iron ore deposits and for its timber.[24]

One thing that the Romans did achieve, however, was the creation of an extensive network of roads throughout Kent. This system has been thoroughly investigated and reported by Margary. One of these roads left Watling Street at Peckham and went to Lewes via Titsey Hill, Limpsfield, Crockham Hill, Edenbridge and Holtye, and thence to Hartfield and over Ashdown Forest, then a true forest. This was a properly constructed Roman road, about 14 feet wide and with a hard stone or iron-slag surface. It may have been built by military engineers, but it had a purely economic purpose, primarily to open up access to and from the Wealden iron deposits, but also to connect London with the grain-producing areas of the South Downs and to improve communications generally. It was probably built about A.D. 100 and its entire route is now known. It passed about one and a half miles west of Mark Beech. It was also carried on a bridge, probably wooden but possibly of stone, over the Eden at Edenbridge, and for a long time this was the only bridge over the Eden or the Medway south of Rochester.[25] Indeed Edenbridge was once known as Villa Pontus Edelmi, though any authority for this name is obscure.[26]

In addition to the purpose-built roads the Romans also adopted and improved many of the existing tracks including the road eastwards out of Dry Hill through Mark Beech. This road now formed a crossroads at Gilridge with the new north-south Roman road. It has been firmly identified by Mr. K.P. Witney as one of the important Roman Iron Ways, superimposed upon the existing Iron-Age road we have noted already. The purpose of this road system was mainly to provide access to the iron-bearing parts of the Weald and to enable the finished product to be removed from the area.[27]

It is disappointing that despite the existence of the Roman roads so few artefacts have been found in the Mark Beech area to show the Roman presence. A substantial Roman villa, that is, a farm house and a temple, have long been known beside the Roman road at Titsey, about ten miles north of Mark Beech, a hill-fort and a bath-house have been found at Hartfield, six miles to the south, and there is a small Roman burial site in north Edenbridge.[28] In or near Mark Beech, however, there is very little; in 1810 a beautiful Roman gold intaglio ring was found at Dry Hill Camp and this is now in the British Museum;[29] and a century later a Roman coin was found in a nearby field.[30] At Ludwell's Farm, Cowden, which lies across the Roman road, an incomplete third-century statuette from the Allier region of France has been found,[31] but that is everything, apart from the claim by two authorities that Mark Beech Church, built in the mid-19th century, was erected on the site of a Roman or Romano-British camp.[32] This is an unlikely tale for which there is no evidence, and it appears that there has been a confusion with Lingfield Mark Camp, especially as one writer attributes the discovery of the intaglio ring to the Mark Beech site.[33]

The one activity which assumed major proportions during the period of Roman occupation was the exploitation of the Weald's considerable iron deposits. This was more extensive than at any other time before the 16th century. Around Mark Beech Hill alone there are the remains of at least six mines; there are many others on Mount Noddy, and the fields around the village are pock-marked with such remains, as any walk or a large-scale map will show. A notable series of ponds lies not quite, but more or less, in a straight line from Cobhambury Wood through Mark Beech to Newtye Hurst on the north side of the road. This may be because a rich seam of iron ore lies along this line, but it is more probably explained by the easy access from the road as there are also several ponds on the south side of the road. Those that have not been land-filled in recent times are now full of water and usually surrounded by trees. Some may be of a later date, particularly the 16th and 17th centuries, and some may have been dug for marl[34] or for clay for bricks; a few of the smaller ones may be bomb craters from the Second World War, but their existence demonstrates the large-scale development of the Roman iron industry in the Weald. This evidence is augmented by the uncovering of bloomeries, the means by which iron ore was smelted until the 16th century. Roman bloomeries have been identified at Mount Noddy, where the workings are very extensive, at Pyle Gate (Pilegate), and at Castle Hill, Holtye, although it should be noted that they are not all recognised in the most recent monograph on the subject.[35] Clinker is frequently dug up near the bloomeries and there is certainly much of it to the east of Rickwoods.[36] Thus Mark Beech was quite clearly an area where one of the major economic activities of the Roman Kent and Sussex Weald was pursued vigorously.

Our ideas about what agriculture there was to supplement such obvious forest activity as hunting must be entirely speculative. It is reported that Caesar was impressed by the number of farm-buildings and the large number of cattle which he saw in Kent, although he was, of course, describing east and north Kent.[37] Parts of Roman Kent were settled by farmsteads, farms and a few estates of the wealthy, but again this was principally in east and north Kent and up a few river valleys, not in the forest of the south-west.[38] Any economic or social decline created by the threats from Germanic tribes from outside the Empire seem to have been only gradual in Kent. However, starting in 383, the Emperor began to withdraw troops from Britannia and the last legionaries were withdrawn in 407 for good, despite a major Saxon attack in 408, and the people of the province, ruled by their Romanised leaders, were left to establish their own defence.

III

The Jutes[1]

BY ABOUT A.D. 425 it was clear that no significant help in the defence of Britannia was going to come from Rome. Saxons had been raiding the east coast of the province from across the North Sea since the third century and as these attacks became more intense the imperial authorities established the 11 great forts between the Wash and the Isle of Wight which formed the defence system of the Saxon Shore. Four of these fortresses were in Kent and the troops manning the line were augmented by Germanic mercenaries or *foederati*.[2] This was a common practice on the frontiers of the Empire, as it declined, and was one which the Romano-British leaders took up after the *de facto* departure of the legions.[3] Such mercenaries were settled around Canterbury in the second quarter of the fifth century,[4] but a truly fateful decision was taken by one of the British leaders, Vortigern, when he invited a band of Germanic tribesmen led by Hengest to settle in Thanet in 449.[5] According to legend, Hengest may, ironically, have landed at Ebbsfleet, where St Augustine was to arrive nearly 150 years later.[6]

Our two problems are, first, that sources for the early period of English settlement are the likes of Bede's *History of the English Church and People* and *The Anglo-Saxon Chronicle*, which are not contemporary and, therefore, do not always distinguish between fact or truth and legend or myth, and, secondly, that some historians of Kent have been too 'patriotic' and have tended, perhaps, to exaggerate the differences between Kent and the rest of Anglo-Saxon England. So our knowledge of the early years of Jutish settlement may be coloured by what has been called the 'Kentish origin myth'. It should be remembered that long-accepted details of the names and dates of early Kentish history rest on one uncorroborated tradition.[7] Moreover, the history of the early kingdom/county must be seen within a national framework rather than a purely local one. Nevertheless, the arrival of the Jutes in Kent was almost certainly the result not of invasion but of invitation. It seems that there was no sudden, large-scale incursion, but a slow drip of settlers, including women and children, so it was about five or six years before Hengest could muster, it has been suggested, about a thousand warriors.[8] He probably had his own agenda, which was not to be kept in subordination nor to be coralled permanently in the extreme east of Kent, but to conquer and rule territory for himself and his people so that the invitation to settle was a classic example of the Trojan Horse syndrome.

A possible scenario is that, starting in about 455, Hengest attacked westwards and by the time of his death in 488 had conquered Kent and Surrey, taken London and founded the kingdom of Kent and, so the tradition states, the dynasty, the Eskings, named after his son and successor, Oisc, that was to rule it for the next 300 years.[9] The custom whereby the monarchy passed to one of the king's sons and failing that to a male of royal kinship was established, but there was no system of primogeniture. Suitability was the prime criterion, plus royal kinship.[10]

According to Bede, and there is some other evidence to corroborate it, the Jutes conquered and settled not only Kent, but also the Isle of Wight, the coastal territory across the Solent, and the area around Hastings which became part of the kingdom of Sussex.[11] The present consensus among scholars is that the Jutes came from Frisia and the mouth of the Rhine, having migrated in earlier generations from Jutland. Frankish influence has long been discerned in Jutish culture and customs, but it is now thought this was the result of contact with and influence by the Franks rather than the Jutes coming from the Rhineland. It is also just possible that it was the Jutes who, in certain respects, influenced the Franks.[12] Old English more closely resembled Frisian than any other of the Germanic continental dialects.[13] Once it was thought that most of the existing British population were killed or enslaved or fled westwards, but it is now believed that much of the British peasantry remained in place.[14] With the exception of Canterbury, the Roman towns retain their Latin names, although Rochester is heavily anglicised, but most Celtic and Latin names were expunged. Names of rivers, such as Darent, Rother, Stour, Medway and Eden (originally Averne or Avon), which are Celtic, survived.[15] Out of about ten thousand names in Kent it is possible that only around sixty, including the rivers, are of pre-English origin.[16] In the early decades of settlement the Jutes replicated the pattern pioneered by Celts and Romans and dictated by topography and occupied mainly east and north Kent and the river valleys. Thus west Kent, particularly the forested region of the south-west of the kingdom, which included Mark Beech, was relatively neglected.[17] It has been suggested that Limpsfield may be a name with Celtic origins,[18] but one of the few definite surviving Celtic names, and one which was important for Mark Beech, was Wallington, now in Surrey, which means 'the settlement of the Welsh or British'.[19] The new frontier of the Cantiaci was now much further to the west than the Roman one and, therefore, further from Mark Beech; most of what is now Surrey was part of Kent or rather subject to Kentish jurisdiction. For example, when in 666 Edwald, the first abbot and later bishop of London, founded Chertsey Abbey, King Egbert I of Kent gave the new institution an endowment.[20] However, within less than 10 years, west Surrey at least had been lost to Mercia and, ultimately, to Wessex.[21]

The kingdom of Kent was one of the seven kingdoms which came to constitute England. It was one of the smallest and, therefore, weakest, but it enjoyed certain advantages which gave it greater influence and enabled it to retain its independence for longer than might be expected. It was the part of the island closest to the Continent and was open to cultural innovations and the building of political links and alliances as well as a conduit for foreign ideas.[22] From the time St Augustine arrived in 597 Kent became the base for the conversion of all England to Roman Christianity. The metropolitan see was established at Canterbury and, even though the original intention of Pope Gregory and of Augustine was that it should be in London, the kings of Kent expended all their energies, influence and diplomacy to keep it there. In 604 bishoprics were established at Rochester and at London and Kent thereby became the only English county to have two dioceses until the 19th century. By these means Kent acquired much influence and prestige. Finally, in a political game with seven players, who often tended to divide on a fifty-fifty basis, the seventh participant could enjoy a balancing role. The kingdom enjoyed a true independence for about three hundred years.

In 668 control of west Surrey seems to have been lost to Wessex and the rest of Surrey was detached by Mercia in about 674.[23] This situation was formalised by a treaty between King Whitred of Kent and King Ine of Wessex in 694 and the present boundary between Kent and Surrey, about three miles west of Mark Beech, was established.[24] By the second half of the eighth century Kent was controlled by Mercia. The last king of Kent is said to have been Baldred, probably of the Mercian royal house, who was expelled by King Egbert of Wessex in about 825. Even the most nominal difference was removed in 927 when Aethelstan, King of Wessex and Mercia and also of Sussex and Kent, and grandson of King Aelfred, was recognised as the first King of England.[25]

There were several features which distinguished Kent from the rest of England from the time of the Jutish settlements, although, as already indicated, these should not be exaggerated. In the first place, Kent was sub-divided from quite early on into political units, known as lathes, which were unique, although they do bear a likeness to the rapes of Sussex. Initially Kent may very well have continued to be divided, as in Roman times, into western and eastern kingdoms based on Rochester and Canterbury. Indeed, even if the centre of power was in east Kent, west Kent may have been ruled by junior or sub-kings and the people of west Kent are sometimes referred to distinctively as the Ceasterware.[26] Only four lathes are attested for the early period, but eventually the whole kingdom may have been composed of twelve lathes. These lathes were disposed from west to east and all the ones in the west and centre lay like sausages in thinnish bands of territory from the Thames in the north to the boundary with Sussex in the south, although that border remained inde-terminate until as late as the 10th century. Even bearing in mind the qualification implied above, it is probable that for a long time there was no political capital of Kent, as a whole, and each lathe had a royal town or court or *vill* in the north, which gave its name to its lathe, and the king and his court moved from *vill* to *vill* administering the kingdom as they went.[27] Except for survivals from the Roman period, and a few ecclesiastical buildings, there were no structures of stone or brick and even the king's palaces were of wood, lath and plaster with thatched roofs. This is why the remains of none have been found.[28]

Most lathes, therefore, consisted of a royal *vill* in the north, surrounded by settled areas and good farmland, with possibly some marsh and salt-pans, an area of downland pasture and, to the south, the forested areas of the Weald and the High Weald, where the lathes had their commons.[29] Mark Beech lay in the most westerly lathe of Wallington when places like Croydon, Purley, Warlingham, Caterham, Godstone, Lingfield, etc., as well as Wallington itself, were in Kent. It was the western half of this lathe that was ceded in 694 and the rump of Wallington was merged with the lathe of Sutton-at-Hone by 995 at the latest, although probably much earlier.[30] The lathe was initially an agricultural unit, but it quickly assumed administrative and judicial functions.[31] The hundred, a territorial sub-division which was smaller than the lathe, was a later imposition by Wessex. Mark Beech was, and indeed still is, in the hundred of Somerden, although a small part of Cowden was in the hundred of Edenbridge and Westerham, and a small part of north Hever was an enclave of Ruxley. It may be that the hundreds in this part of the Weald, including Somerden, which means summer pastures, were established during or soon after the reign of King Aelfred, that is, around 900.[32]

Local historian the late Herbert Knocker, a solicitor in Sevenoaks, claimed that Mark Beech was also in what was known as Holmesdale. However, even if the dens and later the manors were linked with or held by manors to the north, Holmesdale never reached to the Sussex border as Knocker asserted. A more recent historian has defined Holmesdale as being the strip of land only three to four miles wide, but about 60 miles long, between the North Downs and the Greensand Hills. It includes, therefore, places like Westerham, Sundridge, Brasted, Otford, Wrotham, etc., but not Mark Beech.[33]

A second distinguishing feature of Kent was probably the different character of property law. Inheritance was by what was known as 'gavelkind', although it must be understood that there is no certainty that this was a general Kentish custom until the 13th century, and there are hints that a system of partible inheritance may have existed in, for example, East Anglia, but just as, it seems, the monarchy did not pass by primogeniture neither did property.[34] In Kent property passed equally to all sons and, moreover, if there were no sons to all daughters equally. This was unique in England and there is a known example of property passing by gavelkind in Mark Beech as late as the second half of the 19th century![35] This peculiar Kentish practice, which was not abolished until 1926, may have originated from an ecological rather than an ethnic basis. That is to say that this system of partible inheritance probably developed as a result of the Inland/Outland patterns of settlement.[36]

Initially all land was held by the king and the lathe has been described by Mr. K.P. Witney as a sort of single, vast agricultural estate with the king as sole lord, although he may have exaggerated the extent of lathes in the earliest days.[37] Seven lathes are mentioned in Domesday Book and there are few references to lathes in pre-Conquest documents, and those only from the 10th and 11th centuries. There are, however, a few references in eighth-century charters to some names similar to those of lathes.[38] The land of Kent was informally divided into the Inland and the Outland, the former being in the north and the latter on or to the south of the North Downs. The Inland consisted of the king's own demesne and parts of the king's estates, which were let to tenants, known as *laets*. The Outland was occupied by free *ceorls* in their own right, but the king retained large areas of royal forest along the southern part of the Weald. Originally the Outland was the dependent pasture of the Inland estates, but there was a tendency for it gradually to break away from the parent estates. The *ceorls* were possibly the descendants of Hengest's warriors, and *ceorls* and *laets* alike owed rents and services to the king or to the Church, but to them alone.[39] It was the estates to the north, by whomsoever they were occupied, which possibly as early as the late fifth century, that is, in the earliest days of the Jutish conquest and settlement, acquired access to the commons of the forest, to the *daens*, *dennes*, *denns* or dens of the High Weald where Mark Beech was situated. Over the passage of time, of course, the king alienated land to both ecclesiastical and lay tenants so that a layer of intermediary land-holders was created, who could, naturally, let to their own sub-tenants.[40]

One of the characteristics of Kent was that the Church was granted much land, and in west Kent, even though it was in the diocese of Rochester, a large amount of land was granted to the Archbishop of Canterbury or to ecclesiastical institutions in that diocese. For example, by the ninth century, within the lathe of Sutton-at-Hone, which was adjacent to Wallington, the estates of Otford, Chevening, Sevenoaks, Sundridge and Darenth were held by the arch-bishop, and those of Eynsford and Farningham by his servants, and in Wallington the archbishop or his servants held Bexley and Brasted, the church of Rochester held Bromley, Christ Church, Canterbury held Orpington, and St Augustine's, Canterbury held Plumstead, most of which, as we will see, had connections with Mark Beech, which, itself, came to be in ecclesiastical hands.[41] The Church, as landlord, was less inclined than lay lords to allow the cutting of trees, especially large ones like oak and beech, and that is one reason why deforestation was slower in the Kentish Weald than in the corresponding parts of Sussex.[42]

Two further possible distinctive marks of Jutish Kent were the superior status enjoyed by freemen compared with elsewhere, although again this is not definitively attested until after the Conquest, and the individualistic attitudes of the population.[43] This factor, combined with the property laws, led to both a more idiosyncratic culture and to different landscapes and farming practices, although if Professor A.M. Everitt is correct it could have been the other way round; in his view it was the landscape which was the initiating or determining factor.[44] The typical Kent settlement was not a consolidated village, surrounded by land cultivated collectively by the community, as may have been the case in other parts of England and western Europe, but isolated farms and homesteads, where the individual occupier and his family had much greater control.[45] This kind of community can still be discerned in the late 20th century as places like Mark Beech, Hever and, even, Chiddingstone, although not so much Cowden, are still not nucleated villages as that term would be understood elsewhere. The culture led to a robust assertion of individual rights and, no doubt, the constant sub-division of land, generation by generation, by gavelkind inheritance, reinforced this tendency, although it would also produce tenancies that were not economically viable.

The existence of the lathes, the distribution of the royal demesne and forests, the other developing estates, the individualism of the people and the very existence of the Weald forest itself, created or perpetuated another Kentish peculiarity which is very pertinent to the history of Mark Beech. This was the existence of dens in the forest of the Weald and, particularly, the High Weald. 'Den' is an Old English word peculiar to Kent, meaning a pasture. It may also imply a degree of clearance in the forest and can also mean a wild beast's lair.[46] They are of very ancient origin and, a pattern of transhumance may very well have predated Jutish settlement.[47] As we have seen, every estate in the north of a lathe customarily had dens in the Wealden forest. These were areas in the forest where there were rights to hunt the deer, the wild boar and other animals, and to gather brush-wood, but, above all, to graze domesticated animals, particularly pigs, to which the Jutes usually referred as swine. This customary right was known as 'pannage', and every year herds of swine were moved southwards along well-established droves to eat the pastures of the forest, especially for pigs the acorns, and at the time of the Domesday Survey 60,000 pigs were being sent into the forest each year.[48] Cowden was obviously a pasture for cattle, but most dens were used by pigs, and their names were usually derived from topographical features or from the names of individuals or kin who had the rights to graze there or had, occasionally, settled there.[49] In and around Mark Beech, surviving den names apart from Cowden include Shernden, Frienden, Oakenden, Somerden, Pigdown (Pigden), Birchden, Crippenden, Ridden, Lullenden, Puttenden, Barden, Hadinden, Henden, Timberden, Culverden, Dornden, Claydene, Oakdene, Sylvandene and Den Cross. The right of pannage could only be exercised for seven weeks a year from the Autumnal Equinox (21 September) to the Feast of St Martin (11 November), but for most of the rest of the year the forest was fairly empty, except perhaps for waggoners in the spring and a few cowherds in the summer.[50] The early dens, which were derived from the commons, were not created by royal grants, but through regular and undisputed occupation by the free *ceorls* until eventually they were absorbed into manorial estates. These dens, therefore, passed through three evolutionary stages: first, the forest was regulated by the king in the interest of all; then 'manorial' (manor is strictly a post-Conquest term) lords began to assume these obligations; finally, the lords tried to convert the obligations into property rights.[51]

The droves into the Wealden forest criss-crossed each other so there was no simple situation of manors in the north of a lathe having a straight route southwards. Over a long period of time the droves became the basis for the road system, which is why in this part of Kent there is still today a preponderance of north-south over east-west roads. These droves have been most thoroughly researched by Mr. K.P. Witney and by Professor A.M. Everitt, who have reconstructed elaborate plans of the routes and, thereby, provided clues to a detailed pattern of settlement in the forest.[52] The dens belonging to Westerham were intertwined with those of Bromley, Lewisham and Cudham.[53] The Surrey manors of Limpsfield and Titsey had land on both sides of the border.[54] In particular, the Wallington droves to Cowden and Mark Beech crossed spectacularly with the major drove from Sutton-at-Hone.[55] Between the eighth and 10th centuries so many grants of land were made, especially but not exclusively, to ecclesiastical tenants-in-chief, that the commons were beginning to break up, and by the Norman Conquest the same jumbled medley of ownership had been created in the forest as in the uplands, and the division into manorial dens was almost complete.[56]

Nevertheless, most dens go back prior to the Conquest, and many of them possibly to the earliest Jutish settlements or, perhaps, even earlier.[57] It is at this point that we can begin to be more specific about the precise origins of Mark Beech. We must be exceedingly careful because Mark Beech was probably not a settled place at any early date. There are at least three factors we have to consider and the first is etymology, from which quite a bit can be deduced.

The study of Old English names in order to determine the pattern and date of settlement is long-established. In sequence, it would seem that names which included *ham*, *ingas* and *ing* are amongst the earliest names in Jutish Kent.[58] Witney has concluded that *ham* names were formed in the period 450-700 but we have also to consider that *ton* names, such as Tonbridge, were still being formed as late as the 13th century.[59] Ham, which in Kent denotes a group or constellation of settlements, started to be used from the period of migration. They are not very common in the main part of the Weald, but a few do occur even in the environs of Mark Beech. A name like Wester*ham* could probably not have come into use until the chopping off of the western half of the lathe of Wallington in the late seventh century, although it also denotes the most westerly settlement at the end of the river Darent, which rises just south of Squerryes Park, almost at the top of the northern slope of the Chart Hills and about five and a half miles north of Mark Beech.[60] To the north of Edenbridge we find Crock*ham* Hill, Coak*ham* and Brox*ham*, but nearer to Mark Beech are found such names as Ock*hams* Cob*ham*bury and Prink*ham*, and just across the then non-existent border with Sussex Withy*ham* and Black*ham*, which may all be of an early date. This may demonstrate that some small-scale settlement occurred in the Mark Beech area quite early on. Of the *ing* type of name there is the obvious example of Chidd*ing*stone, as well as Wall*ing*ton with its Celtic overtones.

The name Mark Beech or Markbeech, however, does not follow these patterns, although it is quite simple to understand from Old English even if the date of its first use is less easy to establish. In 1893 members of the Kent Archaeological Society made one of their annual summer tours of the county. They were shown a large beech tree growing out of the eastern ramparts of Dry Hill Fort, which, they were told, was known as the Mark Beech.[61] There are so many trees there now that this particular tree cannot be identified. Dry Hill is three miles from Mark Beech, as we have seen, so this cannot be the origins of the village name, although this example provides confirmation, if it is needed, of its meaning. In Old English the word mark (*mearc*) means a border, a boundary, a frontier, and in the forest it has implications of a place of mystery, a sinister location, one which Pagans would associate with the habitation of spirits and goblins. It is the waste or wilderness part of the forest, situated between two more settled places. From the word is derived our modern 'murky', which may indicate that, for Jutes, the word was not pronounced mark, but murk. Beech (*beoc* or *bece*) is the Old English word for a beech tree, so in Mark Beech or, probably more correctly, Markbeech we are looking for a prominent beech tree, possibly among oaks, which marked a division between one area and another.[62] Within Andreasweald there was a tendency, as between oaks and beeches, for the oak to predominate on the heavier clay soils and the beech to do so where the soils were more sandy or chalky, as, for example, at Crockham Hill. As the soil within hundreds of yards of Mark Beech crossroads is heavy clay it is entirely plausible that there was a prominent isolated or semi-isolated beech tree, among the oaks, at just the right point on the boundary of the estates, indeed beside the long-established road, which would have been easily recognisable by the early drovers and settlers. A slightly different spelling, Mearc-bece, is defined precisely as 'a beech tree which forms part of a boundary'.[63]

This poses the question as to what boundary was being identified and this leads us to consider other kinds of evidence. The type of boundary to be identified would be the division between an estate, later a manor, or a parish or both. The earliest charter granting a Wealden den is that of King Whitred in 724,[64] but that comes from Minster in east Kent. The earliest charter to describe the boundaries of a den is a charter of King Cenwulf of Mercia in 814,[65] delineating a Bexley den, an Orpington den and the Plumstead den in Hever of Plum Paddock, which still exists as the name of a house in Uckfield Lane. Uckfield, incidentally, as found in Uckfield Lane and Wood, is an ancient field name.[66] Uckfield Lane is the road which goes north, down the hill, to Hever from Mark Beech crossroads, and the wood is about half way down the lane on the western side. The dens named here are all around the manor of Hever Brocas (meaning a brook), which probably tapered southwards to the road along the High Weald ridge through Mark Beech.[67] There is a further charter of King Aethelbert in 862,[68] which describes a field, Gleppanfelda, probably now Clatfields on the border of Cowden and Edenbridge. In a forested area such as the High Weald there would inevitably have been swathes of uncolonized and unappropriated woodland between identifiable dens. These came to be used as intercommunable pastures and boundary lands or 'marks'. Professor Everitt has demonstrated that settlements on estate/parish boundaries are a particular feature of Kent and that there are a number of such settlements in our area, including Scarletts, Basing, Gilridge, Buckhurst (probably Old Buckhurst), Bramsells, Mark Beech and Horseshoe Green.[69]

Now the history of the precise evolution of parishes in Kent is obscure. The Jutes were, of course, Pagans, existing within a belief-system of polydeities, of whom the most popular seem to have been Woden, the god of knowledge and wisdom, Thumnar, the god of thunder, and Tiur, the god of war. They considered certain wells, stones and trees sacred and assigned magical properties to certain animals, including boar.[70] Although there is some evidence for the survival of Celtic Christianity in Kent before 597, in that year Kent began to be converted to Roman Christianity, though its survival became uncertain following the death of King Aethelbert I in 616, when, for example, the bishop of Rochester abandoned his see and fled abroad.[71] The competition between Roman and Celtic Christianity was resolved at the Synod of Whitby in 664, and with the arrival of Theodore of Tarsus as archbishop of Canterbury in 668 serious institutional developments of the Church began to be put into effect. There is evidence in 'Theodore's Penintentials' that he initiated the formation of parishes, although this process probably did not proceed far for some time.[72] It is, in fact, not possible to assign responsibility for initiating the formation of parishes to one ecclesiastical personage or one generation. As one historian has written, 'all that can be certainly said is that by the 12th century the system was an accomplished fact.'[73]

It would be a mistake, therefore, to suppose that before the Conquest there was some sort of correlation between the existence of a village or settlement and the provision of a church. In east Kent the rituals of the Church were provided for the population by the seven minsters at Reculver, Lyminge, Minster-in-Thanet, Dover, Folkestone, Minster-in-Sheppey and Hoo.[74] It was ecclesiastical houses, the king and, increasingly, lay lords, who founded churches for themselves, their families and their tenants and thereby created the associated parishes. A parish system was, therefore, created slowly on a piecemeal basis in line, naturally, with the patterns of settlement, and this slowness was especially noticeable in the diocese of Rochester in west Kent. The building of churches and the creation of parishes in much of Kent was linked to forest clearance, marshland reclamation, etc., and it has been suggested that most parishes had come into existence by about 1070 at the latest. In the High Weald churches were often built at the junction of main droves emerging from the commons, but where the population was sparse churches were probably not built until at least the 10th or 11th centuries.[75] As we shall see later, Domesday Book did not effectively cover the area of Edenbridge, Hever, Chiddingstone and Cowden in detail so there are no records of churches in that document. However, there is the *Textus Roffensis*, which describes 48 churches not found in Domesday Book, including Cowden and Hever, and the *Domesday Monachron*, which deals with churches subject to Canterbury.[76] Scholars disagree as to the precise date of the first document, but it may have been compiled as early as 1070 and probably describes conditions which existed before the Conquest, although how far back we cannot know.[77] As we have seen, the *Textus Roffensis* mentions the existence of churches at both Cowden and Hever. These buildings would have been small wooden churches with thatched roofs and presumably stood on the same sites as the medieval, stone ones we can see today.[78]

The churches and parishes in this part of the High Weald were created as offshoots or subsidiary or daughter churches of churches in the Weald or further north. Thus Westerham created Edenbridge, Brasted created Hever, Chevening created Sundridge, and Chiddingstone and Shoreham created Otford, Sevenoaks and Penshurst.[79] Dating is difficult and, for example, it is not known when the southern half of Brasted was detached in order to create Hever.[80] Precisely where Cowden fits into such a scheme is unknown also, but presumably the building of a church there could not have been long after the one at Hever.

Another factor to be considered is the hundred, which, as we have noted, was a Wessex imposition on Kent, as was the borough, of which there are several examples around Mark Beech. Hundreds may have begun to be formed towards the end of Aelfred's reign or soon afterwards, *c*.900, and their formation was certainly complete by the Conquest in 1066. The head men of the dens in Somerden met at Somerden Green and these representatives included those from Hever and Cowden. This presupposes that in the 10th century there were settlements to be represented, although whether there were parishes with churches we shall never know.[81]

The upshot is that we do not know precisely when 'parishes' first came into existence here, but the probability is that boundaries marked by Mark Beech were initially of dens and estates rather than parishes. Very frequently the boundaries of estates became the boundaries of parishes (or, sometimes, vice-versa) and this process seems most likely to have happened in this case. In the case of Mark Beech we are identifying, as we shall see in more detail below, the boundary between the manors of Hever Brocas and Cowden Lewisham (and, later, the parishes of Hever and Cowden). Strictly speaking, Mark Beech lay mainly in the latter, and altogether we have 15 charters and five Papal Bulls dealing with the manor of Lewisham, five charters pre-dating the Conquest.[82]

The use of charters is an exceptionally tricky matter as the problem of authenticity is vital and requires expert analysis of form and other techniques. Very few original Anglo-Saxon charters have survived. The vast majority of early charters are preserved only in later copies or summaries. The history of charters is riddled with examples of outright fraud and

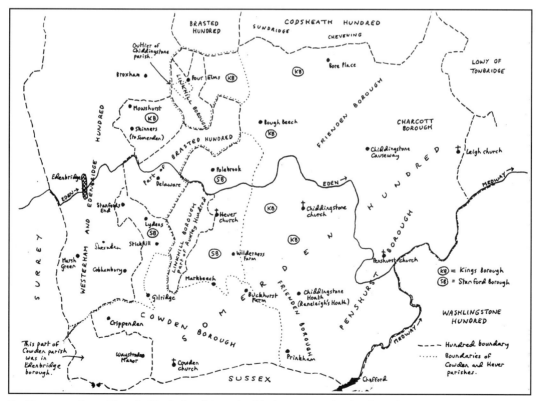

7 *Extreme south-west Kent: the Hundreds and Boroughs of the late-Saxon and medieval periods. (Courtesy of Mr. L.E.W. Cole)*

with retrospective interpolations and the recreation or imitation of charters, that is the rewriting of them retrospectively. As well as deliberate fraud, charters are prone not only to interpolation, but to miscopying. Opperman, who studied the relevant Lewisham charters in the 1920s, conceded the authenticity of only six of them,[83] and Professor P.H. Sawyer's well-known compilation of Anglo-Saxon charters provides a check-list of what other scholars have concluded on the subject.[84]

All scholars are agreed, however, on the authenticity of a charter issued by King Edgar I in 964,[85] and this charter is of supreme importance for Mark Beech. As a result of his quarrels with Edgar's predecessor King Eadwig, the monastic reformer, St Dunstan, spent two years in exile at the Abbey of St Peter and St Paul (Monasterium Blandinium), Ghent, in the late 950s. Ghent was at that time one of the most important centres of monasticism and, on the accession of Edgar, Dunstan returned to England, where he became an adviser and close friend of the king and in 959 or 960 archbishop of Canterbury.[86] The charter of 964 gave the royal estate of Lewisham to St Peter's, Ghent, and we shall see below how important this was for Mark Beech. The estate was very extensive and included not only Lewisham itself, but also Greenwich, Mottingham, Woolwich and Combe as well as, undoubtedly, dens in the Weald. The reason for Edgar's donation or, just possibly, as we shall see, confirmation of Lewisham to Ghent was obviously the result of Dunstan's influence upon him; Dunstan was much influenced by St Peter's and felt that he had a debt of gratitude to that institution. The charter is undoubtedly authentic and represents the first recorded grant of an English estate to a continental monastery.[87] There are five extant copies of this charter and, although it is authentic, Dhondt pointed out that the explicit references to Dunstan in the document are later interpolations.[88]

Before we move on, however, we must consider the possibility that Lewisham was already in the hands of the Flemish abbey before 964. At some time between 893 and 899, Aelthfryth or Elstrudis or Elstrude, third daughter of King Aelfred, married Count Baldwin II of Flanders, whom the *Dictionary of National Biography* describes as a greedy and violent man and whose capital was at Ghent (or Gand). Aelthfryth is said to have been a highly educated lady, as were all Aelfred's children. She and Baldwin had four children, two daughters and two sons, Arnulf and Adelulph, the former succeeding his father as Count in 918 and the latter becoming Count of Boulogne.[89] As a marriage dowry, Aelthfryth was given Wellow in the Isle of Wight and Steeple Aston and Chippenham in Wiltshire.[90] She did not hold these demesnes at her death in 929, but it is possible that she may also have been given Lewisham, a royal manor in north-west Kent, or have persuaded her brother, King Edward the Elder, to exchange it for her original dowry. Aelfred left all his booklands in Kent to his son, but they cannot be identified and there is no record of Aelthfryth ever holding Lewisham.[91] Lewisham was in the northern part of the lathe of Wallington and had, no doubt, long-established rights of access for pannage to the dens in the appropriate part of the High Weald to the south. According to a charter, which purports to be a contemporary record, on the death of Baldwin on 11 September 918, Aelthfryth and her two sons gave the manor of Lewisham to the Abbey of St Peter and St Paul, Ghent, 'for the good of the soul of her lord Baldwin and herself and her sons'. The precise terms were the manor of Lewisham, Greenwich, Woolwich, Mottingham and Combe (hence the modern Westcombe between Greenwich and Charlton), known as the manor of Lewisham, with all its appurtenances, which would include its dens.[92]

This charter was first published in 1842[93] and the oldest extant copy is to be found in the East Flanders State Archive at Ghent.[94] Up to 1914 most historians accepted it as authentic, although in 1907 the English barrister Montmorency expressed some doubt as to the truth of Aelthfryth being the original donor of the manor to St Peter's.[95] Vanden-Haute argued that there were only copies of the charter because the original had been lost, but he accepted its validity.[96] In 1928 Opperman made a thorough study of the St Peter's charters and concluded that the 918 charter represented a real transaction, but that the extant charter copy was one from *c.*1070, which imitated a lost original.[97] However, more recently even this interpretation has been placed in doubt. Dhondt has, *inter alia*, made a careful comparison of the texts of Aelthfryth's charter of 918, the *Liber Traditionum*, which is a register of all St Peter's possessions, compiled chiefly in the 11th century,[98] Edgar's charter of 964 and a charter of William I from 1081. He judged Aelthfryth's diploma to be 'un faux manifeste', fabricated in the 11th century from various sources, but after the *Liber Traditionum*. Dhondt demonstrated that the supposed charter of 918 is an almost exact copy of a gift by Count Wichman, a former Count of Flanders, which is authentic, except for the alteration of a few names, and that the reference to Aelthfryth's charter in that of Edgar is an interpolation.[99] Edgar's charter of 964 says that the gift was made from the Royal Treasury and could not be revoked and, if the bit about Aelthfryth is omitted, then this becomes a gift by King Edgar, not a confirmation.[100] For an insight into the mind of a possible interpolator or forger it may be more than a coincidence that Edgar's second wife, whom he married in 965, was called Aelthfryth and he had a daughter of the same name.[101] In 1908 Duncan pointed out that Cippenham was a recorded spelling for Sydenham, within the Lewisham estate, but this is quite inadequate to show that Aelfred's daughter ever held Lewisham.[102] Grierson also judged it to be a forgery and a fiction of the 11th century.[103] Finally, it should be noted that the 1016 charter of Edward the Confessor, which we will encounter later, made no mention of Aelthfryth/Elstrudis, which it surely would have done had there been any truth in her being the original donor of Lewisham to St Peter's.

The above is not merely esoteric; the charters are important for Mark Beech both for location and, possibly, for date. Another priory was founded at Lewisham, which was a cell of St Peter's, and the manor was to be held by the Flemish institution for nearly five hundred years. As we shall see, the dens attached to this manor can be identified; they are in the most south-westerly part of the High Weald and eventually formed what was called the manor of Cowden Lewisham. Manors, of course, were not generally large consolidated pieces of territory, especially in a heavily forested area such as the High Weald, but parcels of land, often quite small, scattered across the landscape and inter-mixed with similar, contiguous pieces of other manors. In 1281 the manor of Lewisham consisted of some 996 acres plus 120 acres at Greenwich, including forest, and we have no reason to suppose that this was not essentially the extent of the manor in the 10th century.[104]

Ghent lost control of its English possessions during the rule of the Danish kings in the early 11th century and we know that Greenwich was used by the Danes as a base for attacks on London.[105] In 1016, Edward the Confessor, then only an adolescent, but in exile, spent Christmas at St Peter's. It is claimed that on 26 December he promised that if he was ever restored to his English inheritance he would, in gratitude, return the Kentish manor to

Ghent. Edward, it is said, promised the Abbot to restore Lewisham and Greenwich 'with its other appendages, including houses, churches, land, meadows, woods, water-supplies and aqueducts, weirs, seisins and *all* its complete possessions' [my italics and translation from the original Latin].[106] So it is only too obvious that St Peter's had a vested interest in getting their property back and in claiming that Edward had promised to return it to them but, even if the document in our hands today is not totally authentic, there is agreement that it represents a true event.[107]

In 1044, two years after his restoration to the English throne, Edward restored, or so it has been claimed, Lewisham to Ghent. There are nine extant copies of this charter of restoration,[108] but again there are serious questions as to its authenticity. Until the middle of the 20th century historians, including such authorities as Wallenberg and Dhondt, accepted it as authentic,[109] although Stevenson had doubts about it as early as 1914.[110] Since 1945 Harmer and Oleson have both indicated that it must be false on the grounds that the witness list and the date are irreconcilable, especially, for example, that of Eadwine, abbot of Westminster, who did not assume office until 1049.[111] In addition the version known to us is in the same hand as a 12th-century charter of Abbot Herbert of Westminster, and Chaplais concluded that this charter had been forged at the end of the 11th century by Osbert of Clare at Westminster as part of his campaign to get Edward canonised.[112]

We have here another charter which very much serves the interests of St Peter's and, possibly, others as well. The fact that four copies are to be found at Ghent might just attest that it genuinely represents the situation as seen by St Peter's. Forged or not, it surely represents Ghent's actual claims and it is most important for Mark Beech as it tells us for the first time the names of the dens in the High Weald held by Lewisham. It is unlikely to be a complete fabrication and was to be confirmed many times by subsequent kings. It must have been compiled from information supplied by monks from Lewisham or Ghent. Nearly half a century later, Domesday Book provides confirmation that St Peter's held Lewisham with, incidentally, pannage for fifty swine. The prior would have been unlikely to have made false claims to the commissioners, not least because the declared demesne would, unless the abbey possessed certain exemptions, be the basis for taxation.[113]

During the 20th century three historians, Ewing, Ward and Witney, have tried to identify the exact location of Lewisham's dens.[114] The 1044 charter states these to have been Aeschore, Aeffehaga, Wingindene, Scarendene and Sandherste.[115] With one variation these names are repeated in a charter of William I of 1081.[116] Both Edward's and William's charters may be of dubious provenance, and Opperman judged them to be later imitations based on a genuine charter of John of 1209.[117] Some historians have claimed that these dens were additional grants by Edward to the original one of 918 or 964. It is true that the dens had not been explicitly described before, but we know that royal manors like Lewisham had dens and we cannot assume, even if the charters are imitations, that the dens were later additions. It is likely that what had always been the *de facto* situation was being made explicit for the first time. The monks were using their knowledge of the manor's customary rights to get those rights in their fullest extent written out. If these charters were fabricated in or after 1209 they also tell us that the names of the dens were still in use more than a century after the Conquest, but these names cannot have been invented, as they are real places that can still be identified in the 20th century.

8   Rickwoods, 1998. Note the jumble of styles. (Paul Houlton)

There is universal agreement that Aeschore is the Exore mentioned in the Hundred Rolls for 1274, the Essore to be found in a Register of 1281 and in the Lewisham Court Rolls in 1284, the Ashowres in a release of quit rent in 1674, the Ashore in a mortgage deed of 1784, and survived as the field-name of Ashour on the 1841 Tithe Map (field no. 81).[118] It is to be found around Rickwoods and Wickens to the south and west of Horseshoe Green. Aeffehaga is assigned by Witney to Ivelands, around Pilegate, although Ward widened out the area to place it between Mark Beech and Oakdene, the modern Saxbys, known for about three hundred years as Bottings. Ward wrote that Aeffehaga means the enclosure (*hagh/haw*) of Aeffa.[119] Wingindene is the area around Claydene and gives its name to the Wickenden family, who held it, presumably as tenants, throughout the Middle Ages.[120] Scarendene presents slightly more problems: Ewing, Witney and, indeed, Somers-Cocks and Boyson identify it with Shernden and, certainly, the name and the subsequent pattern of tenancies seems to fit. Ward, however, whilst agreeing that Scarendene/Shernden was later held by the Cobham, from whom comes Cobhambury, and then the Burgh families, suggested that in the 10th/11th centuries Scarendene extended to Lord's Land, where Falconhurst was eventually to be built, and on to Hole Farm or the Hole, east of Pyle Gate.[121] This place had already appeared in a charter of 862 as Saengethryg, and Wallenberg and Witney identify it from another charter of 973 as the alternatively named Tryndhyrst and suggest that it was physically linked with Tannera Hole, also named in this second charter, and which it is proposed is Hole Farm.[122] The fact that Lewisham Manor Court was taking rents for Shernden in the 13th and 14th centuries and that, as late as the mid-19th century, it was taking a proprietorial interest in the property now known as Bowlinglands, then an ale house, the *Bricklayers Arms*, provides *prima facie* confirmation that the land on the north-west side of the Pound Crossroads, leading eventually to Shernden, was part of the lands of Lewisham Priory from the earliest times.[123] Saengethryg, Scarendene, Scearnden and Shernden are thus variant spellings of the same place.[124] Sandherste, it is agreed, is the area south of Wickens towards Kent Water, where there is still a Sandfields Farm.[125] The charter of 1081, however, changes Sandherste to Santhrysce, which is either a curious variant spelling or refers mistakenly to Sundridge. The error, if such it was, was by the later imitator because there is no evidence from any other source that

Lewisham held Sundridge dens, which were those of the archbishop.[126] It also looks a bit too much like Saengethryg to be considered seriously as Sundridge.

We have, therefore, now identified the location of the manor of Cowden Lewisham and the position of Mark Beech within it. The dens were transformed in time into farms and the manor encompassed roughly the eastern half of Cowden bounded by Hever in the north, Chiddingstone in the east, possibly, but not certainly, Kent Water in the south, and the Edenbridge-Hartfield road in the west, with an extension north-westwards to Shernden, which has long been mainly in Edenbridge parish (*see* figures 7 and 19). For what it is worth, this corresponds very extensively with the estate that was bought by the Talbots in the mid-19th century, except that Shernden was not included and it did not extend to Kent Water, which may be very significant. There cannot be any doubt that Mark Beech was in the north-east corner of the manor. Ward identified Mark Beech with Aeffehaga, Aeffa's enclosure, and he pointed out that in the Weald it was a tendency for a road and the waste through which it ran to form a boundary between dens or a group of dens.[127] Mark means a frontier and Mark Beech is, therefore, one of the boundaries in the waste of Cowden, recognised by a prominent beech tree. Indeed a much later inventory of 1590 tells us that Mark Beech is bounded on the east and south by the road from Markebeeche to Cowden Cross, via Horseshoe Green.[128] Thus Mark Beech forms the boundary between the manor of Cowden Lewisham and the manor of Hever, especially that part which became Hever Brocas, sometimes known as Linkhill,[129] when the manor was split in the 13th century into Brocas and Cobham. In time it also came to form the boundary between the two parishes. Thus Mark Beech was strictly entirely in Cowden. Strictly, however, is the operative word, because today we can legitimately accept that Mark Beech is partly in Hever as well. Moreover, we must also notice that close to the beech tree, just where the bounds made a 90-degree turn, Mark Beech also included a piece of the manor of Otford Weald or Penshurst Halimote.

Ewing correctly identified six pieces of Penshurst Halimote lying in the parish of Cowden and this is supported by the records of that manor now preserved by the Centre for Kent Studies but deposited at Sevenoaks.[130] Ewing identified the location of five portions, but the sixth is described simply as a 'Copyhold Tenement in Cowden with a Garden and Orchard the property, at his death in 1847, of Christopher Burfoot' in the north-east of the parish.[131] There is often a remarkable continuity in the history of land over the centuries. In the 18th and 19th centuries the bit of land fronting Cow Lane on which the *Kentish Horse* and Old Farm, once known as Mark Beech Farm, stands belonged to the Burfoot family, and indeed in 1861 they had a boundary dispute with the Talbots, now the owners of what had certainly been part of Cowden Lewisham.[132] May we propose that this little enclave of land is the unidentified piece of Penshurst Halimote?

9 *Old Farm, 1998. The oldest building in the centre of village (17th century). (Paul Houlton)*

10 The Kentish Horse *and the church, 1998. (Paul Houlton)*

We have now located Mark Beech, but not dated its foundation and this is extremely difficult. From our charters we can probably assert that Mark Beech was a term and a place which certainly existed by the 10th century. However, the northern estates had driven their swine to their dens from a much earlier date and, therefore, it is quite possible that the drovers identified a beech tree, which they could recognise every year on their return, within the waste on the northern side of their dens at a much earlier date, although how much earlier is impossible to tell.

There is an oral tradition in the village that its name has another origin: in the Middle Ages Cowden, like other communities, established a pound for stray animals from which they had to be redeemed by their owners. The records do not tell us when this pound was established. A new pound was built in 1797, although whether this was on the site of an old one is not certain, though it is probable.[133] At what is still called the Pound Cross Roads, or just The Pound, there was a Pound House, now raised, occupied by the person responsible for the collection of the fines and the release of the animals.[134] In order to eliminate fraud, it is said, there came a requirement for the animals to be taken a 'lady's mile' to the beech tree to be marked independently, hence Mark Beech. This cannot be the origin of the village's name for two reasons: firstly, the Old English word *mearc* does not mean to make a mark, but a frontier or boundary; secondly, the origins of the name undoubtedly pre-date the time when Cowden could have established a pound.

By the time of the Conquest Mark Beech was still an area of very small population and deep forestation. The population remained sparse, but no doubt drovers constructed wooden shelters in the forest for their autumn sojourn and a few may have taken up semi-permanent settlement, although no archaeological remains of such structures have been discovered.[135] Nevertheless, there seem to have been settlements at least at (Old) Buckhurst and at Bramsells.[136]

The Duke of Normandy and his cronies arrived in 1066. What difference would this disruption make to Mark Beech?

IV

The Norman Conquest and Beyond

THE NORMAN CONQUEST probably made very little difference to Mark Beech and any people living there, despite the fact that the Conquest led to the most extensive transfer of land ownership in English history, as King William rewarded his followers, secured his new kingdom and treated it as a land for plunder and subjugation. Norman French was the language of the new élite, but charters and other documents continued to be written in Latin and even occasionally in Old English. With the passage of time Old English and French fused to form a language closer to the one which we now understand and use, although the ruling classes continued to use French until the later 14th century and in the 16th century Henry VIII wrote some of his love letters to Anne Boleyn in French, though there may have been particular reasons for that.[1]

Most of the English landowners were dispossessed, although, apart from those who had died in battle and a small number who continued violently to resist the new régime, few were killed by the new masters. The Battle of Hastings occurred on 14 October 1066 and the victorious Normans first went eastwards to Dover and Canterbury. More than a month later they advanced on London and a detachment of the army passed close to Mark Beech at Bletchingley, Godstone, Tandridge, Oxted, Limpsfield, Titsey and Westerham, causing considerable devastation as it did so.[2] Before going around London to the south and west, William advanced to Lewisham, Camberwell and Battersea, but there is no evidence of molestation of the priory at Lewisham as the Normans generally respected church property and, in any case, Flanders was William's ally, the Conqueror being married to a daughter of the Count of Flanders, Baldwin V (although the count's sister was also married into the family of King Harold!). As we have seen, most of the land around Mark Beech was held by ecclesiastical tenants-in-chief so the Conquest would have involved little change. However, Mark Beech lay in the area of strategic importance between London and Normandy, so many of William's closest supporters were installed in Kent and Sussex. These men included William I's half-brother, Odo, bishop of Bayeux, who was created earl of Kent, and Robert, Count of Mortain, whom we shall meet again, his father's cousin Robert, Count of Eu, and his cousins William de Warenne and Roger Montgomery, all of whom were given extensive amounts of land in the two counties.[3] For Mark Beech the most important person was the king's second cousin, Richard, known as Richard of Tonbridge or Richard, son of Count Gilbert, or Richard

FitzGilbert, who had fought with William at Hastings. This family eventually acquired land all over England and later adopted the name of Clare, from their land in Suffolk.[4] At the key strategic position of Tonbridge, where a bridge had been or was built across the Medway, a castle was erected, of which Richard was made the custodian. Richard and his descendants were given a large quantity of land around this settlement, which was to be known as the Lowy, from the French *lieu/banlieue*, of Tonbridge.[5] This was an area over which the Clares exercised a jurisdiction separate from that of the hundred, in which it was situated, and was to be the cause of endless disputes with archbishops of Canterbury. Perambulations of its boundaries in 1259 and 1279 show that the Lowy extended no nearer to Mark Beech than Charcott and Speldhurst, about four to five miles away,[6] but Domesday Book tells us that in 1086 Wallington, long in Surrey, held a wood in Kent, which was tenanted by Robert the Latin and held 'as of the king' by Richard of Tonbridge and that Richard had expelled a 'rustic' from a virgate of land with a wood in Somerden.[7] K.P. Witney has identified this wood as being part of or adjacent to what was to become the manor of Cowden Leighton, from Robert the Latin, and which with Cowden Lewisham constituted the two most important manors in Cowden.[8] Cowden Leighton, around Crippenden, was to the west of Cowden Lewisham as described in chapter three above.[9] The Clares held considerable amounts of land in Surrey and in Kent outside the Lowy of Tonbridge and evidence that they had interests round Mark Beech is provided by the fact that, in 1314, Gilbert de Clare reclaimed the advowson of Cowden from John de Uvedale.[10] From 1217 the Clares were earls of Gloucester and Hertford, and Gilbert, who was to be killed at the battle of Bannockburn in 1314, was a nephew of King Edward II, his father having married the king's sister, Joan. A John de Ovedale was a Clare sub-tenant at Titsey and was certainly the same person as above.[11] A successful reclamation of the Cowden advowson implies that the Clares had a prior right to it, although how far back in time this right went we do not know and their interest in it is recorded in the relevant Inquisition of Post-Mortem after Gilbert's death in Scotland.[12] A further holding of the Clares was Filston-by-Shoreham, which, by 1171, had been detached from Otford and assigned by the archbishop to them. This is important for Mark Beech as this manor's appendages included Tyehurst in Chiddingstone, which extended to Newtye Hurst, part of which is in Mark Beech.[13] Tyehurst itself first appears as Tryndhurst, a pig holding, in a charter of King Edgar in 966.[14]

It has often been said that Domesday Book did not include the area around Somerden. It is true that the commissioners made no detailed survey of the area because it was very lightly settled and was still heavily forested, but some information on the area is included with manors to the north, with which it was associated. At the time of the Conquest it has been estimated that the population of Kent as a whole was about 40-50,000.[15] Darby calculated that the Mark Beech area had one of the lowest population densities at the time in England south of the Mersey and Trent and that only two other areas, in the extreme west of Cornwall and a pocket in Herefordshire on the border with Wales, were comparable.[16] Yet though the area was undoubtedly very sparsely populated it may not have been as sparse as Darby maintained since the population of the Wealden dens was included without distinction from that of the manors of north Kent. Nevertheless, Domesday does contain snippets of information on the area: it tells us, for example, that the king himself held the manor of Dartford, and St Peter's, Ghent, held Lewisham. Domesday says that the manor of Dartford had 'eight small and three large dens' in the Weald. It distinguishes the dens of the archbishop's manors at Sundridge from the Dartford dens, which included Oakenden at Chiddingstone Hoath and Frienden on the borders of Chiddingstone and Cowden, both of which are just outside Mark Beech.[17] Unfortunately Domesday does not describe the Lewisham dens, but it does tell us that the priory at Lewisham had the right of pannage for 50 pigs, although without more detail we cannot know whether this was at Sydenham and Forest Hill or in the High Weald, and that the whole manor having been worth £12 in Edward the Confessor's time was now worth £30. It includes the earliest recorded name of any place in Mark Beech, except, perhaps, for the churches at Cowden and Hever in the *Textus Roffensis*.[18] The Surrey Domesday section records Bramsells, meaning a 'miry place where there are brambles', as one of the tenements of the manor of Limpsfield, which itself was held of Battle Abbey which also held tenements at Brook Street, Clatfields, Cobhambury and Gilridge.[19] Battle Abbey had recently been founded by William I on the site of the Battle of Hastings. Bramsells is in Hever, but only just, and would today be considered within Mark Beech. It is on the north side of the ancient road which passes through Mark Beech and forms the boundary between Cowden and Hever about four hundred yards west of Mark Beech crossroads.

Over the following three hundred years or more the names of other places in or close to Mark Beech appear in documents for the first time. Such places included Buckhurst in 1232 (this is probably what is now known as Old Buckhurst, but it might be the Buckhurst between Bramsells and Jessups), Bramsells for the second time in 1240, Leighton Manor in 1260, Blowers Hill in 1278, Crippenden in 1278, Tyehurst again in 1292, Brocas in 1297, Bassetts in 1323, Hoppers Bank in 1323, Rickwoods in 1420, Pyle Gate in 1511, Cole Allen in 1545, Hole Farm in 1589 and Edells in 1622.[20] We have suggested that the name of Mark Beech itself goes back to not later than the 10th century, but the first written record of the village occurs in a lease document of 1461, where it is recorded as Markebeche. This document is so important for Mark Beech that it is worth quoting it in full:

Thomas Wykenden of Cowden

Grants

Walter Durkynghall

John Hamond

& Richard Saxpayse

a piece of land Elveland in Cowden,

to the highway Cowden Cross to Edenbridge E,

to land of road of Rd. Saxpayse, land of

the Prior of Mechilham W, land of Thomas

Wykenden called CLENDEN N. 3s 5d rent

Which sd. Rd. Saxpayse, the tenant of

WIKENDEN annually paid for lands called

REDENE, BLOWERSHILL, MARKEBECHE & COWKESCROFT

in Cowden

Witnessed [large number of witnesses]

Dated at Cowden 29 Sept. 39 Henry VI [1461] [21]

The first observation is that this document is in English, demonstrating that by the 15th century English had become the official, as well as the demotic, language, at least at this level of transaction. (It will also be noted that there is no consistency of spelling within quite a short

11   Bramsells, 1998.
(Paul Houlton)

piece.) Secondly, it would seem that four bits of land are involved: the bit called Elveland, the land of Richard Saxpayse, the land around Clenden, and the land called Redene, etc. Thirdly, the document shows that Mark Beech was regarded as an area of its own. Finally, it mentions two families, who were prominent in the history of Cowden, namely Wykenden and Saxby, whose name is preserved in the large house to the east of Cowden crossroads.

Of the places mentioned in this lease it is possible to identify with certainty all but one. Elveland appears in many documents, although usually with different spellings such as Elvyelands, Iveylands, Ivelands and Ivylands.[22] As we have already seen, it is at Pyle Gate.[23] Clenden cannot be other than Claydene. Redene causes slightly more difficulty: on other documents are to be found Ealderedene [Old Redene], Riddens, Rydden and Riddings. From the 1841 Tithe Map we find that Old Ridings and Ridings are fields to the south-west of Waystrode Manor. Upper Riddens is a field on the eastern side of Spode Lane, due west of Claydene. More likely, however, is Riddens, which is a field on the east side of Wickens Lane, just past the entrance to Rickwoods.[24] Blowershill and Markebeche retain the same names today. The only real problem is Cowkescroft, which has not been found in any other document from the 15th century to the present day. Cocksredene, Cockestands and Cockelands are names to be found in the area. Of other possibilities Calves Croft is a field due south of Crippenden, Cowfield is on the western side of Spode Lane, not far from Upper Riddens, and Coxland is a field at Friendly Green. Of all the alternatives, however, the one which does look very interesting is Cowden Croft. This, as late as the mid-18th century, was the name of the field on the south side of the Mark Beech-Pound road, upon part of which Mark Beech church now stands, the rest of which is now known as Church Field. Indeed it was the name still used for this field in the mid-19th century. On the grounds that the name contains the word 'croft' (meaning an enclosed piece of, usually arable, land) and that it fits geographically with the other places mentioned, we can propose that this is the Cowkescroft in the 1461 document, right in the heart of Mark Beech, as we know it today.[25]

At the time of the Conquest it was essential that the Abbey at Ghent and its offshoot at Lewisham should get their estate confirmed formally by the new rulers. There are extant

11 post-Conquest charters, which confirm St Peter's in possession of the manor of Lewisham and its appurtenances, or purport to do so.[26] The post-1066 charters raise the same problems of authenticity as the Saxon ones, and Opperman, for example, suggested that all the charters which predate that of King John in 1209 may be imitations of this 13th-century document.[27] Only the charter of William I, one of the most dubious, repeats the detailed naming of the dens which was included in Edward the Confessor's charter.[28] Thereafter, the Norman and Angevin charters conventionally deal with the matter in such terms as 'the manor of Lewisham and its appurtenances'. Typical, for example, is the confirmation of the manor of Lewisham to Ghent by Henry II in 1160, which states that with the manor went 'its dens in Andreswald with their customs and assigns' [translation from the original Latin].[29] Authentic or not, it is important to note these charters and they are, in chronological order: William I in 1081;[30] William II at 1087-91;[31] Henry I at 1103-05;[32] Henry I in 1109;[33] Henry I at 1114-16;[34] Stephen in 1136;[35] Henry II in 1160;[36] John in 1209;[37] Henry III in 1229;[38] Edward II in 1317[39] and Edward III in 1374.[40] In addition there are five Papal documents, issued between 1145 and 1246, which effectively support St Peter's claims, and thereafter the Papacy seem to take no further involvement in the matter of St Peter's rights in Lewisham for nearly two hundred years because it had no need to do so.[41] This sequence of charters represents very clearly a concerted effort by Ghent to establish its rights and an unequivocal indication that the Crown, through the legal system, recognised St Peter's tenure of the manor of Lewisham and its appurtenances in Cowden, which included Mark Beech, over a very long time.

On at least two occasions in the 13th century, St Peter's had to defend its claims against interlopers, but each time its rights were upheld. The second and more serious case, against Robert de Bampton, son of Walter de Douai, lord of the manor of Lee, was settled by Henry III in favour of the abbey in 1222.[42] Popes Eugenius III in 1145 and Alexander III, at a date between 1160 and 1180, confirmed Lewisham to Ghent,[43] and in 1226 Honorius III twice threatened to excommunicate anyone who interfered with the abbot's property.[44] On 25 September 1246 Innocent IV granted protection to Ghent's properties.[45] In the meantime the manor of Penshurst Halimote, with its tiny enclave in Mark Beech, continued to be held by the archbishop.

The State Archive of East Flanders at Ghent is the depository for many documents concerning the Abbey of St Peter and St Paul and its cell at Lewisham, in England. Many of these documents have been published by Saint-Genois, Lokeren, Fayen, Opperman and others, and they exemplify the extent to which Ghent maintained its connections with Lewisham and, thus, to Cowden and Mark Beech throughout the Middle Ages. It would be a mistake to imagine the priory at Lewisham as one might conventionally imagine such an institution. This priory, like its mother house in Flanders, was a Benedictine house of black monks, but it did not possess a priory church and conventual buildings, nor a monastic community which elected its prior.[46] The prior was appointed by the abbot of Ghent and lived in a manor house, probably at Rushey Green, and he supervised a small number of monks, who had also been sent over from Flanders.[47] There was probably a chapel within the manor house and the priory appropriated the parish church at Lewisham towards the end of the 12th century, after long disputes with the bishop of Rochester, although in 1376 it was to lose its advowsons at both Lewisham and Greenwich.[48] Ghent was interested in its Kentish properties only as a source of revenue, and one historian has described the manor as merely 'a local rent-collecting station'.[49] This is most revealing for the attitude of Ghent towards its English possessions, including those in the High Weald. In 1281 a lengthy register was compiled which listed all the possessions of the abbey, including the lands in England held through Lewisham. This register indicates that Lewisham held 996 acres plus another 120 acres at Greenwich, and this includes land held in the forest. The inventory repeats many of the places first mentioned in the charters of 1044 and 1081 and lists the tenants there. These included three at Essore—William, Martin and Sampson, two at Scarendene—Roger and Nicholas Sroppe, one at Wigindenn—William—and one at Elyslegghetre, undoubtedly Elysland, another William. There are also several references to Westrhide, which must be the modern Waystrode, which is not usually associated with Cowden Lewisham.[50] In addition to this important register there are inventories and other documents which mention Cowden Lewisham's properties in 1336, 1343 and 1376.[51]

The presence of an alien priory and foreign monks, particularly at such a sensitive place as the approaches to London, led to rising suspicion on the part of English kings, especially as war with France became endemic from the late 13th century. There was increasing xenophobia and talk of spies. On three occasions—in 1295, when the prior was sent to Oxford, in 1310 and in 1327—kings took the manor 'temporarily' within their direct control, and in 1337 alien houses were forbidden to send money abroad, although Lewisham may very well have ignored this order and got away with it.[52] The properties were always returned to Ghent, but with the renewal of the French wars in 1369-70 Edward III again sequestrated the estate, even though he acknowledged St Peter's ultimate claim to the manor in 1374.[53] In connection with this event, another inventory was drawn up in 1370 by the king's escheator, Johannes de Bishoppeston, which revealed the large number of sub-infeudations that had occurred in the previous century. It showed that the manor had been reduced to a mere 100 acres with 58 remaining at Greenwich.[54] During the reign of Richard II (1377-99) a petition was delivered to the Crown regarding the Priory's land, and there is also an extant receipt of rents for these properties.[55] In 1396 a further report on Ghent's Lewisham property was made by Gilles Delapporte,[56] but despite alien houses being restored in 1399 by Henry IV, in 1402 the Commons petitioned for the seizure of all such institutions that could not prove their independence. Once again Lewisham seems to have escaped the consequences of such a policy.[57]

What all this demonstrates is that St Peter's rights to Lewisham, including the Wealden extensions, were recognised by authority throughout the period from the Conquest to the early 15th century, although, as the main interest of Ghent was rents, a great deal of sub-infeudation into mainly secular hands took place from at least the 13th century, if not earlier. In Lewisham proper six sub-manors—Bankers, Brockley, Catford, Bellington, Shrafholt and Sydenham—which, in themselves, shows the large geographical extent of the manor, had come into existence by 1290-91,[58] when the statute of *Quia Emptores* made such infeudation illegal.[59] This process undoubtedly occurred within Cowden Lewisham also and this probably explains a puzzle respecting Mark Beech and its neighbourhood.

We have seen that the lease of 1461, in which Mark Beech is mentioned explicitly for the first time, mentioned lands held by the Prior of Michelham.[60] Since at least the publication of Hasted's *History of Kent* in the late 18th century, it has been assumed that the manor of Cowden Lewisham was held by the Priory of Michelham, in Sussex, although in his *Villare*

Cantianum Philipott correctly wrote that Lewisham was held by St Peter's, Ghent, citing the Charter Rolls for 1225.[61] Clearly it is impossible for Ghent and Michelham to have held Cowden Lewisham simultaneously *in capite*. Thus some reconciliation must be found, if there is one, and it is here that we must introduce Agnes de Montacute.

Agnes de Montacute was married in about 1220 to William de Montacute or Monte Acuto or Montagu, but by about 1232 was a widow.[62] It is often very difficult to establish the familial origins of married women from non-aristocratic but landholding backgrounds in the early medieval period because no records survive, or have been found, which provide the information, and such is the case with Agnes. We do not know from which family Agnes came, but it was probably a Sussex one. That she came from the upper levels of the land-holding community is shown by her own holding of land and her marriages to Montacute and, secondly, to Nicholas Malemains, one of the knights of the Warennes, earls of Surrey, who were of national importance and who held, *inter alia*, the great castle at Lewes and that at Reigate.[63] Malemains's immediate son was a royal household knight. Agnes's first mother-in-law was a Warenne, and it is just possible, although unlikely, that she came from this family too. An alternative is that she came from the Dene or Sackville families, who held land in Hartfield, although neither Salzman's nor Phillips's large studies of the Sackvilles, provides confirmation,[64] or else from the De Aquilas family, lords of Pevensey, who held land in the southern end of Hartfield. The most reasonable guess, given the situation of land which may have been her marriage dowry, as we shall see below, is that she came from the de Brom family, leading land-holders in Hartfield during the reigns of Edward I and Edward II.[65] Her name as William de Montacute's wife, as his widow and as the wife of her second husband, Nicholas Malemains, occurs in several documents, but there is never any clue as to her antecedents and this problem remains a matter for further research.[66] Her first husband, by whom she had two daughters, Margaret, who married Sir William of Etchingham, and Isobel (Isabelle),[67] was descended from Alvred, the butler of Count Robert de Mortain, already mentioned, who was rewarded by the Conqueror with the Rape of Pevensey. By 1086 Alvred held land in Buckinghamshire, Cornwall, Devon, Dorset, Northamptonshire, Nottinghamshire, Sussex and Yorkshire, as well as an estate at Montacute in Somerset, where his neighbour was Dru de Monte Acuto. He had, therefore, risen in the hierarchy of the new Norman establishment. By the early 13th century his descendants were using the name Montagu, even though they seem to have had no blood or marriage connections with the Somerset Montagus, a family which became very important at the court of Edward I, II and III, holding from 1337 the title of earls of Salisbury.[68] The Sussex William married Agnes in about 1220 and, although they were peripatetic around their estates, their base was in Sussex. As was customary with such landed families, the Montagus were generous to the Church; for example, in 1226 William and Agnes gave land in Northamptonshire to the Priory of Daventry in return for which the prior agreed to provide them with a chaplain whenever they were in residence at Preston, Northamptonshire.[69] Just before his death, probably in 1232, William gave the chapel at Jevington, near Eastbourne, and all its appurtenances to Michelham Priory, which had been founded as an Augustinian house in 1229 by William de Aquilla/Acquilas, now lord of the Rape of Pevensey.[70] Agnes had no doubt received a marriage dowry and this is how she was able, soon after her husband's gift, to give all her demesne in Hartfield and Cowden to Michelham. At dates unknown over the following 90 years, although probably in the mid-13th century, two other pieces of land in Cowden or Hartfield were given to Michelham: these were Greggeslond, given by Sir Walter de Letton and his wife, Gunnora, of Cowden Leighton, and Warefield, given by Thomas Wickenden.[71] Greggeslond, at least, must have been donated before 1261 because in that year Roger, Prior of Michelham, brought a case against Sir Walter de Letton and Gunnora.[72] These four gifts were confirmed by a royal inspection of Michelham, which is incorporated in a charter made at Windsor on 20 November 1320.[73] An *Inspeximus* involved the inspection and confirmation of earlier charters and it is noticeable that, as well as confirming Michelham's demesne in 1320, Edward II had already confirmed Cowden Lewisham to Ghent in 1317.[74] A second inspection of Michelham was undertaken in 1412;[75] this confirms the charter of 1320 and one from a bishop of Chichester. The document of *Inspeximus* then lists 11 letters patent issued between 1281 and 1392, all of which are relevant to Michelham, but not one mentions Hartfield or Cowden, although they probably would not have done so as all the letters are concerned with mortmain and Michelham was a corporate entity which did not die.

The land held by Agnes de Montacute in Cowden has been identified as being Upper and Lower Priory (now Cross) Farms on the north-west quadrant of Cowden crossroads. Indeed a list of Cowden Church Marks drawn up in 1542 explicitly describes these tenements as 'lands sometyme of Michelham'.[76] Greggeslond and Warefield are both to be found in the extreme south of the parish along Kent Water, which, as we have seen, was almost certainly not in Cowden Lewisham, and Agnes's land in Hartfield was Holywych Farm, just across Kent Water in Sussex.[77] It is also very suggestive that about three hundred yards from Kent Water on the Sussex side there is a farm once known as Gunnore, now called Nore Farm.[78] It is very difficult to see how Agnes de Montacute could have become the tenant-in-chief of Cowden Lewisham in place of St Peter's, Ghent, without documentary evidence, of which none has been found, and in the light of our other evidence it seems unlikely. After the Statute of Mortmain of 1279 a Licence of Mortmain, granted by the Crown, could provide us with the means to discover the information, including Agnes's origins, but this is too late, nor do the Inquisitions Post Mortem provide any clue as to how Agnes acquired her demesnes. No evidence of such a transfer to her has been found and, moreover, we have seen that kings confirmed Ghent's possession by charter not only in 1229 and 1317, but also in 1374, and there are priory documents referring to the land in the Weald in 1281, 1336, 1343, 1370 and 1376.[79] In 1371 and 1399 there is evidence that Shernden, which included Clatfields and Cobhambury, was held by Lord Cobham of the abbot and monks of St Peter's, Ghent, Lords of the Manor of Lewisham.[80]

We must conclude, therefore, that Agnes de Montacute never held the manor of Cowden Lewisham as tenant-in-chief. There are three possible explanations: one, the land given by Agnes was her own demesne and not part of Cowden Lewisham and that, therefore, Cowden Lewisham never extended to Kent Water; two, the land given was part of the manor of Cowden Leighton, as were the gifts of Sir Walter de Letton and Thomas Wickenden, and it is most significant that in 1419 a representative of the prior of Michelham attended the Manor Court of Cowden Leighton, the prior having been declared in default six years earlier, and never, at any time, as far as is recorded, did so for Cowden Lewisham;[81] three, Agnes was a tenant of Lewisham—we have noted the sub-infeudation—and it was her tenancy of part of Cowden Lewisham, presumably to the south of the parish, near the

boundary with Hartfield, which she gave to Michelham. Some credence is given to the third
explanation by a document of 1671 called 'The Tytle of Lewisham', which shows that the
tenants at that time, and by inference therefore their predecessors, were copyholders of the
manor of Lewisham, not lords of the manor,[82] but the evidence concerning Leighton is so
compelling that we conclude that the second explanation, or possibly a combination of the
first and the second, is the most likely.

The view that Michelham never held Cowden Lewisham is reinforced by the records
of Lewisham Manor Court, which, like the inventory of 1281, contain many references to
the High Weald and the Mark Beech area, especially to tenancies and related matters. To
take a few examples: in 1284 Isabell of Essore pleaded before the court; in 1299 William
of Shernden, William Wygenden, Richard Cosin and Osbert Rakke de Wald were twice
recorded as being in default of payments to Lewisham; in 1413 Thomas Wygenden paid
heriot of 16s. 9d. on the death of his father, William; in 1420 the abbot of Battle, Reginald
Cobham and William Wygenden failed to attend the court, although whether they were
liable to do so at that date is unlikely, as we shall see.[83] Most interesting of all is a list of
rents paid 'in Walda' in 1320 and which runs as follows: William of Assher 16s. 6d., William
Wygenden 9s. 7d., Martin of Asshere 9s. 9d., Sampson of Asshere 3s. 11d., William and
Roger of Shernden 3s. 9d., Nicholas Scripp 6d. and William of Shernden 11d.[84] It is
noticeable that this list is contemporaneous with the royal inspection of Michelham and
that most of the names are the same as those in the inventory of 1281. A 40-year gap is
a large one, but it does seem that rents and other payments were being made to Lewisham
and not to Michelham.

Nevertheless, severance of the connection between Ghent and Lewisham came 120
years before the Reformation. As we have seen, the manor was restored by the Crown in
1399, but in 1402 the Commons petitioned for the seizure of all remaining alien houses that
could not prove their independence.[85] Somehow Lewisham escaped, but in 1414, at the so-
called Leicester Parliament, the Commons again petitioned Henry V to sequestrate irrevocably
the estates of all alien priories, although the spontaneity of this must be doubted, and this
was achieved by Act of Parliament.[86] The following year the Lewisham demesnes were settled
by the king on his newly-founded Carthusian abbey at Sheen, Surrey, and this transfer
included 'the priory with the manor of Lewisham and Greenwich in the county of Kent,
being the alien appendages of the Abbey of St Peter of Ghent in Flanders' [my translation
from the original Latin].[87] Thus, for a brief time Mark Beech passed into the Lordship of
Sheen, although Henry V's action was the subject of much protest by the abbey at Ghent
to the Carthusians and, eventually, the Papacy. In 1433 Pope Eugenius IV declared in favour
of Ghent,[88] but the decision could not be enforced in the face of the English king's (by now
Henry VI) lack of co-operation. Ghent tried again, but in 1455 Nicholas V declared in favour
of Sheen.[89] So Mark Beech remained in the hands of Sheen and the archbishop, as Lord of
Penshurst Halimote, with Michelham a tenant in the south, until all the land in Cowden
in ecclesiastical hands was alienated to the Crown in the 1530s.

The economy and landscape of the territory over which these monasteries had control
evolved gradually throughout the Middle Ages. Clearly there were a growing number of
settlements in Mark Beech, although the population must have remained very small. It
remained, naturally, an area primarily of pastoral agriculture. Before the Conquest this

involved principally the maintenance of pigs with, perhaps, a few cattle. Increasingly swine were replaced by sheep, although how far this was so in Mark Beech is uncertain because sheep-rearing required clearance of the forest and the creation of open pasture.[90] The woods of the Weald and of the High Weald were progressively cleared over a period of about three hundred years after the Conquest, especially in the 12th and 13th centuries, and major clearance and colonisation had probably occurred by the third quarter of the 14th century. Nevertheless, it is likely that a part of the forest as remote as Mark Beech may not have been cleared entirely until the 16th or even the 17th century.[91] Meanwhile some arable farming had been introduced with the cultivation of oats and some wheat.[92] Professor Everitt has suggested that it is a myth that Kent, other than the parishes close to London, was ever a very prosperous county before early modern times, and even before the onset of the Black Death the High Weald remained the poorest part of the south-east of England.[93]

As the exercise of the rights of pannage declined to be replaced by other forms of agriculture the practical, if not the legal, links between the northern manors and the dens atrophied and the old Jutish system began to fade away.[94] Subordinate manors began to be formed, and this process is exemplified by the Hever part of Mark Beech, where the evolution of the manor was less complicated than in Cowden. In the pre-Conquest period Hever existed as the inter-mingling of the dens of Bexley, Brasted, Orpington, Plumstead, Limpsfield and, possibly, others.[95] The Brasted dens had included Brasted Lands, Delaware and Stanford's End, and as late as 1156 the Plumstead den of Plum Paddock was still described as a swine pasture,[96] but this phenomenon was getting rarer. By the early 13th century a string of manors was beginning to form along the banks of the river Eden and the Delaware family, for example, had been established on the Hever-Edenbridge border with their own demesnes.[97] Delaware had been formed from Brasted dens, but by 1274 knights' fees had been created by the archbishop out of dens which had once belonged to Bexley.[98] Thus was created the manor of Hever, at that date held jointly by William and Sir Ralph de Hevre. In about 1350 another William de Hevre was in sole possession of the manor and he built a new manor house. William died leaving two co-heiresses, Joan, who was married to Reginald Cobham, and Margaret, married to Sir Oliver Brocas. The manor was thus divided again, the two halves being known as the manor of Hever Cobham, which included what was to become the castle, and the manor of Hever Brocas.[99] In 1383 Sir John Cobham was granted royal permission to castellate his manor house and thus came into existence the fortified manor house known as Hever Castle.[100] The two manors, though retaining their distinct names, were reunited in the early 15th century when Brocas was alienated to Reginald, Lord Cobham. In 1462 these manors were sold to Sir Geoffrye Bulleyn (or Bullen or Boleyn), a wealthy London mercer and lord mayor in 1457-8, who already held land in Norfolk.[101]

Mark Beech lay predominantly within or adjacent to Hever Brocas, although the small manor of Bramsells, for example, remained an independent enclave until the 17th century and Buckhurst lay within Hever Brocas. The divide between Cobham and Brocas lay along Pigdown (Pigden) Lane and Uckfield Lane, and a tongue of Cobham went east of the present crossroads and over Mark Beech Hill to Horseshoe Green. It has been suggested that a road provided the eastern boundary between Hever and Cowden,[102] and in the 19th century there was a road which went south up the hill from a point just east of the present site of High Buckhurst. There was a gate at the bottom and physical inspection still shows the remains of this road today, but it only proceeds to a very large and deep pond on the north-east corner of the hill and there is no visible sign of it continuing over the top to the south side of Buckhurst Wood.[103] In any case the route of this road does not correspond to the parish boundary. Possibly the road and the pond date from the revival of the Wealden iron industry in the 16th century.

The building of the stone churches represented a further important change in the area. At both Hever and Cowden the building of the new churches, essentially much the same today, dates from the turn of the 11th and 12th centuries.[104] We have seen that wooden churches probably existed at both places as early as 1000, but, if so, they were replaced by new stone churches about three hundred years later. Apart from the *Textus Roffensis*, there are documentary references to the church at Cowden in 1115, although there are references to the place from 1100, and to the church at Hever in 1200.[105] At the latter date Walter de Hevre granted the advowson of Hever to the Priory of Cumbwell (or Combwell) near Goudhurst, which had been founded during the reign of Henry II, between 1154 and 1189, and the prior provided Hever's first rector, Le Neve.[106] The implication must be that Walter or his predecessor were tenants in Hever and held the advowson before 1200. The nave and chancel at Hever began to be constructed in 1292.[107] The church at Cowden was built in the first quarter of the 14th century, Ewing suggesting that it was started by Gilbert Clare soon after 1300.[108] This is possible, but it is the opinion of Dr. Jennifer C. Ward, who is an expert on the Clare family and their estates, that this is unlikely on the grounds that the Clares were notably parsimonious, that Gilbert was a minor until 1312, and that it was more usual for the nobility, including the Clares, to patronise monastic houses rather than parish churches.[109] The first recorded Rector of Cowden is Henry Bonzi in 1322.[110]

The 14th and 15th centuries witnessed considerable instability in England caused by the frequent wars with France between 1337 and 1453, weak rule in the early and late 14th and the mid-15th centuries, and a semi-anarchic situation at the bottom of society created both by the foregoing and by such events as the onset of pandemic plague which changed the bargaining power of labour in its favour and created an atmosphere of insubordination.[111] The manorial system seems to have been very badly damaged by the famine of 1314-16, when excessive rain ruined the harvests,[112] and a further destabilising twist was created by bubonic plague, which reached England in 1348 and is thought over the next few years to have killed between a third and a half of the population.[113] Many English villages eventually disappeared, although this was a long-term process. One such may have been Frienden just outside Mark Beech.[114] After the plague reached Kent in spring 1349 it became one of the worst affected counties.[115] We have no records of the plague specific to Mark Beech, other than the tantalising speculation regarding Frienden, but we would be wrong to suppose it was less severe in rural than in urban areas. The ancient bishop of Rochester survived, having moved to Trottiscliffe, but within his entourage deaths included four priests, five squires, ten household servants, seven young clerks and six pages.[116] The Archbishop of Canterbury died and was replaced by Thomas Bradwardine of Cowden, but he died immediately upon his return from Rome.[117] The aftermath of the plague was a dire shortage of labourers to cultivate the land, a shortage of priests to serve the churches and, later, a general atmosphere of rebelliousness. As for priests, it was not that so many died, but many fled to places they thought would be safer.[118] At Michelham seven out of eleven of the brethren died.[119]

An air of discontent pervaded the later Middle Ages, epitomised by the three disturbances of 1381, 1450 and 1471. The first two were peasants' revolts, those of Wat Tyler and Jack Cade, but the third involved the nobility and the towns to a greater extent. Kent took a prominent role in all three uprisings. Tyler's affair in Kent and Essex was largely confined in Kent to the north and east of the county so did not involve Mark Beech.[120] The second revolt was a much more widespread matter and there was a major military encounter between the rebels and royal forces which was won by the former at Solefields, Sevenoaks, about eight miles from Mark Beech, on Thursday 18 June 1450.[121] Twenty thousand men descended from Kent on London but were repulsed with great slaughter. Although a general pardon was promised in order to get them out of London, Iden, the Sheriff of Kent, hunted down many of the rebels in Kent and into Sussex and 25 were killed at Sevenoaks.[122] The rebellion centred around Ashford, but participants were drawn from all over Kent, including at least nine men from Chiddingstone and four from Hever, although none are recorded as being from Cowden. The men from Hever included John Clerk, John Cavet and William Wymbyth.[123] There is an oral tradition, unconfirmed by any other kind of evidence, that Jack Cade met some of the local rebels at Truggers Farm, in Truggers Lane, just outside Mark Beech.[124] The lists of those pardoned included William Warde, the Constable of Somerden, but Professor R.A. Griffiths has pointed out that these lists must be treated with great caution. It may be that the less active rebels were seeking pardons as security against future punishment, and the constable may have been acting as an agent for the inhabitants of his hundred by seeking security for neighbours and fellow subjects. It does not mean that Warde was a participant in the rebellion.[125]

Our final view of Mark Beech in the later medieval period provides us with a colourful example of the lawlessness which sometimes prevailed in rural areas in the aftermath of Cade's rebellion. In June 1451 about thirty-five men, including two members of the Saxpays family, two men from Edenbridge, one from Chiddingstone and one, Thomas Crudde, from Hever, caused an affray at Penshurst, about three and a half miles from Mark Beech. They were brought before the King's Bench at Tonbridge on 30 June the king dispensing justice in person.[126] Their indictment claimed that they had assembled 'in riotous manor and arrayed for war'. They were:

covered with long beards and painted on their faces with black charcoal, calling themselves the queen of the fairies intending their names should not be known broke into a park of Humphrey, Duke of Buckingham called Redleaf at Penshurst and chased killed and took away from the said park 10 bucks, 12 sorels and 60 does belonging to the said Duke; against the king's peace and the form of the statute of the parks and fish-ponds lately I issued.[127]

What happened to these men is not recorded, but the ruling classes were ruthless in the protection of their hunting rights and, alarmed at the previous year's events, increased the severity of punishments, so we can guess.[128]

V

From Henry the Eighth to Queen Victoria

THE REFORMATION resembled the Norman Conquest in one respect: there was a very extensive transfer of land, in this case from ecclesiastical tenure to the Crown or to secular freeholders. This was of obvious significance for Mark Beech, and the lands sequestrated from Sheen and from Michelham are laid out in the *Valor Ecclesiasticus*, an inventory of ecclesiastical properties compiled in the 1530s at the time of the Suppression of the Monasteries. However, the Lewisham land at Cowden and Mark Beech is not itemised in this document because Henry VIII had already acquired the Manor of Lewisham prior to the Dissolution.[1] By the 1520s Henry was in the process of moving his main London palace to Greenwich, and in his desire to improve and expand his own place he cast covetous eyes on the adjacent properties which belonged to Sheen but which had once belonged to St Peter's, Ghent. First he tried to confiscate Lewisham on the grounds that it had been granted to Sheen by a usurper, i.e. the Lancastrian Henry V, but when this ploy was defeated by Sheen's appeal to the courts, which upheld the validity of their title, the king in 1530 exchanged Lewisham for land in Buckinghamshire, which had come to the Crown on the downfall of Wolsey.[2]

For a period of time Mark Beech came under the direct control of the Crown for the first time for about six hundred years. Henry's well-known association with the area arises, of course, from his courtship and marriage to Anne Boleyn, second daughter of the owner of Hever Castle, her elder sister, Mary, having previously been the king's mistress. In 1537, on the execution of Anne Boleyn's brother, Lord Rochford, Hever also was taken briefly into Crown possession so all of Mark Beech was in Henry VIII's hands,[3] but whether Henry ever passed through Mark Beech we shall never know, as there is no surviving evidence. Hever is not far south of Greenwich, but since the attainder of the Duke of Buckingham in 1521 the king had possessed Penshurst, which is about four miles east of Hever, and had made Sir Thomas Boleyn custodian.[4] According to the Spanish ambassador, Mendoza, in November 1528 Henry met Anne at a house about five miles from Hever, but precisely where this was is unknown.[5] It is possible that it was Penshurst. Alternatively, the Boleyns possessed a house at West Wickham, which is about halfway between Hever and Greenwich, but much more than five miles from Hever. Henry and Anne met there on other occasions and it is possible that Mendoza's five miles was a figure of speech or based on inadequate information.[6] Another possible venue was Hammerwood, near Holtye, a royal hunting-lodge about three miles from Hever. A further possibility is Gullege, another Boylen property, later to become part of Anne's marriage dowry, which is at Felbridge, about seven and a half miles from Hever. It is more likely, therefore, that Henry moved around the north, east and west of Hever, but we cannot exclude the possibility that from time to time he came southwards up the hill to Mark Beech, especially as he may have visited the hunting-lodges at Bolebrook, Hartfield or at Hammerwood, which would have taken him through Mark Beech; and we can speculate that Bolebrook, Hammerwood or Gullege might have been the place of assignation in 1528. Nevertheless, it must be noted that Anne Boleyn was not in residence at Hever quite as much as some popular films might suggest. Another of Henry VIII's wives, Katherine Parr, lived at Chiddingstone, her first husband having been the eldest son of Lord de Burgh, Lord of the Manor of Chiddingstone Cobham.

We have seen above how, over a very long time during the Middle Ages, occupation, if not ownership, of land in Mark Beech was consolidated into various individuals and families. The documents do not allow us to link every piece of land continuously with named individuals or families, but in the 16th century the events connected with the Reformation, especially the confiscation of ecclesiastical lands, and the gradual erosion of feudal forms of tenure, created in time a structure of freehold and leasehold tenures. Having passed to the Crown, what we will now call the freehold of Cowden Lewisham passed in 1534 to the king's executioner-in-chief, if not devisor, of the policies of the time, Thomas Cromwell.[7] On his downfall in 1540 it returned to the Crown, and then in 1542 it passed to the earl of Arundel, whose son returned it to the Crown in 1544.[8] Meanwhile Hever was given to Henry VIII's divorced fourth wife, Anne of Cleves, with whom it remained until her death in 1557.[9] After short periods in the possession of the Crown, Cowden Lewisham was conveyed to Richard Sackville and Thomas Winton in 1557, and Hever to Sir Edward and Dame Frances Waldegrave in the following year, with which family it was to remain until the mid-18th century.[10]

The Sackvilles were still in possession of Cowden Lewisham during the reign of Elizabeth I, but in the 17th century the fate of this manor becomes extraordinarily confused because, although there were identifiable lords of the manor, two tenants or copyholders acted as if they were the possessors.

It was claimed that Sackville and Winton had sold the estate in the late 16th century to one of the tenants, William Wickenden, whose grandson divided it equally between two sons in about the 1630s, and that one of these sons had alienated his half share to John Ashdowne. The Ashdowne share passed to the Pigott family, then to John Driver and next to the Streatfields, while the Wickenden half went to the Bassetts and then, via marriage to John Burgess, who held it in 1794.[11]

However, it seems clear that Wickenden and, later, Ashdowne were tenants or copyholders, not freeholders, for James I had granted the lordship of the manor in 1623 to the Ramsey family. In a case that started in 1659, but dragged on for several years, many tenants including Wickenden, Ashdowne, Michael Bassett, Thomas Friend, William Stephens, Edward and Richard Still, John Everest, Richard Jemett and John Streatfield were sued by the Lord for failing for many years to do suit and service at the lord's court and failing to pay due rents.[12] A compromise was reached in 1673 when 19 of the copyholders, including Thomas Gainsford, Thomas Streatfield, William Chapman, Henry Burgess, William Wicken, John Ashdowne and

Michael Bassett, enfranchised their holdings. About ten copyholders, including Edward Still, William Wickenden, William Saxby and Stephen Burfoot, did not enfranchise at that time, although some of them or their heirs did so over the next century or so.[13] It should be noted here that in 1659 the rent rolls had included the names of five Wickendens.[14]

In the Middle Ages the principal landholders included the Lettons, who held Cowden Leighton, but were succeeded there in 1451 by the Cobhams and then, in the 17th century, by the Burghs, who were descended from the Cobhams through a female line. The Cobhams were also tenants of Cowden Lewisham at Shernden from a very early date, but it was the Saxbys and the Wickendens who seem to have been the chief occupants of this manor, and it was the latter who probably occupied the Cowden part of Mark Beech proper.[15] The Saxbys and the Wickendens fade away as major landholders by the early 18th century, but from the 17th century we can begin to observe continuous occupation of many properties in Mark Beech and, inevitably, some other families begin to grow in prominence.

In the 17th century we find that John Ashdowne was the owner of Old Buckhurst, often known until recently as just Buckhurst, thereby causing confusion with the Hever Buckhurst, which is also in Mark Beech. In about 1680 it was actually occupied by Matthew Gainsford. Over the next century it was owned by Ashdowne's daughter, Mary Douglas, and her descendants. By 1796 it was occupied by Obadiah Longley, who had a 21-year lease, and owned by Susannah Payne, née Douglas, from whom it passed to a nephew, John Hargreaves Standen, in 1800, and then to his son, George Douglas Standen. In 1847 it was being farmed by Christopher Burfoot (as tenant), but six years later it was sold to John Saxby, this being the only example of a Saxby holding in Mark Beech by the 19th century.[16]

Broomyfields or Broomfields consisted of four fields on Hopper's Bank at Horseshoe Green. In 1743 it was held by Christopher Burfoot and it passed through Burfoot heirs until, in 1817, it was left to Thomas Kember and Richard Bassett and was occupied by William Bassett, who himself acquired it in 1833.[17] It might be appropriate here to note that for about 30 years in the late 20th century Broomyfields was owned by Dr. Norman Jacoby, who had come to England from South Africa between the two world wars to be a medical student in London and who became Consultant Paediatrician at Pembury Hospital. He wrote an interesting autobiography, but regrettably had nothing to say about Mark Beech.[18]

12 Broomyfields in 1998. (Paul Houlton)

Edells was owned by John Streatfield in 1718, when it was inherited by his daughter Sarah Thorpe, who bequeathed it to her daughter, also Sarah, who married a cousin, William Streatfield. In 1813 it was sold to Charles Brooke, who at that time also owned Claydene.[19] In 1833 it was bought by Colonel, later Major-General, William Woodhouse, of the Indian Army, who knocked down the old timber-framed house and replaced it in 1839-40 with what was described as an Indian-style villa, which we may suppose meant a house with a verandah around it or part of it. Indeed,

marks can still be seen on the wall at the
back of the house which probably indicate
where the verandah was. This was the first
structure in Mark Beech to be built
completely from brick or stone, pre-dating
both Falconhurst and the church by more
than a decade, although the *Queens Arms*
was being built in brick at about the
same time. General Woodhouse's brother,
George, inherited it in 1845.[20] On the same
access road as Edells was Coldharbour Farm,
whose land went down to where the
railway is now. The house no longer exists,
but in 1734 it was held by Alexander
Osborne, tenanted by Thomas Gainsford, and
was sold to William Streatfield. Thereafter,
it passed through the hands of several
Streatfields until it was sold to Charles
Brooke in 1813. In 1833 Colonel Woodhouse acquired it and it was absorbed into
Edells. It had, in fact, never been part of
Cowden Lewisham, but was a copyhold of
Penshurst Halimote and a mare was taken
as heriot on the death of Woodhouse in
1845.[21]

*13   Edells, seen here in 1998, has remained essentially
unchanged since 1875. (Paul Houlton)*

On the other side of Blower's Hill were several farms, of which the largest, at 76 acres,
was probably Wickens, known for a while at a later date as Gainsford's. In 1655 it belonged
to Bernard Hyde of Bore Place, Chiddingstone, and was occupied by Edward Swaysland and
Josias Johnson. In that year it was sold to Edward and Richard Still, father and son, and
remained with their family for 40 years, when it was sold by Bridgett Still, who had married
John Culpeper of Riverhead, to Thomas Wood. The Woods remained for about 130 years,
although as descent was through females the name changed to Bennett, to Sanders and to
Robinson. During this period the tenants included, at various dates, William Piggott, John
Friend, John Banister, John Gainsford and William Huntley. In 1829 it was sold to Joseph
Gainsford. One of the interesting things about this farm is the survival, in Great and Little
Hogfield, of field names which probably link the area to its Jutish past.[22] Nearby, on Mount
Noddy, was Curd's Farm, whose house was burnt down in the mid-19th century. It was only
of eight to nine acres and in 1775 was in the hands of George Wheeler. In 1780 it went
to John Glover, and in 1805 to William Burfoot, in whose family it was to remain for 70
years. By the late 19th century the tenant, however, was Winifrith, probably the publican at
Horseshoe Green.[23] To the south of Curd's lay Coleman's Farm, which in 1602 was held
by John Pelsett, passing to John Ashdowne in 1674, and which in the 18th century went
to the Piggotts and, briefly, to the Drivers, before being bought by Carew Sanders, the owner
of Curd's, in 1786.[24]

Up the road from Curd's lay Coles Farm, now known as Horseshoe Green Farm. This consisted of about 40 acres and in 1752 was held by William and Elizabeth Catt. This farm came to Thomas Potter in 1756, when the tenant was John Glover, and in 1789 it passed to William Cheesman and in 1813 to Mary Luck, his daughter, who married John Killick and whose son William Cheesman Killick inherited it in 1832. In 1841 the tenant was Christopher Burfoot.[25] Below the farm lies Horseshoe Cottage, an amalgamation of two 17th-century cottages. Ownership until the 20th century went with the farm and it was for a time a shop, which is visually obvious, but it is presently occupied by Mr. Peter Rayner, whose wife, Valerie, was formerly a dancer with the Royal Ballet, of which company Peter was for a period manager. He presently organises the Neighbourhood Watch scheme which operates in the village. Right down Blowers Hill, again, near Edells and Coleman's, Brook Farm and the Hole were to be found. The farmhouse for the former was situated near the present Cowden station but was destroyed when the railway was constructed, so the house at the top of Blowers Hill is a substitute and was formed out of two farm cottages. Brook, very small though it was, was divided into four parts, one of which was a small piece of land between Noddies and Curd's; the other three were known as Hayslands, Godmans and Chapmans Fields. Hayslands was owned by three generations of Piggotts from 1761 to 1792, when it passed to the Whatleys. Richard Kenneth Whatley had bought Godmans in 1788 from John Humphrey, it having previously been possessed by Edward Gaynsford. Chapmans Fields had once belonged to John Ashdowne, but from the mid-18th century was Medhurst property. In 1794 it too was acquired by the Whatleys, so from that time onwards the four pieces were amalgamated as Brook Farm. The Hole belonged to the Streatfields from about 1683 until it was sold to Colonel Woodhouse in 1835.[26] It first appears in Cowden records in 1589, but was probably built about a century earlier. It was almost certainly an impressive timber-framed house, but Woodhouse destroyed two-thirds of it, probably because it was in a bad state of repair, to create the Hole Cottage which can still be seen today, although that was further damaged on 7 March 1943 by a German bomb.[27] The Hole had once been in the occupation of the Wickendens, possibly since about 1500, and one of them had even been called Wickenden de la Hole.[28]

Up the other side of the hill from Cowden station is Friendly Green, with Saxbys, known in previous incarnations as Oakenden and as Potters, on the south side of the road. Neither is strictly in Mark Beech, but Friendly Green justifies inclusion if only because it became part of the Falconhurst estate. Part of it was further copyhold of Penshurst Halimote and in the 17th century some of it at least was held by the Saxbys.[29] It was also known as Bartletts, and from 1697 until 1835 it was yet another Streatfield property but was then sold to Colonel Woodhouse.[30]

North of Friendly Green is Pyle Gate (Pilegate), a small farm of 25 acres. For about 140 years it too was owned by the Streatfields and was sold like other bits of land to Colonel Woodhouse in 1835.[31] To the north of Pilegate is Alcocks or Lambert Cottage, which had about 10 acres. This too was Streatfield land until it was sold to the Rector of Cowden, Rev. Thomas Harvey, in 1811, when it was occupied by George Gainsford. It was inherited by Harvey's son, also Thomas and also Rector of Cowden, and sold to Woodhouse in 1836.[32] Adjacent to this small farm was Lords Land, upon which Falconhurst was eventually to be built. This too was Streatfield property until 1835 and we know that this land was let to Thomas Banister in 1674 for 21 years and to Christopher Burfoot in 1741 for 20 years.[33]

14 *Wickens, 1998*
(Paul Houlton).

15 *Horseshoe Green Farm, 1998.*
(Paul Houlton)

16 *Horseshoe Cottage, 1998.*
(Paul Houlton)

17 Pyle Gate (Pilegate), 1998.
(Paul Houlton)

The quadrilateral formed by The Pound/Mark Beech Cross/Horseshoe Green/Cowden Cross was completed in the east by the land upon which the heart of Mark Beech stands. The large quadrilateral was known as Eastlands and Lord's Land, which constituted the major part; the village church was eventually built on its extreme north-east corner and throughout the 18th and the first half of the 19th centuries it belonged to the Streatfields.[34] There were also some small enclaves of land along Cow Lane: first was the piece of Penshurst Halimote, of which the Burfoots were copyholders and eventually freeholders; second was Killicks, which is half of the land upon which the second and most recent vicarage was built. It was once owned by Richard Adgate and occupied by Thomas Killick, but from 1756 it belonged to Christopher Burfoot, who died in 1782 and who was succeeded by his son, also Christopher. The elder Christopher also had Buckhurst, Heathen Street and Jessups, and these went to his other sons, John and William. In 1817 Killicks was sold to Thomas Kember, a son-in-law, and Richard Bassett, with Hoppers Bank, but in 1833 went to Richard Banister and in 1836 to Colonel Woodhouse.[35]

The south-east corner of the crossroads was principally the property known as High Buckhurst. This consisted of Mutton Field (in fact on the west side of the road), the other half of the land of the vicarage, which was tenanted by the Banisters. It was owned by the Streatfields, then by the Woodhouses and, finally, by the Talbots. It included the land upon which the school and cottages were built and the major part of Mark Beech Hill excluding much of its northern slopes and the land to the east. This had belonged in the 17th century to Richard Swaysland and went to Bridget Culpeper, née Still, in 1695. By 1750 it was possessed by the Banister family, who also had a great deal of land in southern Hever, that is within or adjacent to the Hever sector of Mark Beech. High Buckhurst had once been Streatfield land and had been let to John Wickenden, for example, in 1626 for 20 years at £10 13s. 4d. It is this land, incidentally, which provides us with an example of inheritance by gavelkind as late as 1851, when Richard Banister died leaving four sons, three of whom, George, Henry and Edward, were to die intestate and unmarried. The eldest son, Richard, died in 1865, leaving one daughter, Elizabeth. At the age of 37 she married Henry Collins, aged 21, who was illiterate, on 24 February 1868, and gave birth to her first child, Clara, four days later. The Collins were to have at least two other children, Horace Banister, born in 1870, who was to build Woodside, the forerunner of the modern High Buckhurst, and Edith, born in 1871. Elizabeth died in 1886 and Henry in 1890 from consumption, aged only 43, but in the meantime they had inherited the properties that had once been her grandfather's. There is another example of gavelkind in Mark Beech, when this same property was partitioned equally in 1648 by Richard and Stephen Streatfield on the death of their father, Henry.[36]

The Land Tax records, which are very accessible and comprehensive for Mark Beech for the period 1780 to 1832, augment our knowledge of both the ownership and occupation of land in the area. The records for 1780-1, for example, confirm much of what we know from other sources, such as leases, etc. They show that the Streatfields owned Coldharbour, the Hole, Pyle Gate and Lords Land. The last three were all occupied by Burfoots, who themselves owned Mark Beech Farm and Scalefields. Other owners included Driver, Douglas, Woodgate and Banister. The records of 1832 and the Tithe Survey of 1841 reveal relatively little change in these patterns except for the arrival of Woodhouse. Another family to own large amounts of land, although not chiefly in Cowden and Mark Beech, was Woodgate. In the 18th century the Woodgates possessed Sandfields Farm and owned land in Chiddingstone, where they built Stonewall Park, and in Leigh, Tonbridge, Tudely and elsewhere; for a while in the 19th century they owned Claydene and confused matters by renaming it Falconhurst.[37]

In 1745, after the Hever inheritance had passed into the hands of three Waldegrave daughters, the two Hever manors were sold by them and their husbands to Sir Timothy Waldo, and for nearly 200 years this family, latterly known as the Meade-Waldos, became the leading landowner in Hever; as late as the second half of the 19th century their Hever estate extended to more than 2,000 acres.[38] These manors were not intact, however, especially around Mark Beech, and this surely indicates that some enfranchisement or sales had taken place, probably in the 16th and 17th centuries. The Meade-Waldos held all the land north of the road from Stick Hill through Mark Beech to Wilderness Lane, with the exception of the last two fields west of Wilderness Lane, which were Streatfield lands. Thus they held such farms as Jessups, also known as Willetts, once a pig farm, and Buckhurst, but not Bramsells, which had been held by the Saxbys in 1554, was in the possession of James

18   Jessups, 1998. (Paul Houlton)

King in the 18th century, and was bought by the Streatfields in 1812.[39] The Streatfields were probably even greater land-holders than the Meade-Waldos, but, as was usual, most of the land of both families was tenanted. Indeed, when the Meade-Waldos went to live at Stonewall Park on the departure of the Woodgates for Claydene, Hever was let to a series of tenant-farmers, whose number included at one time a junior member of the Streatfield family.[40] In 1597 the Streatfields had acquired Cowden Leighton, and as we have seen, until the 1830s they held large chunks of the former Cowden Lewisham. To the east they held a large part of south-west Chiddingstone, where they lived in High Street House, later known as Chiddingstone Castle, and their territory extended to include Tyehurst and New Tyehurst, which with Low Buckhurst they acquired in 1797, Wilderness Farm, including land on the western side of the lane, and the eastern half of High Buckhurst, that is, the woods on the eastern side of Mark Beech Hill, known as Buckhurst.[41]

The Banisters and the Burfoots were also major landowners in Mark Beech in the 18th and 19th centuries. The Banisters had a sizeable piece of land on the south-eastern quadrant of Mark Beech cross as well as other interests which extended north to Meechland Farm and other places in Hever. The name was sometimes spelt Banister and sometimes Bannister and it is preserved in Bannister's Barn, situated on land which once belonged to them. Sometimes High Buckhurst was referred to as Bannister's Farm (and for a brief time in the late 19th century as Mark Beech Farm). The family are to be found in Hever and Cowden from the late 17th century, and others of this name are to be found at Horsmonden and Downe. It is possible, therefore, that they are related to John Banister of Horton Kirby who, in the late 18th century, wrote one of the most famous texts on agriculture, *A Synopsis of Husbandry*.[42] The Burfoots, who in different generations were a clan of either brothers or cousins, had land to the west of Cow Lane and very considerable interests as either owners or tenants all over the area. Of the principal families in the area in recent times, the Streatfields first appear in 1593, the Stills in 1655, the Burfoots in 1673, the Banisters and the Bassetts in 1674, the Meade-Waldos in 1745, the Gainsfords in 1750, the Drivers in 1783 and the Woodgates in 1788, although they are to be found in Penshurst in 1457.[43]

The evolution of these patterns of land-holding and occupation took place within the context of changing topography and farming practices. It must be remembered that in Kent from earliest times there was little farming of open and communal land and this was especially true of the Weald and High Weald. Fields were enclosed and probably had always been so and they tended to be on the small side.[44] In the mid-16th century Mark Beech remained an area of low population density: in the 1560s the average density in the Weald was 117 persons per 1,000 acres, and the parishes of the western Weald had the lowest densities. Unfortunately the Hever registers for this period are lost, but Cowden had a density of 77 persons per 1000 acres and Chiddingstone had 79. Only Leigh at 70 and Tonbridge at 72 had less.[45] This small population, which, it might be said, is a feature which has prevailed to the present day, was now living in an environment which undoubtedly displayed a much less wooded aspect than in the past and, therefore, an increasing proportion of the land was deployed to arable farming. Deforestation was never complete, but by the 17th century much clearance had occurred and was to continue thereafter. Yet from about 1600 trees began to be planted as well as felled and it would be an error to suppose that all the woods which survive today are continuous survivals from Andreasweald. Some, at least, are replantings after previous clearance. In 1781 about a quarter of the south-east corner of Buckhurst was a field known as Lower Buckhurst Field and most of its western edge encompassed two fields, Higher Buckhurst and Little Buckhurst Fields, but all this area is now wooded. In 1841 the centre of Buckhurst was open, but it is now planted with conifers.[46]

The area around Mark Beech at the extreme western end of the High Weald has, at 32 ins., one of the highest average levels of annual rainfall in the south east of England.[47] In the 16th century deer were still very plentiful and at Northfrith Park, Penshurst in 1541, for example, there were said to be at least 350 of them.[48] In the 17th century Wealden settlement remained primarily hamlets and scattered farms. Traditionally this was an area of mixed farming, with animal husbandry predominating. Cattle rearing was the principal activity, but sheep were also important, especially in the High Weald, even if the climate and the wet, clogging soils were not entirely suitable. A trade off with land usage had to be struck. During the period 1350 to 1600, in particular, cattle predominated, although the growing of grain, particularly oats and wheat, was a feature.[49] There is evidence that in the later Middle Ages, after the 1348-9 plague, there was some contraction in grain production, and slowly over time the amount of oats cultivated diminished, wheat correspondingly increased, and small quantities of barley began to be grown.[50] The chief instrument of cultivation remained the ox-drawn plough and the ox was not entirely replaced by the horse until, maybe surprisingly, the 1840s, if then.[51] Two collections of old photographs from the High Weald show oxen ploughing Weald clay in the 1890s and a team of four oxen drawing a timber cart near Wadhurst in 1906. The last working team of oxen is said to have been at Ditchling, Sussex, about 20 miles from Mark Beech, in 1938.[52] Though even southern England was climatically marginal for vines, some had always been cultivated since Roman times. The vineyards at Penshurst had failed to flower in 1345 and 220 years later the vine had disappeared altogether from the area.[53] If the vine, as a cultivated crop, vanished until the second half of the 20th century, it was more than replaced by its near cousin, the hop. Hops were introduced into Kent and Sussex from the Low Countries in about 1430, had become established in the High Weald by about 1500, and by the mid-17th century there were hop-gardens throughout the region, including, it is known, at Chiddingstone.[54] (These dates have interesting implications for the derivation of Hopper's Bank, which name is found as early as 1323, i.e. a century before hops were introduced to England, so it must have some other derivation.) With its enclosed fields, suitable climate, plentiful supply of coppice wood for poles, and proximity to the important market of London, Kent became a centre for production of beer. One historian has averred that the hop exerted an influence wholly disproportionate to its acreage and eventually became 'at once the saviour and the blight of High Weald agriculture'.[55] Although the main centres of production always remained in the Weald, particularly in central Kent and down the Medway valley, we find some hops being grown in Mark Beech. At the time of the Tithe Commutation in 1841 there were a number of hop gardens in the area, as the Tithe Files for both Hever and Cowden attest. Special documentation had to be drawn up for this crop, and for this reason we know that at least one of the parties to the agreement, William Burfoot, was illiterate and had to make his mark rather than sign his name.[56] By 1841 Cowden as a whole had nearly 75 acres of hops, distributed in 23 separate gardens, two of which certainly were in Mark Beech as the fields below the site of the last vicarage were a hop garden by the 19th century, and a second hop garden was situated at Curd's.[57] As we shall see, a third hop garden was, ten years later, undoubtedly part of the farm immediately around Falconhurst. The acreage of hops in Cowden doubled between 1821 and 1875, but the area, including Mark Beech, always remained one of relatively low hop density.[58] If the characteristic round oast house, which did not develop until the first half of the 19th century, is rare in Mark Beech, examples are to be seen at Pyle Gate and at Wickens, and this must indicate that there were hop gardens there too. There are others close to the village, if outside it, such as in Truggers Lane, Chiddingstone and, of course, the famous, photogenic ones at Chiddingstone.

Livestock and arable remained the chief farming activities then, and a clear picture of the area in the first half of the 19th century can be discerned. In 1840 about 64 per cent of the cleared land in Cowden was arable, and about 36 per cent pasture.[59] About 20.9 per cent of the High Weald was woodland or hedgerow, although Mark Beech may very well have had a higher proportion, and Buckland, writing in 1845, confirmed that the area was densely wooded.[60] In 1801 the proportions of arable land devoted to various crops were wheat 45 per cent, oats 42 per cent, peas 6 per cent, turnips and rape 3 per cent, barley 2 per cent and potatoes and beans 1 per cent each.[61] A four-course rotation system was employed, and at any one time a typical situation was that of Hever in about 1840 when 15 per cent of the land was fallow, 25 per cent to wheat, 10 per cent to barley, 15 per cent to oats, 25 per cent to clover and 10 per cent to turnips.[62] The general problem was the nature of the soil and the lack of drainage. We have noted already several damning comments on the character of the former, and at the time of the surveys for the Tithe Commutation in the 1840s one commissioner, Matthews, wrote of Chiddingstone that it had 'a cold, hungry clay which for want of good drainage is generally wet and retards the ripening of crops ... the 4 courses [of rotation] could produce much more. The hop gardens would benefit from drainage, the crops being very uncertain.'[63] Cowden was not very different and the commissioner there, Woolley, stated that matters were even worse on account of the shaws. 'There is a good deal of land', he wrote,

> of a very good quality ... which if less shaded would grow wheat and beans of good quality—and with effectual under drainage and high farming would be by no means unproductive ... The surface is very undulating and uneven. The Inclosures are small and shaded by the Shaws which surround almost every one of them ... All the grass is upland—for the most part very poor hungry Pasture intertwined with Arable land. A considerable part of the Northern and North Eastern [i.e. Mark Beech] extremity of the Parish is of this character ... With the exception of a trifling quantity of good free working land east of the village all the Ploughland is cold Weald clay of a character which as it requires more than others to have the full benefit of the sun and drying wind is seriously injured by the Shaws which surround every inclosure.[64]

Similarly, Commissioner Browne wrote of Hever that the parish was 'undulating, the subsoil chiefly clay. The land appears to be of an average quality. The course of husbandry is irregular ... There is some gravelly land in the parish. The pasture is indifferent.'[55] Of the cattle in Cowden about a third were now dairy cows, and in 1847 there were 52 farms, *in toto*, of which 29 were less than 50 acres, 14 were between 50 and 100 acres, and the remaining nine between one and three hundred.[66] Fields were small, as Commissioner Woolley had noted, and the earliest large-scale Ordnance Survey maps show, for example, that the quadrilateral bordered by Mark Beech, Horseshoe Green, Friendly Green, and The Pound, altogether an area of about 300 acres, was divided between no fewer than 71 fields plus a number of shaws.[67] About 75 per cent of farmers in the High Weald were tenants and their lords tried, through the detailed particulars of leases granted, to control their practices. In 1711, for example, a lease by John Ashdowne and Henry Pigott to John Bridgland and Richard Burgis, both of Cowden, stipulates that there is a penalty rent of 40s. for every acre not particularly named to be ploughed or sown, which the tenants shall plough, break up or sow with any manner of corn or grain. The lessees covenant to spread all dung, etc. arising from the premises and not to sell or carry away hay, straw or fodder, but to lay 250 loads of marl, each load being of 12 bushels, on certain specified fields.[68] An earlier lease of 1626, as we have noted in another context, by Henry Streatfield to John Wickenden for land at High Buckhurst, Mark Beech, provided 20 acres for 12 years at £10 13s. 4d. per annum with a penalty clause for sowing more than six acres of oats.[69]

Such conditions were still imposed in the 20th century. In 1918 the Leppard family, who had been in the area since at least the middle of the 19th century, assumed the tenancy of Wilderness Farm. The tenancy agreement of 18 January 1918 included a clause which stated that

> The Tenant shall farm the Arable Land properly, and consistently with good husbandry, and keep and leave the same clean and in good heart and condition, but shall not in any one year have more than half thereof in white strawed corn and in the last year of the tenancy shall farm the arable land upon the four course system, that is to say: one fourth wheat, one fourth barley or oats, one fourth fallow or roots, one eighth peas or beans, one eighth clover ley, so that on the farm being given up to the Landlord or next succeeding tenant there shall be a proper proportion not less than half the arable land coming in due course of average quality in clean condition and in a fit state to be cropped with white strawed corn.

Another clause stated that

> the Tenant shall consume upon the said premises, in a husbandlike manner and for the benefit thereof, all the hay, straw, haulm and fodder, roots and green crops, which shall be there produced or made, except hay and wheat straw and roots, which may be sold and carried off the farm upon the tenant bringing back and expending in the same year on the premises hereby let an equivalent in good dung, bone manure or feeding cakes, the tenant to produce when required vouchers of such hay and wheat straw and roots sold off and of dung and cake brought back in lieu thereof. This permission to sell shall not extend to the crop of the last year of the tenancy.[70]

In April 1930 the tenancy was renewed by a similar agreement.[71]

Although farming remained the main economic activity, the 16th century saw a remarkable revival of the Wealden iron industry. The forest provided plenty of wood for charcoal, the fuel for smelting the iron ore, especially after the Reformation had removed the inhibitory controls of ecclesiastical landlords. Iron production continued into the 18th century, but the revived industry was at its peak during the century 1570-1670, and the High Weald became 'the workshop of the Tudor armaments industry'.[72] Around Mark Beech, however, it never properly recovered from the difficulties experienced during the Civil War, when two rival ironmasters in Cowden, one Parliamentarian, the other Royalist, only succeeded in destroying each other's businesses.[73] The revival of the industry was most profitable for some, and one of the large masters, the Titchbornes, were able to reconstruct Crippenden, where the barrel of a Civil War canon made in Cowden is to be seen. Iron production now demanded not primitive bloomeries but furnaces, which required a considerable head of water. This explains the construction of two artificial lakes behind man-made dams on Kent

Water at Cowden. For Mark Beech, therefore, the revived industry meant solely the provision of ore and we have speculated already that some of the pits around the village may date from this period rather than from Roman times.[74]

There are, finally, two further activities, which were to be found around Mark Beech in modern times. Edenbridge was noted as a centre of the leather industry, and a tannery, owned by the Whitmore family, existed there from at least 1673 until the 1970s. For about a hundred years from the mid-19th century it was the largest employer in the town and the hooter summoning the workers in the morning was a familiar sound; it was said to be a more reliable time-check at 8 a.m. than the church clock.[75] In the 18th and 19th centuries outwork was placed in the surrounding villages and Cowden was noted for its glove-making.[76] Secondly, Kent was always a county prized for its cloth. The centre of this industry was to the east at places like Tenterden, but weaving went on all over the county for, after all, one of Kent's major activities was sheep-rearing, and not just on Romney Marsh. In the Weald cloth manufacture was, after iron working, the second most important industry of the area. Tonbridge and Chiddingstone were regarded as important local centres for woollens and Cowden too was a village well-known in the 17th century for its broad cloth and its dressed cloth.[77] The latter implies the existence of a fulling mill, but no records of such seem to be extant.[78] Writing as late as 1868, Rev. E. Turner said that he could remember, as a boy in the adjacent parish of Hartfield, the spinning wheels humming away in the houses.[79]

Prior to the reforms of the 19th century local government, and indeed for most of the population most of the time government itself, revolved around the parish. The institutional unit was the Vestry, which had responsibility for such matters as basic law and order, the maintenance of roads and bridges in the parish, and, above all, the administration of the poor law. By the 18th century maintenance of roads by unwilling locals was proving quite inadequate, particularly in this part of England where, as we have seen, observers had for a long time deplored the condition of the roads. Turnpike trusts were considered by some to be a panacea and two examples ran through Mark Beech. The first was the Southwark to Ashdown Forest turnpike, which was started in 1723 but part of which became the Westerham to Edenbridge turnpike in 1765. The other was the Cowden to Penshurst turnpike. Unfortunately the records of both these enterprises have been lost, but turnpikes did not prove to be the universal solution that some had thought they would be. There was considerable resentment at the paying of the tolls, especially on the part of those, like farmers, who had always had 'free' access to the roads and to whom they were vital. Furthermore, it was often naively assumed that, having put a road into good order, there would be little more expenditure and the income would just roll in as profits. The Westerham-Edenbridge turnpike, for example, found that its income never covered even its accumulating interest payments and its mortgage charges, and in 1835 it defaulted with debts of over £50,000.[80]

An important matter to note is that the modern main road up to The Pound crossroads follows a different route to the historic one. The present straight road from Brook Street up Stick Hill to Hever Lane is a 19th-century creation. At the point at the bottom of Stick Hill where the modern road turns slightly to the right to go up the hill it will be observed that the remains of an old road, which is now a public footpath, continue more or less straight on. The original main road joined Hever Lane at a point lower than now, and then either went up to The Pound on its present track or continued southwards to Jessups, running parallel to

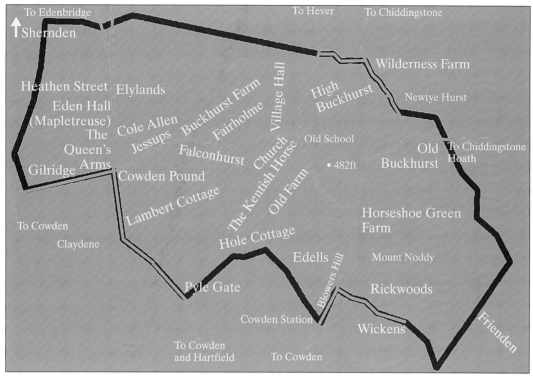

19   Mark Beech in 1999. (Paul Houlton)

but about 200 yards west of the modern main road. This may explain why there is the
otherwise inexplicable boundary between Hever and Cowden at this point, which, we can
suggest, went down the middle of the old road.[81] More likely, however, is that the boundary
is a watercourse which marked the division between Hever Brocas and Hever Cobham and/
or the boundary between Somerden Hundred and an enclave of Ruxley (see figure 7).

    One of the consequences of the Reformation was that the needs of the poor, which
had previously fallen on the Church, but especially the monasteries, now fell on the parish.
Starting with the Elizabethan Poor Law of 1601, central government charged the parish with
responsibility for its own poor. To that end the vestries elected Overseers of the Poor, whose
function it was to conduct the day-to-day administration of the system and to help collect
the Poor Rate, which financed it, although the Overseers were under the jurisdiction of the
Justices of the Peace, whose functions were administrative as well as judicial. Indeed the
Justices from all over the county would meet in Maidstone or Canterbury four times a year
in Quarter Sessions to constitute a sort of pre-modern County Council. Both Cowden and
Hever took their responsibilities seriously and provided both outdoor relief and almshouses.
Indeed Cowden anticipated statutory regulation by starting to look after its poor from
1599.[82] For more than two centuries the names of members of the leading families in the
area such as Saxby, Pigott, Wickenden and Burfoot recur as Overseers, but within the
Cowden and Hever records it is impossible to identify a great deal which is specific to Mark
Beech. Dr. C.W. Chalklin, however, has shown that there was considerable poverty in
Cowden and Hever during parts of the 17th century.[83] After the Poor Law Amendment Act

of 1834 was passed, the parishes of Cowden, Hever, Chiddingstone, Penshurst and Leigh united to provide a Penshurst Workhouse, which was built at Bough Beech, the existing properties eventually being sold. The Penshurst Union did not, however, commend itself to the Poor Law Commissioners in London, who required a large, central workhouse for the whole Sevenoaks district.[84] A workhouse was provided on St John's Hill, Sevenoaks, but this proved to be quite inadequate so a new Union was duly constructed between Ide Hill and Sundridge. This was a monstrous structure, which housed 500 'inmates' and cost £12,000 to build. It was completed in 1845 and from that time all people seeking public assistance in Mark Beech were removed to this institution because the whole rationale of the new system was to eliminate outdoor relief, that is, assistance to the poor outside the work-house.[85] Unfortunately, most of the Sevenoaks Union Records for the 19th century have not survived and much was probably destroyed by 'weeding' when they were deposited at Sevenoaks Library in 1949.[86] Nevertheless, a few such records survive and from them it appears that the admissions from Mark Beech in the 1840s were very infrequent, although again it is often difficult to ascribe any specifically to Mark Beech.

The second political and administrative entity that impinged on the population was, of course, parliamentary representation. Parliament was responsible for enacting the laws and levying the taxes, most of which affected all the population, whether an individual was part of the small minority who possessed the franchise or the majority who did not. Prior to the introduction of Income Tax, first during the French Wars of 1793-1815 and again after 1842, the main taxes were Customs and Excise, which touched all in some way or other, or the Land Tax, which was of special interest and vexation to landowners. Until 1832 Mark Beech was represented in the Commons as part of the two-member constituency, which embraced the whole of Kent. After the First Reform Act Mark Beech became part of the new two-member constituency of West Kent. There is little profit in trying to assign parliamentary candidates to parties, at least to organised political parties in the modern sense, before about the time of the French Revolution, if then.[87] Nevertheless, the ballot was open until 1872 and a combi-nation of the small electorate and enterprising newspapers and book producers led to the publication after most elections in most constituencies of Poll Books, lists of electors and those candidates for which they had voted. In time these books became ever more sophisticated and often included such details as addresses and occupations.[88] The number of electors was small and was as follows: 1754: Chiddingstone 17, Hever 12, Cowden 14; 1790: Chiddingstone 23, Hever 8, Cowden 15; 1802: Chiddingstone 18, Hever 7, Cowden 19; 1835: Chiddingstone 24, Hever 20, Cowden 21; 1847: Chiddingstone 28, Hever 23, Cowden 32. Names, familiar to us in other contexts, such as Bannister, Bassett, Burfoot, Harvey, Longley, Woodgate, Streatfield, Meade-Waldo, Driver, Still, Killick, Hunt, Gainsford and Talbot, appear on the lists.[89] In 1835 two Longleys and two Burfoots, Richard and William, voted for the Liberal candidates, the Harveys, father and son, voted Conservative, and Streatfield, Gainsford, Bannister and Stephen Burfoot did not vote.[90] In 1847 the non-voters included Richard Streatfield, Bassett, Christopher Burfoot and James and Obadiah Longley. Two Bannisters and Henry Streatfield voted Liberal, and the Conservative supporters included William, John and Richard Burfoot, Meade-Waldo, Gainsford, Harvey, Killick and Henry Longley.[91]

Being in a county constituency Mark Beech was always represented, as legally it had to be, by landed gentlemen of substance, and by the late 18th century they were usually those who described themselves as Tories. However, in the 1820s they tended to be Independents, in the 18th-century sense of that term, who did not necessarily support the Government of the day, even though those of Liverpool, Canning, Goderich and Wellington were Tory, whether liberal or ultra. This demonstrates the degree to which party loyalties and disciplines were still loose in the early 19th century. The election of December 1832 initiated a short period of time when West Kent was frequently represented by Whig/Liberals. Whig/Liberals won both seats in 1832 and the Tory/Conservatives did so in 1841, but the two groups shared a seat each in 1835, 1837 and 1847.[92] In English counties before 1832 the franchise was limited to adult males owning freehold property worth at least 40s. per annum, and the Reform Act added adult males who were either seized of copyhold land worth at least £10 per annum or who leased or rented land worth at least £50 per annum. Given the small population, chiefly of landholders and agricultural labourers, the number of electors in Mark Beech was exceedingly small, being only six in number in 1832 and growing very slowly over the next 20 years.[93] Most Mark Beech electors usually voted Tory/Conservative, if they could be bothered to vote at all or were able to get themselves to Maidstone for the hustings, but there were always a number of Liberal voters, as we saw above. The M.P.s for West Kent between 1832 and 1852 were T.L. Hodges (Liberal), 1832-41 and 1847-52; T. Rider (Liberal), 1832-5; Sir W. Gearey (Conservative), 1835-41; Sir E. Filmer (Conservative), 1841-52; Lord Marsham (Conservative), 1841-7.[94]

Other national events between 1530 and 1850 seem to have largely passed Mark Beech by. As far as we can tell, the Reformation caused few ripples in the area apart from the changes in land-holding; there were no recorded public protests, and at both Cowden and Hever the incumbents seem to have accepted the frequent ecclesiastical and liturgical changes without resigning or being expelled. For example, Richard Chapman, rector of Cowden, and Thomas Cyttes, curate at Hever, seem to have had no difficulty in 1534 in renouncing Papal authority in England,[95] and a century later Rector Aynscombe of Cowden retained the living throughout all the ecclesiastical changes that occurred between 1633 and 1668.[96] However, between 1627 and 1647 several members of one family at Hever were fined 18 times for recusancy.[97]

The Civil War was slightly different; most of the population was not directly involved, but among those that were there were sharp differences of view and of behaviour. A problem was that Kent, particularly west Kent, was not owned, controlled or dominated by a small number of prominent landowning families, and therefore the leadership of society fell to a group of twenty to thirty gentry families.[98] We have seen that the two iron masters in Cowden, though not gentry, took opposite sides, and in the immediate vicinity of Mark Beech we find that the one aristocrat in the area, Lord Cobham of Starborough Castle, was a royalist, whereas the Seyliards of Delaware in Hever and the Derings at Squerryes Park, Westerham, were parliamentarians.[99] At some date between 1643 and 1648 there seems to have been a minor skirmish near Delaware Farm, on the border of Hever and Edenbridge, between parliamentarians and royalists, and in 1648 Starborough was destroyed by parliamentary troops.[100] Sir Thomas Seyliard of Delaware served on the County Committee, established by Parliament to rule Kent.[101]

Sevenoaks was a key place in the struggle for the allegiance of the population and was in parliamentary hands more often than not. In August 1642 Parliament sent an expedition under Colonel Edwyn Sandys there to scotch the pro-royalist machinations of Sir John Sackville, and Knole House was sacked.[102] In 1643 a Kentish rebellion against Parliament's attempts to impose the Sacred Vow and Covenant centred on Sevenoaks. Four thousand 'rebels' occupied the town and made contact with the king. Their supporters included the Streatfields of Chiddingstone.[103] Another parliamentary force, including 1,200 dragoons commanded by Colonel Browne, was sent via Reigate, but on their approach most of the rebels fled southwards. They were killed or captured at the battle of Tonbridge in July, although a few escaped to Winchelsea.[104] A royalist army finally prepared to advance from the west, and earth ramparts dug at Squerryes were manned by 400 troops as the first line of defence for Sevenoaks, where 800 horse and the 1,200 dragoons were placed, but it was defeated at Alton in Hampshire in December.[105] By 1644, 4,000 parliamentary troops were stationed at Sevenoaks, but in 1645 another royalist plot was hatched centred on the town, although this plan was thwarted.[106] In 1648 another royalist scheme led to the seizure of Tonbridge, but in August 1649 they were suppressed in a skirmish at Tunbridge Wells.[107] By this time Lord Lisle and Algernon Sydney of Penshurst had declared themselves Republicans and served on the County Committee for Kent.[108] In these ways the English Civil War flowed around Mark Beech, although we have no evidence of military or political activities in Mark Beech, itself.

The era of the French Revolution and wars left little trace in Mark Beech, although it is said that the several straight rows of oak trees which can be seen today between the land belonging to High Buckhurst and Jersey Cottage, and which certainly seem to be about 200 years old, were planted during the panic that took hold in Britain at that time concerning the prospective shortage of timber for ships for the navy.

Our survey of Mark Beech during this very long period ends with a local example of the incendiarism which swept southern England, but particularly Kent, in 1830-2. These events accompanied the two-year national crisis which emanated from the attempt to reform Parliament and, incidentally, coincided with revolutions in France, Belgium and Poland. It was caused by the dissatisfaction of farm labourers with the operations of the Poor Law, the low level of wages, and the introduction of labour-saving technology such as the threshing machine.[109] It led to the destruction of threshing machines, the firing of haystacks, barns and other property, and the issue of minatory letters to landowners and farmers, often over the pseudonymous signature of 'Captain Swing', who gave his name to the affair.[110] The perpetrators were usually afforded sympathy and security by those labourers who were non-participants, and sometimes too by tenant farmers and a few magistrates.[111] This outbreak of lawlessness continued from January 1830 to September 1832 and Kent was the English county with the most cases of arson, with 61, followed by Sussex with 34, Surrey with 23 and Norfolk with nineteen.[112] In August and September 1830 an orgy of destruction spread across west Kent, including Orpington, Brasted, Shoreham, Otford and Sevenoaks. On 17 September, *The Times* reported that the latest victim of 'Swing' had been Rev. Thomas Harvey, Rector of Cowden, who, besides Alcocks, owned parts of Furnace House, Woolcombs and Shoebridges Farms in south-west Cowden. His barn and corn stack had been burned to the ground.[113]

Twenty years after these events Mark Beech was to be transformed utterly by the arrival of the Talbot family, the building of a church and the creation of a parish, and by the construction of a railway with a station in the village.

<h1 align="center">VI</h1>

<h1 align="center">The Arrival of the Talbots,
The Church and the Railway, 1850-88</h1>

ON 16 APRIL 1849, Hon. John Chetwynd Talbot (1806-52) saw an advertisement in *The Times* for the sale of an estate near Edenbridge in Kent.[1] Talbot was the fourth son of 2nd Baron Talbot, who was head of a cadet branch of the earls of Shrewsbury whose seat was at Ingestre, near Stafford. J.C. Talbot went to Charterhouse and to Christ Church, Oxford, from where he graduated in 1828.[2] At the age of 20 he had been to Russia to attend the coronation of Tsar Nicholas I, his uncle being the head of the British delegation which attended it.[3] In 1830 he married Hon. Caroline Jane Stuart-Wortley-Mackenzie (1809-76), daughter of 1st Baron Wharncliffe, and they had two sons, John Gilbert (1835-1910) and Edward Stuart (1844-1934). As a younger son he was unlikely to inherit land, so in the 1830s he began to practise at the

Parliamentary Bar, where he became very successful on account both of his considerable abilities and good luck; he started his career when railway construction was getting under way, for which the promotion of parliamentary legislation and other legal processes was required. He lived in Great George Street, Westminster, became very wealthy, and was acquainted with the rising politician, W.E. Gladstone (1809-98), who had been at Christ Church from 1828-32, and his young family.[4] In 1834 he became Recorder of Monmouth and in 1836 that of Windsor. In 1843 he became a Q.C., in 1846 he was elected Deputy High Steward of Oxford University, and in 1849 he became Attorney-General to the Prince of Wales.

Within months of seeing the advert in *The Times*, J.C. Talbot had bought in 1850 what we will call the Edells estate from Mr. G.F. Woodhouse. Edells had already been

20   Hon. John Chetwynd Talbot, M.A., Q.C., (1806-52), the effective founder of modern Mark Beech.

offered for rent in 1847, when it was described as being 'in a highly respectable neighbour-hood' and 'in a romantic situation, approached by a carriage drive, through an avenue of trees',[5] a description which still pertains today. In 1849-50 the house was still for rent, but Talbot bought it as well as the land and in buying it he acquired not only the house known as Edells and the farm that went with it, but Coldharbour, Friendly Green, Pyle Gate, the Hole, Lord's Land, Eastlands and Killicks.[6] In the years to come his successors were to buy additional pieces of land, namely Alcocks in 1854 (although Lambert Cottage and its garden was sold off in 1911), Old Buckhurst and Coles in 1858, Mutton Field in 1875, Mark Beech corner in 1893, and much of High Buckhurst, Broomyfields, Wickens, including Colemans and Curds, and Brook Farm in 1909, so that by 1914 what we will now call the Falconhurst Estate extended to more than 600 acres and the family had become the dominant landowner in Mark Beech, at least south of the High Weald ridge road.[7]

Talbot had a vision and did not wish to remain merely an estate owner, however extensive; he aimed to replace Edells with a grand country mansion, to found a church at Mark Beech and to turn this old Kentish hamlet into a proper village. To the first two ends he appointed the architect David Brandon (1813-97) to design and build a large country house and a church.[8]

Brandon had been a partner of Thomas Henry Wyatt (1807-80) and together they had designed, for example, the *Rundbogenstil* church of St Mary's, Wilton, Wiltshire during the 1840s. The designs for Talbot were Brandon's first independent commissions and, although he was to go on and design St Mary's, Wantage, Berkshire in 1866, and a private chapel at Bayham Abbey in 1870, Brandon specialised in designing country houses, particularly in the Jacobean style, five of which he designed in Kent, including the one at Mark Beech.[9]

Talbot's house was built on Lord's Land, on a site about a third of a mile west of the crossroads, but tucked back from the road and with magnificent views over the Kent and Sussex countryside to the south. It was called Falconhurst, mainly because the Rector of Cowden told Talbot, erroneously, that the wood nearby was called Falconhurst Wood.[10] Construction was well under way by August 1851, when Lord Hardinge, a former Governor-General of India and a friend of the Talbots who lived at Penshurst, visited the site and pronounced that 'we have made no blunder in our house', which was already 'well forward'.[11] In 1913 a considerable addition was made to Falconhurst to a design by John Duke Coleridge (1879-1934), a former pupil of Sir Edwin Lutyens.[12] In 1943 the original part of the house was found to be very seriously infested with dry rot. Plans were drawn up to restore the house but, in view of the expense, they were never executed and this part was pulled down in 1960-1.[13] Thus what is to be seen today preserves very little of Brandon's original, which was completed in 1852, so that for the next several decades Falconhurst became the focus of the life of the estate, of which it was the centre, of much of the life of the village, and of a wider circle of national and international interests through the Talbot's extensive familial and other connections. Today the house is still occupied and the estate run by J.C. Talbot's great-great grandson, Charles J. Talbot (b.1947).

Brandon's church, named Holy Trinity, was completed at the same time. This church is part of the Gothic Revival and is in the Early English style, 'timidly' so according to Pevsner.[14] It is constructed in Kentish ragstone, but with hard-stone facings with a tiled roof. The design was for a simple church consisting of a nave, a semi-circular chancel at the east

21   Falconhurst from the south, 1877. (Charles Talbot)

22   Falconhurst, from the south west, 1998. The 1852 house was attached left. (Paul Houlton)

end and a small tower on the north, capped by a pinnacle with shingles, and a single tolling bell. It survives after nearly 150 years, its external appearance little changed. There is room for a congregation of 120 people, and the foundation stone was laid by the founder's eldest son, John, on Easter Monday, 3 April 1852.

The Talbots, husband and wife, would certainly have commissioned a church at the village which had become their new home, but their resolve was confirmed by the Evangelical style of worship they found at Cowden. They were singularly unimpressed by the Rector's habit of climbing into the pulpit and slapping a five-minute egg-timer on the edge, determined to complete his sermon before the timer expired.[15] Both were pious and enthusiastic Tractarians, although John Chetwynd had been at Oxford before the movement started, and the precise reasons for his commitment is unclear.[16] Possibly they were influenced by Gladstone, although we cannot tell whether Talbot participated in the famous Convocation vote at Oxford in February 1845, which divided along Evangelical and Tractarian lines, because no record is taken of such votes.[17] We know from Gladstone's diaries that he took the Tractarian line,[18] becoming a convinced Tractarian after an Evangelical upbringing. During his lifetime he was probably regarded as the most prominent and influential lay churchman.[19] Gladstone and his wife became very friendly with the Talbots and were later related by more than one marriage. At Mark Beech the Talbots started a tradition which survives today in the ritual employed in the church, and which also continued in their

23 Left. *Mark Beech Church from the south east, 1998. (Paul Houlton)*

24 Above. *Interior of Mark Beech Church, c.1935. (Mrs. Barbara Penman)*

family. Their second son, Edward, was to become the first Warden of Keble College, Oxford, a contributor to the noteworthy Anglo-Catholic publication, Gore's *Lux Mundi* (1889), and, after a short period as a parish priest in Leeds, as High Church as Victorian society would permit, successively bishop of Southwark, Rochester and Winchester. In 1874 and 1875 he attended, as a High Anglican representative, along with Henry Liddon, Malcolm MacColl and Christopher Wordsworth, the Bonn Reunion Conferences, organised by Ignaz von Dollinger, where they discussed possible 'Catholic' reunion with liberal Roman Catholics, Old Catholics and Orthodox colleagues.[20] Gladstone wrote of him that, 'His whole manner of performing Divine Service is quite admirable: but I am afraid he overfeels'.[21]

The construction of the church took 253 days at a cost of £1,250 plus architect's fees, which was met entirely by the Talbots,[22] and was consecrated, ironically perhaps, by the Evangelical Archbishop of Canterbury, John B. Sumner (1780-1862), with whom, it was said, the Talbots had nothing theologically in common,[23] on 14 December 1852. From the beginning there were pews, a pulpit and a font and, underneath, a crypt which was intended as a burial vault for the Talbots but which has never been used for that purpose. From early days it housed the boiler for central heating, originally coal-fired but oil since the 1960s. All the chancel windows and some of those in the nave were fitted with stained glass, produced by William Wailes (1801-81), a pupil of Augustus Pugin who ran one of the largest factories to produce such glass in Victorian Britain at Newcastle-on-Tyne.[24] These windows were paid for by the vicar's two sisters and by Lady Montagu of Beaulieu, Caroline Talbot's niece, among others.[25] One that was fitted in the nave at a later date was said to be very striking, depicting an angel with a flaming sword and the words 'the angel of the Lord standeth around those who fear him', which is said to commemorate an alarming meeting of two spinster ladies with some labourers in nearby woods.[26] Several of the windows in the nave had to be removed in the 1920s on account of severe weathering, and others there, and one in the chancel, were removed, somewhat arbitrarily it would seem, by the then vicar in the 1950s, and all are now lost.[27] There was also a barrel organ with only eight melodies, although a second one with another eight was acquired early on.[28] The church plate was given by Rev. Thomas Bowdler, about whom little seems to be known.[29]

Whilst Falconhurst was being built the Talbots lived at Edells. Unfortunately, however, John Chetwynd Talbot did not live to see the completion of either his new house or of the church. He had worked very hard all his adult life and was suffering from what the Victorians called 'consumption', which in his case was certainly tuberculosis. In summer 1852 he went to an hotel in Brighton for a recuperative holiday but he died there suddenly of a heart-attack on the night of 26 May, just short of his 46th birthday. He was buried at Ingestre, but on the death of his widow in 1876 his remains were removed to Mark Beech and they were buried together. Staying in the same hotel at the time was Gladstone's wife, Catherine, née Glynne (1812-1900), who was convalescing after a miscarriage. Catherine showed such sympathy and care to the widowed Mrs. Talbot that the two women now became the closest of friends, a friendship only broken by Caroline's death 24 years later.[30] Talbot's dreams had to be fulfilled by his widow and his eldest son, who had wanted to be an Anglican priest, but who, after finishing his schooling at Charterhouse and going to Oxford, devoted his life to his family's affairs and to public business.[31]

In 1851 the Talbots had gone to Rome, accompanied by their younger son, Edward, and servants, although there was never any question of conversion to (Roman) Catholicism; it was simply a holiday to an historic city, to several in fact. They travelled by train, sea and carriage via Dover to Calais, Paris, Dijon, Geneva, Turin, Genoa, Livorno, Pisa, Florence, Sienna and Rome, returning via Sienna, Pisa, Spezia, Marseilles and Paris.[32] While staying in an hotel in Florence they met Robert Shapland Hunt (1817-1904).[33] Hunt was born in Kilkenny and is said to have retained a marked Irish accent to the end of his life, but he went to Charterhouse, like Talbot, and to Exeter College, Oxford in the late 1830s, just as the Oxford Movement was taking off. Despite an age difference of 25 years, Hunt was said to be friendly with John Keble (1792-1866), and to have worked for a while for Edward B. Pusey (1800-82), two of the leading figures in the movement. As an ordinand he was trained at Chichester Theological College, one of the main institutions for training

25 *Rev. Robert Shapland Hunt, M.A. (1817-1904), the first vicar of Mark Beech, 1852-1904.*

Tractarian priests, and at the time he met the Talbots he was a curate at Cuckfield, Sussex. To them he seemed to possess the precise qualifications, background and character they needed for an incumbent at Mark Beech, although they were not ready to offer the post then.[34] Their journey home coincided with the *coup d'état* which transformed Louis Napoleon Buonaparte from President of the Republic to Emperor Napoleon III, and Talbot was briefly detained in Provence as a 'spy'.[35] Incidentally, Louis already had a connection with our area: in preparation for an earlier attempted *coup d'état*, he had lodged some of his supporters at Brasted Place under the care of Mary Edwards, known as the Comtesse d'Espel, who was his mistress at the time, and he visited Brasted more than once.[36]

It was left, therefore, to Mrs. Talbot to oversee the completion of the church and the new house. It was left also to Mrs. Talbot to invite Hunt to take the living at Mark Beech, which was at £50 per annum plus a vicarage, and he duly did so.[37] He was to remain for 52 years, until his death, and the first vicar of Mark Beech was admired by those who knew him for his piety, sincerity and sanctity. He remained unmarried and lived at the vicarage with various siblings, particularly his sisters, Mary Jane and Theodora, who predeceased him, and in 1893, on the 40th anniversary of his ministry at Mark Beech, he was made a Canon of Canterbury Cathedral.

Having provided the land on the south-west corner of the crossroads for a church and a churchyard, the Talbots handed it to the Church Commissioners and retained only the rights of patronage and of access to the crypt. Once Mrs. Talbot and her two children had

removed to Falconhurst they gave Edells as the vicarage to the Church Commissioners also, while remaining the ground landlords. In 1853 in memory of his father, John Gilbert Talbot gave a clock and mechanism to the church, which was installed in the tower. This clock was made by Bernard Lewes Vulliamy (1780-1854), who was of Swiss descent and was the Queen's clockmaker. It was his clock number 1495, the last, and cost £71, including the face.[38] It was a 30-hour clock so somebody had to climb the tower daily to wind it, for which in 1915 £1 per annum was being paid, but it kept good time until it was electrified in 1960, although a renovation in 1997 seems to have been an improvement. The last

26   Bob Mattin, c.1978 (John Topham Library)

person to wind the clock by hand was Bob Mattin, a retired labourer from the estate, who lived at School Cottages and who died in 1982. Even after electrification he used to mount the tower steps every day to satisfy himself that all was well![39]

The building of a church and the appointment of a vicar necessitated the creation of a parish. As we have seen, Mark Beech had been divided since the original creation of parishes in the area between Cowden and Hever, with the historic centre of the village in Cowden. Indeed, the new church was in the parish of Cowden, if only just. On the north side of the church was and is a large beech tree, which some locals claim is on the site of the tree by which Mark Beech was given its name by the Jutes, and on the south side are two cypress trees, said to have been grown from seeds brought from Palestine by Lord Medway.[40] Before his death, J.C. Talbot had sketched the putative boundaries for a parish, which encompassed all his estate and more, but when the actual territory was carved out of Cowden and Hever it was not as extensive as he had envisaged.[41] Not many inhabitants today seem to know the exact boundaries of the parish and, therefore, of Mark Beech, and they may be astonished to discover what it does not include, rather than what it does. Strictly, therefore, Mark Beech does not include Wickens, nor Saxbys Mead, let alone Saxbys itself, nor Friendly Green, nor Dyehurst, nor Wilderness Farm, although the occupants may be surprised to learn it.

Reference has been made to the intention of the Talbots to expand the village, indeed to create a nuclear village for the first time. They never quite succeeded in achieving it, and their estate included a large number of scattered farmhouses, which remained largely tenanted for the first century of the estate's existence. However, hardly had the church and Falconhurst been completed than Mrs. Talbot embarked on the building of a school and schoolhouse, which were finished in 1854 and 1856 respectively. Two pairs of semi-detached labourer's cottages were planted round the corner in Cow Lane in the 1860s, and in 1911 a terrace of five more cottages was placed beyond them, the one nearest to the road accommodating the post office, which had previously been at Jessups. Other cottages were built around the estate, such as those at the Grove, above the Hole, and below Pilegate.[42]

The arrival of the Talbots in Mark Beech, the building of a church and the creation of a parish were undoubtedly major events in the history of the village, but the most important thing to happen in the second half of the 19th century was the appearance of the railway. British railways date at least from the 1830s, and by the 1860s an extensive network of lines had been put in place throughout the country, but, writing of his childhood in his memoirs towards the end of his life, Bishop Edward Talbot said of Mark Beech that, although it was less than 30 miles from London, the place was remote and backward.[43] We have seen how small the population was in mid-century and the same was true of the larger area around Mark Beech. At the 1861 census Edenbridge, Westerham and Crowborough all had fewer than 1,000 people each. East Grinstead had about 4,250, Sevenoaks about 4,900 and only Tonbridge and Tunbridge Wells were of any size, with a combined population of 21,000. A little further away, Uckfield had 2,000 people, Eastbourne 6,000, Lewes 9,000, Maidstone 23,000, Hastings 28,000, and Brighton and Hove 87,000. To the north, the whole area of what was to become outer, suburban London, including Beckenham, Bexley, Bromley, Chislehurst, Orpington and Sidcup, contained only 17,000 people, Bromley being the largest place with 5,500.[44] So this part of south-east England was an area of low population and mainly agricultural employment. Industry or commuting to London hardly existed, and this part of extreme south-west Kent and the adjacent bits of Sussex and Surrey formed an enclave where railways were effectively non-existent.

By 1863 the London, Chatham and Dover Railway controlled the lines along the Thames littoral to Gravesend, Dartford, the Medway towns, Canterbury and Dover, with branches from Swanley to Sevenoaks and from Faversham to Margate. In 1841 the London, Brighton and South Coast Railway[45] opened a line from London to Brighton via Croydon, Redhill and Haywards Heath. This company then started pushing eastwards along the Sussex coast from

Brighton and opened a line to Hastings via Lewes in 1846, with branches from it to Newhaven in 1847 and to Eastbourne and Hailsham in 1849. In 1855 the company started the penetration of the Weald with a line from Three Bridges to East Grinstead, and in 1858 an independent company built a line north from Lewes to Uckfield which the L.B.S.C.R. bought in 1864.[46]

Meanwhile, in 1842, the South Eastern Railway had built the line which came closest to Mark Beech for many years, through the valley between the North Downs and the High Weald from Redhill to Ashford via Edenbridge and Tonbridge. This line was extended to Folkestone in 1843 and to Dover in 1844, with branches from Paddock Wood to Maidstone in 1844, from Tonbridge to Tunbridge Wells in 1845 and from Ashford to Canterbury, Ramsgate and Margate in 1846. Until the extension of the London and Chatham system in the 1860s this route was the only way of getting from London to Canterbury and the Channel ports by train. In 1851-2 the South Eastern pushed its line from Tunbridge Wells to Hastings via Wadhurst and Robertsbridge and built a line to link Hastings and Ashford via Rye. In 1856, the company extended its line to Maidstone northwards to Strood.[47]

By about 1860 or so, then, the South Eastern controlled much of west Kent and the extreme east of Sussex, while the L.B.S.C.R.'s area was the axis from London to Brighton and the coast of Sussex east and west of Brighton. This left a vacuum in the area encompassed by East Grinstead, Edenbridge, Tunbridge Wells and Uckfield, in which, of course, Mark Beech was situated. Despite the lack of population and industry and despite an agreement between them in March 1864 not to encroach on each other's territory,[48] the two companies wanted to construct new lines which would link the towns of the area and enable them to compete on the routes considered to be most lucrative, such as those between London and the south coast. The L.B.S.C.R., in particular, planned to try to outflank its rival. The clue to this was the construction of a complex pattern of lines from Croydon to East Grinstead, from Oxted (Hurst Green) to Groombridge via Edenbridge, from Groombridge to Uckfield via Crowborough, from East Grinstead to Groombridge, and from Groombridge to Tunbridge Wells, as well as some other lines.[49] This would provide a more direct route to Lewes, Eastbourne and Hastings, create a new cross-Channel route to Dieppe from Newhaven, and give the possibility of running rights to the north-east through Tunbridge Wells. So to this end there was founded in 1865 the Surrey and Sussex Junction Railway Company which, though ostensibly an independent enterprise, was nothing more than a front for the L.B.S.C.R. The two companies shared several directors and, by August 1866, the L.B.S.C.R. held £125,000 out of £150,000 of shares.[50] The Three Bridges-East Grinstead line was extended to Tunbridge Wells in 1866 and in 1868 a single track line was opened from Groombridge to Uckfield.[51] Now all that was needed was the line northwards.

The well-known civil engineering contractors, the Waring Brothers, who had built railways, harbours and other works all over Britain and in Belgium, Portugal, Argentina and India, were appointed to construct the line through Mark Beech,[52] and between December 1865 and July 1867 more than £240,000 was spent on the project, about £162,000 on the works and around £80,000 on the purchase of land and compensation of landowners.[53] In Mark Beech this included payments to the Meade-Waldos, for land and disturbance on the north side of a tunnel, and to the Talbots, particularly regarding Edells, Coldharbour, Brook Farm, which was to be razed, and Wickens, for which altogether the Trustees of J.C. Talbot received £2,070 and Mead-Waldo £420.[54]

From the start construction of the railway went badly: the works cost more than anticipated and they got seriously behind schedule. Warings argued later that the engineering problems were more difficult than expected and that, surprisingly, or so they claimed, there was a shortage of labour. The Board of Directors of the L.B.S.C.R. became very alarmed as early as February 1866 and decided to formulate new agreements with the Surrey and Sussex and the contractors.[55] Eventually it was agreed on 18 May and was confirmed by the Board on 29 May that the two companies would merge and that the L.B.S.C.R. would pay all the Surrey and Sussex's debts and acquire those shares it did not already hold.[56]

Ironically, it was just at this moment that the *coup de grace* was given to the project because, first, on 11 May 1866, the great London brokers, Overend, Gurney & Co., who dominated the railway market, collapsed sending depressive shock waves through the whole British economy.[57] Secondly, by the early summer of 1866 one of the major engineering works was now in hand: digging a mile-long tunnel through the escarpment of the High Weald. Passing just west of the centre of Mark Beech and under the land of the Meade-Waldos and of the Talbots, this tunnel, starting in a cutting in Hever at about the 300 ft. contour, would drop about 50 feet as it proceeded southwards and emerge near the bottom of Blower's Hill, where a station for Cowden would be built; there was to be a station for Hever about half a mile north of it. Over the tunnel were to be three shafts or vents, which can still be seen sitting incongruously in the middle of fields and from which, until the 1960s, steam would emanate as trains passed below.

The construction of the railway had brought hundreds of workers and camp-followers to the area, as was usual in the era of railway building, and they posed problems of public health, lack of recreation, food supply and law and order.[58] Between 700 and 1,000 men were employed on Mark Beech Tunnel, mainly English but with some French-speaking engineers and supervisors. This was probably the consequence of Waring's previous contracts on the Continent, and over time French-speaking labourers were introduced until, by April 1866, it was said that there were four to five hundred of them.[59] Whether these people were replacing English workers or augmenting them is unclear, but a very explosive situation was created by the rumour or allegation that the French (they were probably a mixture of French, Belgians and Luxembourgers) were being paid between a third and a half less than their English counterparts and that it was company policy to replace English workers with cheaper, foreign labourers.[60] Inevitably this created an explosive, xenophobic situation, likely to boil over at any time.

The Kent Constabulary had been formed under the Borough and County Police Act of 1856 and had already had to deal with much petty crime in the area in association with the railway workings, frequently deploying men around Mark Beech above the normal establishment. On Sunday 5 August 1866, Superintendent Richard Dance from the divisional headquarters at Tonbridge had spent the day at Mark Beech with a sergeant and several constables. He was very alarmed at the heavy drinking in the two public houses, the *Kentish Horse* at Mark Beech and the *Victoria Arms* at Horseshoe Green, and the threatening language which he heard, and he ordered several of his men to return with him to Mark Beech the next morning.[61] He was too late because, in what was obviously a premeditated conspiracy, that very evening at Mark Beech Tunnel yard many English workers started to smash windows, break into huts and assault Frenchmen. Fourteen French workers were hustled out of Brook Farm, probably the original farmhouse, not the present one, and windows, furniture and crockery were broken.[62]

John West, the occupant of Brook Farm, hastened to Cowden to summon the two resident policemen, Police Constables William Solly and George Bassett. Waring's Inspector of Masonry, William Stanbrook, was also spending the night here.[63] The two policemen went to the station yard, but, hopelessly outnumbered by scores of taunting, aggressive and drunken Englishmen, Bassett rode off to Tonbridge to summon assistance while Solly observed from a safe distance. It must have been like the Wild West as Bassett thundered off on his horse into the night for reinforcements. He did not return with Dance and twelve other constables until 5 o'clock on Monday morning, when it was decided to summon more help and to inform the Chief Constable, Commander Ruxton.[64]

Ruxton hurried to Mark Beech and a company of infantry were put on standby at Shorncliffe Barracks, Folkestone, from where they could easily have been brought up the railway line to Edenbridge.[65] By now the French workers had fled to Hever and to Edenbridge, pursued by the English, and the Chief Constable proceeded there in his fly.[66] At Edenbridge the inhabitants bolted their doors and boarded up their windows as French workers scurried up and down the High Street seeking sanctuary, usually in vain. Nearly one hundred police were now present, but it seemed as if the English attackers were about to effect a final reckoning near the site of the new Edenbridge Town station, where the foreigners had congregated. The presence of so many police had a sobering influence though, and the whole riot now came to a rather tame, anti-climactic end.[67] Rumours that some people had been killed, or even very seriously injured, proved to be untrue. There is an oral tradition in the village that a small brick structure behind the *Kentish Horse* and abutting the churchyard wall was built as a mortuary for those killed, not so much in the riots, but during the course of constructing the railway, but the church burial registers provide no confirmation that anyone was killed at the railway workings. Such dead could have been buried elsewhere, of course, but only one two-and-a-half year old child is specifically identified in the register as being connected to the workings.[68] However there are two very intriguing entries in September 1866, that is about a month or so after the riots. On 13 September there occurred the funeral of Michel Smidt, aged 29 (Smidth and aged 39 on the death certificate), and on 17 September that of Franz Smidt (Smidth), aged 34, undoubtedly Michel's brother. They had both died on the days of their respective funerals from cholera, which in 1866 was enjoying its fourth great assault on the population and which killed 18,000 people in the United Kingdom.[69] They were described as railway labourers and their address is simply given as Mark Beech.[70] Their names have not been found in any other document. They were unequivocally working on the railway, but were they German, in which case all the workers could not have been French or French-speaking? Were they Flemish? With their names spelt as they were, they were almost certainly Alsatian, which was, of course, part of France. It is interesting and alarming, but not unexpected, to find an outbreak of cholera in the 1860s, especially in the kind of conditions which would undoubtedly have prevailed on the railway workings, for cholera certainly occurred in England as late as the 1890s. The men seem to have been buried with some haste, and it is sad to reflect that two brothers died so far from home. It is most unlikely, given the highly infectious character of cholera and the living and working

27 *Death Certificate of Michel Smidth, from cholera, 1866.*

conditions of these labourers, that these were the only cases of the disease amongst the workers on this construction project and further investigation of the matter certainly seems necessary.

On 9 August two magistrates enrolled a large number of Edenbridge citizens as Special Constables to accompany the full-time police who went to Mark Beech to make arrests.[71] Ten men were arrested and appeared at Tonbridge Magistrates Court on 11 August.[72] In October, at the Quarter Sessions in Maidstone, seven of them were imprisoned for a year with hard labour.[73]

Thus concluded the one event for which Mark Beech has any claim to fame in the outside world, the so-called Mark Beech Riots.[74] They helped to end the first phase of the building of the railway through Mark Beech. The Board of the L.B.S.C.R. were very dissatisfied with the contractors, with the prospects for the line and with the rising costs of the project. Although the line from East Grinstead to Tunbridge Wells via Groombridge had been completed on 21 February 1867, the Board decided not to be responsible for any more expenditure on the Croydon to East Grinstead and the Hurst Green to Groombridge sections,[75] and on 26 March any further work was abandoned.[76] The half-completed works were left until the 1880s, when the L.B.S.C.R. decided to revive the scheme. In 1884 the line from Croydon to Oxted and East Grinstead was opened, that to Edenbridge and Eridge and to Tunbridge Wells, via Mark Beech, four years later, and in 1894 the track was doubled between Eridge and Uckfield.[77]

Stations were opened at Cowden and Hever and these were extremely important for the local economy and the lives of the people in the area. Here was a double-track line with passenger trains taking about an hour direct to London. At Cowden the Talbots had a key for themselves and the staff at Falconhurst which gave them direct access to the London-bound platform. Both stations had extensive sidings and storage sheds, and up to the First World War and beyond they were used to bring in coal, building materials and other products, and to despatch milk and other agricultural products.[78]

Thus by 1890 at the latest Mark Beech was on the brink of potentially the most momentous changes in its history. It now had good communications with the outside world; it had a church, was an established ecclesiastical parish with defined boundaries, and had a school; a nuclear village seemed to be in the process of creation; and it had a family who owned much of the land in the village and were ambitious to put the place on the map. For an optimist the future looked good.

VII

The Evolution of the Village,

1850-1918

AS AGRICULTURE did and still does play such an important part in the life of the community it seems entirely appropriate that we should start our analysis of the village between the middle of the 19th century and the end of the First World War with a look at the farming activity during the period. Despite the removal of the Corn Laws between 1846 and 1849, British farming was generally prosperous during the third quarter of the 19th century.[1] This was as true for areas in which corn growing was not predominant as it was for those areas where it was. A growing population with a rising standard of living, plus the excessive cost of transporting food in bulk from abroad before the arrival of trans–continental railways and large steamships, created economic conditions in which British farmers could compete effectively in their own market.[2] The High Weald, of course, had never provided the ideal conditions of climate and soil, especially the latter, for successful farming in a market economy, but Kent had always enjoyed the close proximity of London, which was already the largest city in Europe by the end of the 18th century, and the metropolis had an insatiable demand for food.[3] But the road system around Mark Beech was not good and, as we have seen, there was no railway until the late 1880s. Consequently, it was the farmers of north and east Kent who were the chief beneficiaries, and the Mark Beech area did not share in the prosperity of farming even of other parts of Kent. This remained true up to the time of the First World War.[4] Indeed the High Weald had always been the poor partner of Kentish agriculture. Of all the regions of Kent in about 1840 it had the second lowest output of wheat, at 24.4 bushels per acre, the lowest yield of oats, at 33.6 bushels per acre, even though Cowden was a parish of above average oats production, and the lowest yield of clover at 19.5 cwt per acre.[5] It was an area where there was little incentive for inward capital investment, despite the example in Mark Beech of the Talbots, which, anyway, was investment in land *per se* rather than in new farming methods.[6] There were few incoming farmers and attitudes were con-servative and unreceptive to innovation.[7] One French observer, comparing the whole of the Weald to one of France's second-rate provinces, wrote in 1865 that the farmers were 'men without capital, and as ignorant as they were poor'.[8]

The so-called Great Depression of 1873-96 was not, therefore, something which especially affected the area as it was already in a depressed state. Between 1840 and 1875 the proportion of cultivated land in Cowden devoted to arable decreased from 64.1 per cent to 52.3 per cent, and in the area designated by Dr. Short as Hartfield, which included Cowden, it decreased further to 27.9 per cent in 1887 and to 23.55 per cent by 1913.[9] Even though the amount of hop growing in Cowden did increase to more than 107 acres in 29 gardens by 1875, thereafter it declined.[10] There was also a decline in corn growing.[11] In the long hot summer of 1851 (the year of the Great Exhibition), the hops and other crops suffered severely. 'The earth is baked to a cinder', wrote John Chetwynd Talbot, and 'it is something to be asking for rain in the middle of harvest', but, he complained, 'My poor hops suffered bitterly from the blight & I shall get all round about 1/3 of the crop which under kindly seasons I should have had. This is a loss of some hundreds, but must be endured.' The implication of this is that at least in the early days of their residence the Talbots were farming the home farm themselves, although the precise location of these hops has not been identified. There were, however, compensations for, 'In return the hot sultry weather bakes the life out of the weeds and I shall be able to clear our land to great advantage so that we must take the rough with the smooth.'[12] Naturally, a decrease in arable farming meant an increase in livestock and there were modest increases in the numbers of sheep, but more particularly in cattle.[13] Also some land was turned over to fruit growing, chiefly apples in this area.[14] Nevertheless, this was not within one of the five main areas of fruit growing in Kent identified by Dr. Harvey, and the number of orchards was always small.[15] Fruit growing, especially without the outlet of a railway, and livestock could not compensate for the loss of arable. It would be a mistake, however, to conclude that an extension of grassland was automatically a mark of agricultural poverty, because dairy farming and poultry required an increase of grassland and this part of the High Weald was never especially suitable for corn production.[16] To make corn-growing viable in the High Weald corn prices had to be at about 56-60s. per quarter and such prices were only achieved in the 1850s and between 1866 and 1874.[17]

The outbreak of large-scale warfare in Europe in 1914 temporarily changed the prospects for agriculture.[18] The military took over land in places like Crowborough and Ashdown Forest, Maresfield and Edenbridge, soldiers being encamped in Stangrove Park, but Mark Beech was not directly affected.[19] There was much ploughing up of pasture during the war and, therefore, a reversal in the decrease of land devoted to crops which had been taking place over the previous half century. The proportion of cultivated land under the plough increased to nearly 30 per cent of the total.[20] In Hartfield, Withyham and Cowden the acreage of cereals, which had dropped from about 1,270 in 1875 to only 360 in 1914 now increased again to nearly 700 acres by 1918, and potato production, which had been virtually static at about 50 acres between 1875 and 1914, increased to 127 acres by 1918.[21] In Mark Beech during the war, a part of High Buckhurst, near the crossroads, was converted to chicken farming, and a wooden house, which still survives as Ashtrees, was erected to accommodate a manager, Miss Dean, the daughter of the owners of High Buckhurst. The poultry farm itself has long disappeared.[22] Hop growing, on the other hand, declined markedly and the amount of livestock remained unchanged.[23]

During the war we see the first glimmerings of modern-style mechanisation, but at the same time a degree of rural depopulation. The population of Kent had already increased by at least 100 per cent in the century before 1851, but it continued to do so over the next 60 years.[24] For Mark Beech, it is more useful to take the area of the post-1889 administrative county, rather than the old geographical county. In 1851 the former had a population of 486,000, and this had increased to 869,000 by 1911, an increase of 79 per cent.[25] We might legitimately ask whether this was reflected in any way in the tiny example of the village. In 1851 Mark Beech had a population of 236. For two decades it did increase to 289 in 1861 and 301 in 1871, but thereafter it declined again and then hovered around plus or minus 250 so that the population was 216 in 1881, 248 in 1891, 268 in 1901 and 246 in 1911, an increase of only 4.23 per cent over a 60-year period.[26] This very slow growth, even compared with Kent as a whole, is undoubtedly explained by the fluctuations within a poor agricultural economy, but what is most striking is that the 1891 census, the last to which we can presently gain detailed access, reveals a high degree of multi-occupancy in the houses which existed at that time and, though so near to London, Mark Beech remained a rural and agricultural place. To take but one example of crowding, although there are many others, in 1891 what is now known as Old Buckhurst and is occupied in 1999 by two people, had 19 inhabitants, although it was slightly larger than the present structure.[27]

It is worth pausing at this point to make an analysis of the 1891 census. The population comprised 74 adult males, 79 adult females and 103 children, making a total of 256, with children constituting 41.2 per cent of it. Of the adult males 36 were agricultural labourers, six farmers and three gardeners, so 60.8 per cent of the total were involved in agriculture in some way. There were four bricklayers, two blacksmiths, one carpenter, one gamekeeper and one bailiff. Some of the six male servants, unspecified, were probably gardeners too. The balance was made up by two bakers and a miller, a railway porter, the stationmaster, Charles R. Daniels, a coachman (to the Vicar) and a police constable, George Bates, who lived in one of the cottages at Mark Beech Cross. Five men were described as being of independent means, including three from one family, the Woodhouses, at Lambert Cottage. There were 19 female servants, cooks, chambermaids, laundresses, and the women included the school teacher, Jane Scott, her assistant and niece, Agnes Scott, and a 35-year-old governess at Mapletreuse, employed by Ernest Baggallay J.P. for his children, called Miss Kate Freeman. There were five widows and three widowers and only one man described specifically as retired, although a few others were over 65 years of age. Three of the widows were described as being the head of their household. The evident conclusion is that, only about 100 years ago, Mark Beech was a community whose population was on average much younger than it has become today, with a large proportion of children, which was still overwhelmingly agricultural, with very few middle- or upper-class inhabitants.[28]

The church of Holy Trinity continued to be a major focus for much of the life of the village. Annual summer garden parties were held, usually in the grounds of Falconhurst, for fund-raising.[29] In 1893, to mark the 40th anniversary of the founding of the church and of Hunt's ministry, George Frederick Bodley (1827-1907), who had been a pupil of Sir Gilbert Scott and was one of the leading Victorian architects of the second generation of the Gothic Revival and a close friend of Edward Burne-Jones, Dante Gabriel Rossetti and William Morris, was commissioned to redesign entirely the sanctuary.[30] This he did, with tiles on the floor and a carved, stone reredos behind the altar. With Bodley present, the new chancel was consecrated by the Archbishop of Canterbury, Edward W. Benson (1829-96),[31] and in 1908, after Hunt's death, the reredos was painted in his memory.[32] This was part of extensive repairs and alterations to the church in 1907-8 under the supervision of the architect George H.

Fellows Prynne, when the opportunity was taken to build a vestry over the entrance to the vault/boiler room on the southern side of the chancel.[33] These works were executed by Hope Constable of Penshurst at a cost of more than £384.[34]

On the 50th anniversary of the foundation money had been raised by public subscription for the replacement of the old barrel organ with a pipe organ made by Henry Bishop of London and Ipswich, and this was installed in 1903. The cost was £216 13s. 6d. and the organ fund finished the project with a surplus of nearly £15 which was transferred to general funds.[35] A considerable coup was achieved when Sir Walter Parratt (1841-1924), Chief Professor of Organ at the Royal College of Music and Master of the King's Music, who later became Professor of Music at Oxford in 1908, was persuaded to come to Mark Beech and 'open' the new organ.[36] This organ had hand/foot bellows, but was supplied with an electric air-pump in 1952 after the church had been connected to the electricity supply in 1949; electric lights were installed to supplement the candelabra.[37] The organ had to be repaired and cleaned in 1923 at a cost of £38 16s. 0d. and this has been done several times since, including a major overhaul in 1952-3.[38] In the early days the organist was blind and he walked the six miles or so from Edenbridge and back twice each Sunday.[39] He was not a very proficient player and it has been written of him that 'his playing was incredibly bad; for the thunder of "Lo, He comes" he doubled his fists and rolled them up and down the keys; we never achieved the response to the 10th commandment or the charge to "Let the earth" in the Benedictus without a breakdown'.[40]

The other chief matter to do with the church, apart from the transfer of the parish from the diocese of Canterbury to that of Rochester in 1905,[41] was the provision of a vicarage. After the Talbots had moved to Falconhurst, Edells became the vicarage, as we have seen, and Robert Hunt lived in the Woodhouse's villa for more than 20 years. However, in 1873-5 Joseph Clarke (1819-88), the architect and surveyor to the Canterbury diocese who was responsible for the building of about 50 new churches, was appointed to make great alterations to Edells.[42] This he did, doubling the size of the house, removing the verandah, and installing features that were appropriate to a vicarage, such as carved crosses on some of the stone lintels and a little bowed stained-glass window over the front door, which is still known as the vicar's oratory,[43] although it now has clear glass. This typical red-brick Victorian house can still be seen, and careful scrutiny reveals that the two halves of it, which otherwise blend together well, are in different styles. The augmented vicarage was paid for by the Church Commissioners and Queen Anne's Bounty, but Mrs. J.C. Talbot bore some of the cost, particularly by supplying bricks to the value of £214 and by paying the final outstanding balance of £129, and the vicar himself paid for the black, cast-iron fireplaces, most of which can still be seen, at a cost of almost £13.[44] The bricks were produced on the estate at a site between Falconhurst and Alcocks, just as they had been in 1851-2, probably in connection with the building of Falconhurst.[45] Nineteenth-century maps and some other evidence show that there were two other brickworks in Mark Beech; one was to the north-east of Buckhurst Farm, and the other was about a quarter of a mile north of the village crossroads on the east side of Uckfield Lane.[46] The total cost of altering Edells, which was done by William Kesterton, was £1,623 plus fees of £117 for the architect.[47] The vicarage had extensive stabling and Hunt appears to have kept several horses and a carriage and to have employed a full-time coachman.[48]

By the turn of the century, however, Hunt was getting old and infirm and was finding it difficult to get up the hill to the church. It is said that there was a stone footpath all the way from the vicarage to the church across the fields and that it has been seen within living memory,[49] but it now seems to have disappeared and its exact route is, therefore, unknown. There was also a walkway parallel to the road from Falconhurst Lodge to the church so that the Talbot family and the servants at and around Falconhurst could walk to church without going on the road. This was known as Church Walk, but is now disused and overgrown, although it was certainly still being used up to 1939.[50] It is the reason why the fields on the south side of the road do not abut on it, there being a strip of overgrown land about 20 yards wide all the way from Falconhurst to the church.

In view of Hunt's aged condition, John G. Talbot, since the death of his mother in 1876 the owner of the estate, agreed to build a new vicarage in Cow Lane. The architect appointed was John Duke Coleridge (1879-1934), the grandson of Lord Coleridge, Lord Chief Justice of England, 1880-94, who was, as we have noted, a pupil of Sir Edwin Lutyens.[51] In 1904-5 a vast Lutyens-style house was built in Cow Lane along with two cottages for gardeners, etc. and a coach house.

This house can still be seen, divided now in two, and is known as the Old Vicarage. The builders were Hope Constable of Penshurst, now Butchers, and the cost of £2,400 plus architect's fees was met by J.G. Talbot.[52] There is a tradition in the village that the new vicarage was financed by public subscription but this was not the case, and what seems more likely is that some of the internal fittings were paid by public subscription. After completion the new vicarage was given to the Church Commissioners and Edells was returned to the Talbots, dilapidations of £307 having been first charged on it.[53]

Coleridge's house was not finished until 1905. Consequently, just as J.C. Talbot had never occupied Falconhurst nor seen the finished church, Hunt never lived at the new vicarage; he died in July 1904.[54] There are several contemporary testaments to the style of ritual that Robert Hunt and his patrons initiated at Holy Trinity, and also to the esteem in which the vicar was held and the saintliness of his character. A very brief one is by Gladstone.[55] Another is by Lady Lucy Cavendish, née Lyttelton (1841-1925), the niece of Mrs. J.C. Talbot and, following her husband's assassination in Phoenix Park, Dublin in 1886, the widow of Lord Frederick Cavendish.[56] She was confirmed in Mark Beech church, gave to it the altar cross and candelabra, and spent the last years of her life at Penshurst.[57] The fullest and most interesting account, however, is by Lady Gwendolen Stephenson, née Talbot (1877-1960), whose words about the blind organist have already been quoted. It is unfortunate that, although Hunt was regarded as an inspirational preacher, only one of his sermons, that which he gave at the Golden Jubilee anniversary, has survived in print.[58] Moreover, as is often the case with sermons and political speeches, it fails to have the same effect on a cold page as it did on listeners. Writing in 1921, Lady Stephenson reflected common opinion in the village when she referred to Hunt's inspirational presence. To her the great event in the church's calendar was Harvest Thanksgiving. The choir boys robed in the porch and, having processed down the aisle, were crammed into the chancel. 'It was our great day in early times,' she wrote, and 'the church was decorated riotously with vegetables and fruit.' Of Hunt, she observed that 'the unadorned church, the deplorable music, the long services, were somehow transmuted by his awe-struck reverence, his depth of devotion, his saintliness, in fact, into worthy acts of worship. His 10 minute sermons were always beautiful, often sublimely beautiful.'[59] He was a difficult man to follow and, for whatever reasons, Hunt's 52-year tenure was followed by three successors over the next 16 years.[60]

We have already seen how the Talbots set about adding houses to the stock in the village. They were not the only ones to do so. In the 1840s and '50s there began to be built the first examples, other than Falconhurst, Edells and the church, which were not timber framed. Buckhurst had already been rebuilt in 1790, but there are a number of examples from the mid-19th-century decades including Dyehurst, several of the properties on the east side of Horseshoe Green, Cherry Tree Cottages and the *Queens Arms*. Jessups was to follow in the 1870s. With the construction of the railway a row of terraced houses was built on the north side of the hill above Cowden station, but there are five impressive new houses of this period, namely, Eden Hall, Rickwoods, the new Vicarage (now the Old Vicarage), High Buckhurst and Fairholme, which were built in 1877-8, 1899, *c*.1904-5 and 1920-1 respectively. In the 1870s and '80s Eden Hall, then called Mapletreuse, was owned by Sir Richard Baggallay, a former M.P., Attorney-General, and from 1875-85 a High Court judge. Sir Richard, who died in 1888, and his wife have memorial plaques in Mark Beech church. He had six sons (his oldest predeceased him) and six daughters. The sons included Claude, a lawyer, Ernest, also a lawyer and M.P. for Brixton 1885-7, Frank Thomas, F.R.I.B.A., Frederick, an Anglican

29   *Sir Richard Baggallay (1816-88), Q.C., Member of Parliament, Solicitor-General, Attorney-General, High Court Judge, owner and occupant of Mapletreuse, 1876-88. (Community of St Andrew)*

30   Mapletreuse (Eden Hall), from the north east, 1878. (Community of St Andrew)

31   Eden   Hall   (formerly Mapletreuse), from the south east, 1998. (Paul Houlton)

clergyman, and Henry, an army officer. One of his daughters, Ada, married Edmund Meade-Waldo and another, Elinor, a Charrington from How Green House. Sir Richard bought Mapletreuse in 1876 and immediately set about building a large country mansion on the front of the old farmhouse.[61] This is the Victorian house which can be seen today, now St Andrew's Convent, and it was certainly finished by 1878. Ernest inherited the house, and after his mother's death in June 1892 he sold the house to Mrs. Charlotte Cubitt for £11,500. She gave it to her son, Thomas Cubitt (1870-1947), the grandson of Lewis Cubitt (1799-1883), the architect brother of Thomas Cubitt (1788-1855), the famous speculative builder, later Lord Ashcombe, on his marriage the following year.[62] Ernest Baggallay went to live in Moat House, Cowden and became Chairman of Cowden Parish Council on its formation in 1894, a position he was to keep until he left the area in 1912.[63] Meanwhile

Thomas Cubitt took up residence at Mapletreuse in 1894, renamed the house Eden Hall and owned it until 1945.[64] Stylistically all these houses are typical of their period and all were large properties, clearly built for wealthy families. Cubitt married Countess Fede Riccardi, whose father was Italian and whose mother was English. In 1904 he was made a Count by King Victor Emmanuel III of Italy, was granted a Royal Warrant in 1905 to use the title in Britain, and thereafter called himself Count Riccardi-Cubitt. Once his children were grown up, he spent half the year in Italy and half the year at Eden Hall, and it is said he owned the first car to be seen in the Edenbridge area, a French Darraq.[65] At the same time a few houses disappeared, such as Curd's, which was lost in a fire in 1856,[66] and Pound House, which seems to have disappeared in the 1880s.

Forty years ago, Professor W.G. Hoskins designated the period 1570-1640 as the era of 'the Great Rebuilding' in southern England and the Midlands.[67] Even if this hypothesis has not entirely withstood the force of subsequent criticism, there are certainly a number of examples in Mark Beech from that period or slightly earlier. From the 15th century come Hole Cottage, Old Buckhurst and Horseshoe Green Farm, and from the 16th and 17th, Pyle Gate, Old Farm, Buckhurst Cottage, Bramsells, Elylands and Cole Allen. One of Elylands recent inhabitants was the daughter of General Sir Reginald Wingate, a distinguished soldier and administrator in Egypt and the Sudan, Mrs. Victoria Dane, who was the last god-child of Queen Victoria. Cole Allen's inhabitants have included Guy Ewing (see below) and Violet Ironside Bax, who died in 1953 and left Mark Beech church a large sum of money which was absorbed into general diocesan funds for the repair of churches. Nevertheless, the real period of house building in Mark Beech was 1840-1920, with concentrated bursts of construction in 1840-60 and in 1875-1920. This period saw the building not only of the properties mentioned on pages 75-6 above but also of the rebuilt Edells (twice), Falconhurst, the rebuilding of Gilridge, the *Queens Arms*, the school and school house, nine cottages in Cow Lane, Jersey Cottage and the adjacent buildings, the Grove, Station Cottages and Cowden and Hever Stations, Ashtrees (originally the Brown House) and a few others. In 1909, after the death of Mr. A.H. Denny of Underriver, the whole of the central part of High Buckhurst, Hoppers Bank and the properties on the eastern side of Horseshoe Green, including the *Victoria Arms*, plus Curd's and Wickens farms were put up for sale. In the auctioneer's sale catalogue the central plateau on the top of Mark Beech Hill was described as a 20-acre building site, which 'occupies a most delightful and healthy position, at a height of between 400 and 500 feet above sea level, and commands on all sides particularly extensive and magnificent views over the surrounding picturesque country', 'affording splendid Sites for the erection of one or more residences'. Messrs. Langridge and Freeman, the selling agent, also indicated a field to the south-east of Wickens as suitable for a mansion.[68] J.G. Talbot bought most of this land and kept it for agricultural purposes so this idea was not fulfilled, but it was potentially very much a straw in the wind for the future of Mark Beech.[69]

It is this period too that sees the emergence of the four public houses in the area: the *Kentish Horse*, known for a while as the *Kentish Arms*,[70] on Mark Beech crossroads, the *Victoria Arms* at Horseshoe Green, the *Queens Arms* at Cowden Pound, and the *Bricklayers Arms* at Heathen Street. The *Kentish Horse* was the brainchild of Christopher Burfoot, who owned the building, which may have once been two cottages. At the time of the 1841 census it was described as an alehouse, but from the 1851 census onwards it became a public house

32   The Queens Arms, *1998.*
The small board to the left of the
door reads: 'Lager not sold here'.
(Paul Houlton)

with Burfoot as the landlord, and the Burfoots were still the licensees as late as 1911, although they seem to have gone by 1922.[71] The *Queens Arms* appears also in 1841; it was built by William Longley from Pound House on the opposite side of the road and he and his descendants were the landlords until the First World War.[72] The *Victoria Arms* became a flourishing inn when the railway was under construction in the 1860s; it was closed down during the First World War, when the first serious attempt was made to curtail drinking hours, but a careful look at the building today reveals that the wrought iron pole, from which hung the pub sign, is still in place. The landlord for many years was Winifrith, who also farmed some of the land around Horseshoe Green, and he was succeeded in 1909-14 by H.C. Skinner, before he moved on to be tenant of Wickens between the wars.[73] The *Bricklayers Arms* was at the top of Stick Hill in the house now known as Bowlinglands. Strictly it was always an alehouse rather than fully licensed premises, and it closed in 1910 through lack of sufficient patronage.[74] When the railway was being completed in the 1880s, or while the lake at Hever Castle was being dug, the workers gave several of the pubs in the area pseudonyms so that the foreman and others did not know where they had gone, and the *Bricklayers Arms* was called by them the 'Barking Donkey'.[75]

As the major landowners and the occupants of the 'big' house the Talbots inevitably continued to play a central role in the life of the village. In addition to their many friends and acquaintances they were part of a large extended family related over the generations to many land-owning and professional families including, *inter alia*, the Lytteltons and Cobhams, the Antrims, Bridgemans, Gladstones, Glynnes, Guests, Streatfields and Stephensons. They brought to Falconhurst and to the church many of these relations and friends, but at the heart of their relationships for much of the 19th century was the triangular connection between the Talbot, Gladstone and Lyttelton families.[76] J.G. Talbot, indisputably head of the family from 1876, stood unsuccessfully at Kidderminster in 1862 and at Malmesbury in 1865, but became Conservative Member of Parliament for West Kent in 1868 and at a by-election in 1878 transferred to the seat for Oxford University on the elevation of another Kent landowner, Gathorne Hardy, to the peerage as Viscount Cranbrook.[77] Talbot was an M.P. for 41 years and spent most of them on the back benches; he was Parliamentary Secretary at the Board of Trade, 1878-80, and in 1885 was considered by Lord Salisbury, the Prime Minister, for the position of minister of education (Vice-President of the Committee of the Privy Council on Education), but was passed over in favour of Edward Stanhope, whose family were near neighbours as landowners at Chevening, on the advice of Balfour.[78] He did not contest his seat in January 1910, but by the end of his parliamentary career he had become Father of the House of Commons, while in 1897 he had been made a Privy Councillor. He was also a Church Commissioner and since 1867 had been Chairman of West Kent Quarter Sessions. From 1889 until his death he also represented the area known as the Ward of Sevenoaks (3) on the new Kent County Council, where he was succeeded by Colonel Charles Williams of Bough Beech.[79] He had a large family of five sons and six daughters, and on his death from pneumonia in 1910 the estate was inherited by his eldest son, George John Talbot (1861-1938). J.G. Talbot had the distinction of being the last Member of Parliament to have a town house in Great George Street, Westminster, and after his death most of it was pulled down. He was buried at Mark Beech and the large number of mourners included Herbert Gladstone, W.E.'s son, who was at the time Home Secretary in Asquith's Government and who had been one of the Gladstone family staying at Falconhurst on Census Day in April 1861. On the same day as his funeral there was a Memorial Service in Westminster Abbey, effectively his parish church in London, to mark his distinguished service to the community.[80]

We have already noted the close friendship between Caroline Talbot and Catherine Gladstone, which had become especially intense after the death of Caroline's husband in 1852.[81] In 1839, in a joint ceremony at Hawarden, Flintshire, which had been the Glynne family home but thereafter became the country home of the Gladstones, Catherine had married William Ewart Gladstone, and her sister Mary (1813-57) had married the 4th Baron Lyttelton (1817-76).[82] On another occasion Catherine's brother, Henry Glynne (1810-72), married Lyttelton's sister, Lavinia (1821-50). Her oldest brother, Sir Stephen Glynne Bt. (1807-74), was the author of *Notes on the Churches of Kent* (1877), which omits strangely any reference

33 John Gilbert Talbot (1835-1910) with his family, 1878. Meriel extreme left, George J. back row left, J.G.T. seated right, Gwendolen (later Lady Stephenson) front right, Mrs. Meriel T. (formerly Lyttelton), front centre. (Charles Talbot)

34 W.E. Gladstone with his family, 1884. Gladstone standing at back, Mary extreme left, Herbert middle front, Agnes (Mrs. Wickham) front row, second from right. (Charles Talbot)

to Mark Beech. This book was published after Sir Stephen's death so he might have made good the omission had he seen his work to the press. The Gladstones paid frequent visits to Falconhurst: Gladstone's diaries show him talking to Robert Hunt, walking the countryside, taking carriage drives to Cowden, to Penshurst to lunch with Hardinge and to other places, and worshipping at Mark Beech and Hever churches. His penchant for physical exercise is exemplified by the long walks he took and the fact that on one occasion he and a son walked the 4½ miles from Falconhurst to Edenbridge (top) station to return to London, the baggage following in a cart.[83] The friendship was so close that, during the parliamentary session of 1858, while Gladstone's house at Carlton Terrace was being refurbished, Catherine remained at Hawarden, but William stayed with Mrs. Talbot at Great George Street.[84] At the time of the 1861 census, when Gladstone was Chancellor of the Exchequer, most of his family, though not W.E. himself, were staying at Falconhurst, and over the years various members of the Talbot family visited his home at Hawarden.[85] At one time it was thought that J.G. Talbot would marry one of Gladstone's daughters, Agnes, but instead he married Meriel Sarah Lyttelton (1840-1925), one of Lord Lyttelton's daughters, and his brother Edward married one of her sisters, Lavinia (1847-1939).[86] Thus the lives of the three families—the Talbots, the Gladstones and the Lytteltons—became completely intertwined in both London and Mark Beech and these relationships were further strengthened by Edward Talbot, Stephen Gladstone and Albert Lyttelton going to prep school together.[87] In 1873 Lyttelton tried unsuccessfully to persuade Prime Minister Gladstone to have his peerage raised to an earldom and, when Lyttelton subsequently went insane and committed suicide by throwing himself down a stairwell, William and Catherine Gladstone insisted on going to inspect the house in Park Crescent, London, to satisfy themselves that it had been suicide and not an accident.[88] Further Gladstonian links with Mark Beech are provided by the fact that for many years in the second half of the 19th century, Oakedene, now Saxbys, was owned and occupied by the Carmichaels, one of whom, Sir James Carmichael, was one of Gladstone's secretaries in the mid-1880s;[89] secondly, in the 1860s, another of Gladstone's secretaries was James Frederick Stuart-Wortley, the son of Caroline Talbot's brother; and, thirdly, Old Buckhurst is today occupied by John Gladstone, the G.O.M.'s great-grandson. It would seem that Gladstone never again visited Falconhurst after 1876, when he attended Caroline Talbot's funeral, but his children certainly did so up to the time of the First World War, the last being his daughter, Mary Drew, in 1917.[90] Nearly

60 years earlier Mary had written one of her earliest surviving letters, to Lavinia Lyttelton, from Falconhurst.[91]

Lord Lyttelton was married twice and had 12 children. Two of his daughters were, of course, married into the Talbot family and a third, Lucy, has been mentioned already. It was Gladstone, inevitably, who had appointed her husband Lord Lieutenant in Ireland. Yet three of Mrs. J.G. Talbot's brothers also paid many visits to Falconhurst. First there was General Sir Neville Lyttelton (1845-1931), who was probably the most distinguished of his family. A professional soldier, he commanded a brigade in the Sudan, 1898-99, and a division in the South African War, 1899-1902, and became C.-in-C. in South Africa, 1902-4. In 1904 he became Chief of the Imperial General Staff and, in 1908, C.-in-C. in Ireland. From 1913-31 he was Governor of the Royal Hospital, Chelsea. Gladstone was one of his heroes, and having attended Gladstone's famous speech on Armenia at Liverpool in 1896, Lyttelton accompanied Mrs. Gladstone at her husband's funeral in 1898.[92] He was a frequent visitor to Mark Beech when his military duties permitted, and on his return from the Sudan in 1899 he was met at Cowden station by the Edenbridge Town Band (which still flourishes) and had his carriage hauled all the way up the hill to Mark Beech, where he spoke to the assembled villagers.[93] In September 1914 he addressed a recruitment meeting in Edenbridge as a result of which nine men enlisted.[94] His brother, Albert Victor (1844-1928), was an Anglican priest of a High Church kind. He ministered at Hawarden and in South Africa, and in old age moved between lodgings in London and his sister's home in Mark Beech. Unmarried, he employed a housekeeper in London, to whom his sister, Mrs. Talbot, would refer as 'Albert's concubine', and on his death he was buried in Mark Beech churchyard, just by the east gate.[95] Another brother, Alfred (1857-1913), played cricket for Cambridge University, Middlesex and

35   Mary Gladstone (centre) at Falconhurst, 1877, with Mary Talbot (left) and Katie Wickham (right). (Charles Talbot)

36   General Sir Neville Lyttelton (1845-1931), as Colonel Lyttelton, 1888. (Charles Talbot)

four times for England against Australia and in 1903-5 became Secretary of State for the Colonies in Arthur Balfour's cabinet. He much enjoyed his visits to Falconhurst and described them in a letter to his sister, Lavinia, as 'sunny little intervals'.[96] Balfour (1848-1930), who had wanted to marry another Lyttelton sister, Mary, 'May' (1850-75), was another visitor to Falconhurst, as was Prime Minister Stanley Baldwin (1867-1947).[97]

Mention of cricket brings us to another prominent Mark Beech activity. The Talbots were keen cricketers, as were the Lytteltons. It was said that Lord Lyttelton had so many children because he wanted to create a family cricket team! Unfortunately, it seemed, he had more daughters than sons, but this did not matter as the females in both families were interested in the game and, moreover, very good at it. Many landed families in the 19th century formed cricket clubs, mainly to provide games for the family and for estate workers, and Falconhurst was no exception. A club was founded in 1854 and has been playing on the same ground ever since. It was called Falconhurst Cricket Club, and until about 1918 was made up mainly of family and estate workers. After the First World War its playing membership broadened so that increasingly it became in effect Mark Beech Cricket Club, although it retains its old name down to the present day. Before 1914 the highlights of the year were an annual match between the estate and the village and a match between two female teams, mainly of Talbot and Lyttelton women, but after 1918 the matches were between Falconhurst and a President's XI on the Saturday and against Chiddingstone on the Monday.[98] The earliest match for which a record has survived took place on 13 September 1860, when Falconhurst went to play Chiddingstone Hoath, a club now known as Stonewall Park. It appears that in those days matches were of two innings per side, as in first-class cricket today. On this occasion Falconhurst won by one wicket, the scores being Chiddingstone Hoath 35 and 44, Falconhurst 33 and 47 for 9.[99] From the late 1880s Meriel Talbot, who was said to have been an outstanding batswoman with a fearsome cover drive, was known as 'Slasher' Talbot and is remembered by a friend as 'a tip-top wicket-keeper',[101] organised two women's teams, and the Streatfields also ran one at Chiddingstone. Meriel's teams were a women's branch of Falconhurst Cricket Club, drawing on family and a few women from the village, and a team drawn from a wider area, which was known as the White Heather Club although why is unknown. The players for the White Heathers included not only members of the Talbot and Lyttelton families, but such ladies as Maude Lawrence, Lady Idina

37 *Ladies cricket match at Falconhurst, 27 August 1886. Charles Baggallay and Bertram Talbot can be seen umpiring.* (Charles Talbot)

38   Miss M. Talbot's XI versus Miss M. Kemp's XI, Falconhurst, 30 August 1889. Most of the teams were drawn from the Talbot, Kemp, Baggallay and Wynne Roberts families. Sir Richard Baggallay is standing at the back, in the centre. (Charles Talbot)

Brassey, Dame Maud Bevan and the composer Dame Ethel Smythe (1858-1944).The players were fully equipped with conventional cricket gear, down to a green cap with a large white figure 'W' on it, the Falconhurst cap being green with 'FCC' on it.[101] Whether Alfred Lyttelton ever played for Falconhurst is unknown, but it is quite possible that he did on a few occasions.

Another feature of life on the Falconhurst estate which must be mentioned is the fire brigade. This was founded in the early days of the estate and was a properly equipped fire-fighting unit with a horse-drawn pump. It was made up of estate workers and its primary purpose was to serve the estate. Nevertheless, they would attend incidents elsewhere and helped to extinguish fires at, for example, Prinkham Farm, Chiddingstone in October 1921, and at Lockskinners Farm, Chiddingstone on 17 March 1924.[102] In 1908 the Falconhurst Brigade offered to give coverage to Cowden village, if a fire hydrant were put in the High Street, but the parish council refused to do this at public expense.[103] This is slightly surprising because the collective folk-memory would surely have remembered the fire in 1657 which had destroyed a large part of the village?[104] Proper drill and practice was taken very seriously, and the Falconhurst Brigade went to competitions all over the county, at which they consistently achieved commendable results against larger, better funded town brigades. In July 1922, for example, the brigade took part in the South East Competition at Gillingham and took second place out of 72 competing units.[105] The unit was badly affected by members going into the armed forces after 1914 but, as we have seen, it survived throughout the interwar period and remained an impressive organisation, at least in the 1920s, in which Sir George Talbot took a close personal interest. It did not survive the Second World War for a number of reasons, including the absence of many of its members during the war and the reorganisation of fire-fighting services as a County Council responsibility after 1945.

Mention has already been made of the village school, considered by Mrs. J.C. Talbot to be her particular responsibility. We have seen that a school and a school house were built in the early 1850s. The school itself had accommodation for 60 children, although actual attendance was usually more in the region of 40, and a divided cottage provided for the head teacher and a library of books and daily and weekly papers and periodicals.[106] Part of one of these buildings was used for a time as an orphanage, this being another of Mrs. Talbot's charitable interests. Mrs. Talbot also founded the Parochial Mission Women's Association and her son the Kent Penitentiary for Fallen Women, the national association having been co-founded by uncle William Gladstone.[107] The school was very much integrated into the life of the church and provided education within a religious context. It was not, however, a National School, having been founded by the Talbots and supervised by them, the vicar and the vestry. In 1900 J.G. Talbot gave the school to the Canterbury Diocesan Board of Education, but everyday control remained in local hands.[108]

The school was for children of elementary school age and was free. Very unfortunately, the Log Books of this school seem to be lost, so it is impossible to provide a detailed account of it, but from other sources we do at least know the names of the teachers. The first teacher was John King, who seems to have been in Mark Beech for about 20 years. By 1871 King had been replaced by William Kibblewight, who was replaced in turn in 1881 by Mrs. Emma Sarah Fox. It is most unusual to find a married woman teaching in the 19th century, unless a widow. Emma, whose maiden name was Robinson and who had been born in Hampstead, was 30 years old and married to carpenter George Charles Fox. At the time of the 1881 census she had living with her in the school house a daughter, Helen Mary, who had been born in Mark Beech on 20 June 1880 (she, not the father, having registered this birth), and two sisters, aged 12 and 15, but there is no sign of her husband, who does not appear at any other address in Cowden or Hever. George may have been the son or brother of Frederick Robert Fox, who appears in Kelly's Directory and in the Poll Books of the 1850s and '60s as the tenant at Falconhurst Farm, but who does not feature in any of the censuses between 1841 and 1881. Where was Emma's husband on Census night 1881? Was he absent for some good reason? Were the Fox's reluctant to be enumerated? Had this been a marriage (which was not in Mark Beech) forced by pregnancy and husband and wife had since parted? Was Emma the recipient

39 *Boys at Mark Beech School, c.1930. Wally Leppard third from left; others unidentified. (Mrs. Walter Leppard)*

of the Talbot's charity? Are there quite ordinary explanations?[109] Here is a possible Victorian mystery about which we could speculate endlessly but are unlikely to find answers. By 1891 we find Miss Jane Scott, with an assistant, as teacher, but she was replaced in 1899 by Miss Mary Jennings, who remained for 25 years and is still remembered by a small number of older villagers.[110] Miss Jennings was assisted, at least at one time, by Miss Gardiner.[111]

As might seem natural and appropriate in a village not far from London in the second half of Queen Victoria's reign, many anniversaries and special events were celebrated in Mark Beech with rituals of one kind or another, both of a solemn and a jolly kind. The major events of the church's calendar were marked by parties for children or special services in Holy Trinity. The anniversary of the founding of the church was always celebrated annually with a special service in early December to which outside preachers or celebrants of a distinguished character were frequently invited.[112] Royal occasions were celebrated too: Queen Victoria's Golden Jubilee in 1887 was marked by the planting of an oak tree, complete with a metal plaque, at the crossroads, and this tree is still flourishing. In 1897, at the Diamond Jubilee, a carved stone plaque was affixed to the outside corner of the school and this survives for later generations to view. It is said that Edward VII attended Garden Parties at Hever Castle,[113] and for the Coronation of George V in 1911 a large party was organised for all the children of the village.[114]

The life of the area was to be changed very much when, in 1903, the Meade-Waldos, who had been living at Stonewall Park for about 70 years, sold Hever Castle and the Cobham half of the Hever estate to the Astor family. The farmers to the north-east of Mark Beech now had new landlords, who brought with them great wealth and the vigour of the New World. The Astors had emigrated in the 18th century from Germany to North America where they became extremely wealthy from the fur trade and then from investment in New York real estate. From 1882-6 William Waldorf Astor (1848-1919) was the American Minister in Rome. In 1890 he inherited from his father a fortune said to have exceeded $100 million (then worth about £21 million and, maybe, about £2,100 million in 1999 values) and decided to settle with his family in England, where he became a naturalised British subject in 1899. He bought Cliveden House in the Thames valley in 1893, but gave it to his eldest son in 1906, having acquired Hever in November 1903. Astor lived some of the time in Italy and one of the consequences was the importation of much classical and other Italian sculpture and the creation of the Italian Gardens at Hever. Hever had never been a substantial, nuclear village, but Astor destroyed some of the houses that did exist, such as the ones opposite the *Henry VIII* public house, because he wished to create a 'Tudor village' within the curtilage of the castle. He also dammed the river Eden to create a large artificial lake alongside the castle and 145 men were employed to dig it by hand. All this work was completed by November 1906,[115] and thereafter the presence of the Astors provided the locality with a considerable amount of new employment, a wider fame for Hever, and a lustre when William Waldorf was created Baron Astor in 1916 and Viscount in 1917.[116] His eldest son, Waldorf Astor (1879-1952), who was married to the famous Nancy Astor (1879-1964), lived at Cliveden, but Hever Castle was occupied by the second son, John Jacob Astor (1886-1971), who was himself raised to the peerage in 1956 as Baron Astor of Hever.[117] His son, Gavin (1920-87), the 2nd Baron, became Lord-Lieutenant of Kent and was much loved and is well remembered in the area.

One very important aspect in the life of any community was, of course, the supply of healthy water and the disposal of wastes, matters that were of supreme interest to the

Victorians. Most of the larger or older houses in Mark Beech, including Bramsells, Buckhurst, Old Buckhurst, Falconhurst, Elylands, Pyle Gate, Edells, Horseshoe Green Farm and Lambert Cottage had wells, as did the school and the cottages around it when they were built in the early 1850s, but others, such as Cherry Tree Cottages and the small houses at Horseshoe Green, were supplied by springs, which are clearly marked on 19th-century maps.[118] An alternative supply was provided from the pond at Marl Pit Shaw via a filter and a pipeline, although this may have been for farm animals. At some time in the late 19th century a bore hole was created on the top of Mark Beech Hill, and a galvanised iron wind-pump erected to supply water to nearby parts of the village; at least three pipes ran from this pump: one down to the crossroads and the houses there, one to a tank, presumably again for animals, in Cow Lane near Old Farm, and the third down to High Buckhurst.[119] This system was discontinued in the 1950s, when the wind-pump was dismantled and most of it left on the ground, where it can still be seen in the woods to the south-east of the village. Until the 20th century sewerage was tipped into pits.

We have already noted the formation of the Sevenoaks Union for the administration of the Poor Law, but the surviving records are not very extensive. It is still difficult, therefore, to analyse the position in Mark Beech in this respect with any precision. At an impressionistic level it would appear that the inhabitants of Mark Beech did not become involved extensively with the system; nearly all the people recorded in the Pauper Index and in the Death and Baptism Registers, which constitute much of what has survived from this period, were from addresses in other parts of Cowden and Hever. There are, however, a few exceptions: in 1872 Ann Chesson, age unspecified, said to be from the Hole, Cowden, which is in Mark Beech, was admitted (although the 1871 census shows several Chessons living in Cowden High Street, there is no Ann anywhere);[120] on 12 November 1881, Ann Fford died aged 79 in the work-house and was buried at Mark Beech. The 1881 census reveals that the previous April, Ann, born in Cowden and a widow of 78, was a member of the household of her nephew, George Collins, agricultural labourer at Hever Warren, not strictly in Mark Beech. Here was a household of seven people and one supposes that Collins could not cope with the presence of his aunt any longer.[121] In March 1867 and in March 1873 two female Collins's gave birth to children in the workhouse, although what precise connection they had with others of that name in the area is unclear.[122] On 5 July 1897 Richard Boakes, a name found frequently in the church registers and in the census returns for Cowden and Hever, was buried at Mark Beech having died in the Union aged 70.[123] Finally, the Servants and Apprentices Book indicates that many of the farmers around about, including one of the Streatfields at Polebrook Farm, Hever, took on boys and girls from the Union, but none appear to have been in Mark Beech.[124]

Mark Beech remained within the parliamentary constituency of West Kent until the county was divided into three two-member constituencies by the Second Reform Act of 1867 and the franchise was again extended, although not by much in the county constituencies.[125] Mark Beech was still in West Kent, but this was now a smaller area as there were West, Mid and East Kent constituencies. Secret ballot was not introduced until 1872, so at least for the 1868 election, won by Gladstone and the Liberals although West Kent was held by two Conservatives, including J. G. Talbot, we can see how the small number of Mark Beech electors voted.[126] One of the Liberal candidates in 1865 and 1868 was Sir John Lubbock, later Lord Avebury (1834-1913), who lived at Downe. Having failed in 1868 to defeat J. G. Talbot by only

55 votes, he became M.P. for Maidstone, 1870-80, and for London University, 1880-1900 (from 1886 as a Liberal Unionist). He was the creator of Bank Holidays.[127]

Under the Septennial Act of 1711 elections for the House of Commons had only to be held every seven years, although they were usually more frequent than that. At the time of the elections during the 1850s and '60s the number of electors in the district (although few of them lived in Mark Beech) was as follows: 1852 Hever 18, Cowden 31, Chiddingstone 26; 1857 Hever 21, Cowden 26, Chiddingstone 20; 1859 Hever 25, Cowden 21, Chiddingstone 23; 1865 Hever 16, Cowden 26, Chiddingstone 22; 1868 Hever 38, Cowden 48, Chiddingstone 43.[128] The number of these electors with addresses or property in Mark Beech did not usually reach double figures until 1867, and the Second Reform Act, which introduced a householder franchise, had minimal effect here. Richard Bannister and James Longley consistently voted Liberal and they were joined by Sir James Carmichael when he moved into the area, but everyone else, if they voted at all and there were plenty of those who didn't, voted Conservative. In 1868 the only Liberal voters were Carmichael and Robert Fox, who lived at Falconhurst Farm.[129] In 1857 West Kent was won by the two Liberal candidates, C.W. Martin and James Whatman, but at all other elections the Conservatives were successful, whatever the national result, and M.P.s included not only J.G. Talbot in 1868 and 1874 but, appropriately perhaps, Viscount Holmesdale, 1859-68, and Viscount Lewisham, 1878-85. Mark Beech was not to be represented by a Liberal again until 1906. By the Third Reform Act of 1883-5 rural Kent was divided into eight single-member constituencies and the farm labourers were given the vote, thereby probably increasing the Liberal share of the vote, although there were other factors accounting for this.[130] Mark Beech was incorporated within the south-west or Tonbridge division and, although some elections were close, the division was won by Conservative candidates at every election up to the First World War other than that of 1906, when it was won by A.P. Hedges for the Liberals. The Conservative M.P.s were R. Norton, 1885-92, A.S. Griffith-Boscawen, 1892-1906, and Capt. H.S. Clay, 1910-18.[131]

Other political developments were the attempts to extend democracy to the level of local government. The Local Government Acts of 1888 and 1894, the first passed by a Conservative government, the second by a Liberal one, abolished both the administration of the county by Justices meeting at Quarter Sessions and the secular functions of parish vestries, and County, District and Parish Councils were put in their place. In 1888 Mark Beech came within the orbit of Kent County Council, the first elections to which were held in 1889, and in 1894 Sevenoaks Rural District and Cowden and Hever Parish Councils were created. Elections for all these councils were infrequent before 1918 and even after then. Party politics did not operate, at least overtly, and all the councillors acted as Independents, a practice which is still observed at parish level. The first meeting of Hever Parish Council took place on 31 December 1894, after a preliminary meeting to elect councillors on 20 November, and the first meeting of Cowden Parish Council was held on 5 January 1895, after a preliminary meeting on 4 December 1894.[132] However, no explicit reference to any matter in Mark Beech is recorded in the minutes of Hever Parish Council before 1918 and, indeed, until later, but at Cowden there is reference to an unsuccessful attempt to get the District Council to widen Blowers Hill at Wickens Lane in 1900-1, and the matter of the Falconhurst Fire Brigade and a fire hydrant in Cowden.[133] In 1933 Cowden Parish Council persuaded the Rural District Council to install a hydrant at Mark Beech, near the school, but this seems never to have been done.[134] Perhaps it should be noted here that the roads in Mark Beech were not metalled until after the First World War.[135] One of the interesting features of Hever Parish Council was that it constituted itself, as it was entitled to do under the 1894 act, as a Burial Authority. A Hever Burial Board had already been established on 23 July 1875, but its functions were transferred to the parish council on 22 August 1895 after a special meeting of the Board had agreed to do this on 6 June.[136] The parish council took within its control and administration the graveyard around St Peter's, a responsibility that it continued to exercise for the next 90 years, although, of course, since 1853 most Mark Beech people were buried neither at Hever nor Cowden, but in the village churchyard.[137]

Mark Beech entered the First World War still a small agricultural hamlet and, apparently, relatively remote despite its proximity to London and the presence of the railway. In the first edition after the outbreak of war in August 1914, the local newspaper, the *Edenbridge Courier*, did not mention the hostilities; Britain had not after all been involved in a Continental war since the Crimea or even since 1815. It devoted the whole of its front page to a detailed description of the previous Saturday's flower show at nearby Marsh Green.[138] The military were an inevitable presence in the area, particularly on Ashdown Forest, but at Edenbridge, too, there was an encampment for both British and Canadian troops.[139] Several Edenbridge women married Canadian soldiers, but the Mark Beech church registers provide no example of someone from the village doing so. It is said that there were times during the war when the artillery bombardments in France, which must have been at least 140 miles away from Mark Beech as the crow flies, could be heard in the area. As we have seen above, the war did provide some stimulus for agricultural production and there was an increase in the amount of land under cultivation. As a precursor to the Women's Land Army of the Second World War, there was local recruitment of at least 15 women under the Agricultural War Service for Women scheme to farms in their own area. Miss, later Dame, Meriel Talbot was the local organiser and most of the women seem to have been employed either by Mr. Bryson at Pyle Gate or Guy Ewing at Claydene.[140] Eden Hall became in 1914-15 a refuge for Belgians, including wounded soldiers, who had left their country after the German invasion. They first arrived on 23 October and there are records of these Belgians being entertained at Falconhurst, of them planting trees there to commemorate their visit and also of some being entertained at High Buckhurst by Mr. and Mrs. Edmund Dean.[141] At least 1,138 Belgian refugees were present in Kent, of whom at least 30 were settled in Mark Beech, and the County Council sent a questionnaire to all Districts to see what help and accommodation might be provided for them. Sevenoaks returned a completely nil return, except for the offer of one hospital bed in the workhouse at Sundridge.[142] Other Belgians were accommodated at the V.A.D. hospital in Pitt Lane, Marlpit Hill.[143] Belgian Refugee Committees were established in many of the villages; at Cowden the leader was Mrs. Burkhardt from Claydene, a daughter of Guy Ewing.[144]

By 1915-16 Eden Hall had been offered by the Riccardi-Cubitt family to the army as a V.A.D. Hospital and it was used by about twenty-five or so wounded and traumatised soldiers brought from the front in France and was rated as a Class A V.A.D. Hospital. Four hundred and eighty-one cases were treated in this hospital and 85 operations were performed.[145] Only one soldier died at Eden Hall and he was buried in Mark Beech churchyard. He was Private John Lewes Behagg of the Bedfordshire Regiment, who died in May 1916, and his is the only military grave in Mark Beech from the First World War, complete with a standard War Graves Commission headstone.[146] Count Riccardi-Cubitt and his son Charles were away at the war, so his wife and three daughters, Vera, Theodora and Monica, became Red Cross nurses and took a full part in the running of the establishment.[147] Many of the soldiers were suffering from shell-shock rather than wounds and Vera wrote to an Australian soldier, who had spent some time at Eden Hall and with whom she had become friendly, that there was a new treatment for such cases: 'To thoroughly tire out their bodies so that they can sleep at night, we organise parties for gardening in the morning; 10 of them are tied to the mowing machines and mowing the lawn.'[148] Another feature of life at the hospital was the concert parties organised to entertain the troops, and one such was held in Edenbridge on 10 April 1918, raising £125 for the two hospitals.[149] In May 1918 there was much excitement when a balloon passed low over the house and the occupants, who turned out to be two British and four American naval officers, were invited to descend and have tea, which they did.[150]

In the early days of the war, when a German invasion was still a possibility, however remote, places in the south-east of England like Mark Beech were in areas subjected to detailed contingency planning for road movements by both military and civilians and also for the total evacuation of the population. District Administrators were appointed who were, in fact, military officers of at least Lieutenant-Colonel rank. On a declaration of martial law, draconian powers were to be given to these men. Detailed instructions were drafted for evacuation of the population at only two hours' notice. The main road from Crockham Hill to Edenbridge to Hartfield, and thus through Mark Beech, was to be reserved exclusively for military traffic. The ordinary, fleeing public would have been compelled to use either the Cowden Pound-Gilridge-Cowden village route or the one to Chiddingstone and Bough Beech. All guns and ammunition, of whatever description, were to be surrendered to the army. Each individual was allowed to take one suitcase and there was a maximum of one carriage, cart or car per family. All wheeled vehicles, machinery and tools were to be made useless to an enemy or removed (within the one suitcase and cart limit and, if possible, within two hours). The army had the powers to move or slaughter any or all animals, which civilians were not allowed to take with them, except for dogs.[151] None of this, of course, proved necessary, but in 1917 the Tonbridge and Tunbridge Wells Relief Committee was established to help those in difficulties, such as soldiers' wives, and to create, through an increased number of Special Constables, a greater degree of police surveillance. Heads of Special Constables were appointed: these were Mervyn Streatfield in Chiddingstone, Rev. S.W. Wheatley in Hever, and C.B. Hausburg in Cowden.[152] At the beginning of the war 75 men from Cowden parish had volunteered as Special Constables, including G.J. Talbot, Guy Ewing, Count Riccardi-Cubitt, Edmund Dean, George Dann (from Horseshoe Green) and Christopher Dean.[153] In the 1920s there was a board in Mark Beech to show who had served in the armed forces, but this has now gone and as there is no war memorial in Mark Beech we have no idea who, if anybody, from the village was killed in the war.[154] There are war memorials in Edenbridge and in Cowden, but they give no clue as to whether anyone from Mark Beech is included in the list of names. Nevertheless, it was without doubt a wonderful relief to the inhabitants of Mark Beech, as everywhere, that the terrible slaughter came to an end in November 1918, although one of the consequences of the restrictions on alcohol consumption introduced during the war had been the irrevocable closure of the *Victoria Arms* at Horseshoe Green.

VIII

Modern Mark Beech,
1918-99

SINCE THE END of the First World War Mark Beech can be said to have truly acquired its modern persona. The population of the administrative county of Kent grew from 938,000 in 1921 to 1,015,000 in 1939 and to 1,494,000 in 1991, an increase of eight per cent between the world wars and of 59 per cent in 70 years; by 1995 it stood at 1,551,000, but that of Mark Beech had grown only to 315 by the outbreak of the Second World War.[1] This is a somewhat strange phenomenon, which undoubtedly requires some explanation. The period between the two wars, like that since 1945, was one during which south-east England in general continued to experience considerable population increase and large-scale prolif- eration of buildings over the countryside. In 1914, in Britain as a whole, only eight per cent of the population lived in owner-occupied houses so even the middle classes lived in rented accommodation. The two decades between 1919 and 1939, but especially the 1930s, saw the growth of building societies and an increase in the number of mortgagees, the construction of new estates, the introduction of council houses, and the appearance of so-called ribbon development in an era when there were very few effective planning or building controls, especially in rural areas.[2] It is untrue, however, to claim there had never been any controls in the past because in 1637 John Wickenden of Cowden had been indicted 'for erecting a cottage at Cowden without four acres of land as stipulated by statute'.[3] From 1894 Rural District Councils had the power to stop development, but where the development was *bona fide* and was well-founded compensation had to be paid, so few interventions occurred. Such 20th-century developments were especially marked around cities like London and, although commuting by rail had existed on a small scale before 1914, the inter-war period saw a rapid growth in the number of workers who did this. Mark Beech had a railway which provided travel to London in less than an hour and, therefore, the question as to why Mark Beech did not develop in the same way as much of the metropolitan region at that time arises. The L.B.S.C.R. was incorporated by the Railways Act of 1921, along with all the others in the area, into the new Southern Railway.[4] This company embarked upon a major programme of electrification, which would encompass the whole system, and the line through Mark Beech was set down for modernisation in 1940, by which time, of course, everybody had other things on their minds and all non-war related investments had come to a halt. After the creation of British Railways in 1947, the electrification of the line was constantly planned to take place 'within the next five years', but equally constantly was for ever postponed and has yet to be accomplished. At the time of writing it is said to be the policy of both Railtrack and of Connex South Central, the train operators, that it should be electrified as soon as possible. The trains remained, therefore, until the 1960s, when they were replaced by diesel units, relatively slow, noisy and dirty steam trains.

Communications were, however, not the only and probably not the deciding factor. We have seen already how as early as 1909 estate agents had identified Mark Beech as an area ripe for development.[5] When the remainder of the Hever estate was sold by the Meade-Waldos in 1919, the large field of 17 acres on the north-east quadrant of Mark Beech cross which was then attached to Greenlands Farm was singled out in the sale catalogue as being ideal for house building, and a further six acres on the south side of Hever Lane, were designated as building land.[6] This sale involved the disposal of 1,015 acres and many farms and cottages in Hever and Mark Beech in 36 lots; the answer to our question must be that none of the principal landowners in Mark Beech, such as the Talbots, the Astors and the Meade-Waldos, particularly the first two, wished to see development occur. Between 1909 and 1919, then, three sites were identified as suitable for house building within Mark Beech, one of them for large numbers of houses, and a fourth just outside the village, yet none were built. Fairholme was built after the war and a few houses were built down Uckfield Lane, but these were very few in number, and with another war in 1939 any possibilities came to a temporary end.

40   *Fairholme in 1998. Note the large windows: Raxworthy's son was consumptive, hence maximum sun and air. (Paul Houlton)*

After 1945 a wholly different legal regime came into existence with the passing of the Town and Country Planning Act of 1947.[7] Mark Beech found itself within the new Metropolitan Green Belt, specifically designed to prevent the proliferation of houses and further spread of London in an uncontrolled way. The idea of a Green Belt had first been proposed by the London County Council in 1937 and was a major proposal within the Abercrombie Report of 1945, but now it was established by statute.[8] The enforcement of the Green Belt was not immediate, but a further inhibiting factor was the shortage of building materials immediately after the war, although Roughitts was built in 1952 (this was for agricultural purposes),[9] a prefab, Riding Light, was erected in 1953-4, four bungalows were built in Uckfield Lane in 1954-5,[10] and in 1958 permission was granted to build a bungalow at Horseshoe Green, between Horseshoe Cottages and the Bakery, which had closed, and which is now known as Little Meadows. Since then it has become almost impossible to build new houses in Mark Beech, other than for agricultural purposes. It is possible to add on to existing houses, and this has been done since 1948 with such properties as Bannisters Barn, Bramsells, Jersey Cottage, Buckhurst Cottage, Rookery Cottage, Summerhill, Outwood, Elylands and Lower Buckhurst, to raise and rebuild on existing sites, which has been done at Old Oak House and Wood Cottage, both in Uckfield Lane, and to convert farm buildings to domestic purposes. Indeed Lower Buckhurst, Bannisters Barn and Barn Platt are early examples of conversions from farm buildings in the late 1940s. In the 1980s and 1990s, as farming needs have changed, there has been a rash of barn and oast house conversions in the area, though the possibilities for this in Mark Beech have been relatively limited. The *Kentish Horse* has undergone two extensive reconstructions, in the 1970s and in the 1990s, and since 1945 Horseshoe Cottage and Cherry Tree Cottage have each been each converted from two cottages to one house. At least two houses, the 1905 Vicarage and High Buckhurst, have been divided in two, but only two entirely new houses on unoccupied sites, Spring Grove and New House, Buckhurst Farm, have been built in Mark Beech since 1958. One of the victims of this policy has been the Church Commissioners, who have failed on three occasions to obtain planning permission to erect a house on an ear-marked site, between Ashtrees and School Cottages, for a replacement vicarage. The District Council granted permission for a house for a resident parish priest, but when the Church tried to vary the conditions to enable any clergyman to occupy the house, including retired ones, the application was refused. As there has not been a separate vicar of Mark Beech since 1965, the District Council seems to have taken the view that to grant permission to build would be to circumvent the otherwise strict prohibitions. Others have also failed to gain permission to build on green-field sites. The controls established by the Green Belt have been augmented by the fact that on 28 October 1983 Mark Beech was declared to be within the High Weald Area of Outstanding Natural Beauty, and on 2 July 1991 found itself made a Conservation Area.[11]

The upshot has been that the area has remained a rural and agricultural one, even though agriculture has been a continuously declining industry in terms of employment, particularly since about 1960. When houses do come on the market, and only a few do, they command high prices and are bought now by people who commute, invariably by car, to Edenbridge, Tunbridge Wells, Sevenoaks, Tonbridge, Oxted, Croydon and London, or are retired.

Once the First World War finished, British agriculture entered a 20-year period of great difficulty.[12] In our area the total amount of cultivated land decreased between 1919 and 1938 by 10.6 per cent and wheat production, in particular, declined from 3.74 per cent of arable land in 1913 to 2.27 per cent in 1938.[13] With agricultural hardship and increasing mechanisation the labour force went down in Dr. Short's Hartfield area from 470 people in 1924 to 330 in 1938, a decrease of 25 per cent.[14] Large amounts of land came on the market, and we have seen already that that part of the Hever estate which had not been sold to the Astors in the Edwardian period was disposed in 1919. The consequence was that a number of houses and gardens were acquired as freeholds, but simultaneously there was some consolidation of farms so that between 1924 and 1938 the number of holdings of less than twenty hectares decreased from 60.4 per cent of the total to 58.1 per cent, those between 20 and 120 increased from 37.7 per cent to 40.1 per cent, while the proportion of those of greater size also fell from 2.3 per cent to 1.8 per cent.[15] The Hever estate itself, however, was increased in 1938 when the Astors bought the estate known historically as Chiddingstone Cobham from the Streatfields; most of this land was, of course, in Chiddingstone, but it did include some in Hever parish, including the fringes of Mark Beech, such as Wilderness Farm. The land remained tenanted until sold in 1983.

In anticipation of war the governments of the mid- to late 1930s did begin again to intervene in agricultural markets with regard to crops such as wheat, milk, potatoes and sugar beet, which began to make an appearance on a small-scale around Mark Beech, but it was the outbreak of the Second World War that created a renewed demand for home-produced food and led to a revival of agriculture.[16] A great deal of land which had not been ploughed for many years was brought into cultivation and there was an increase in the production of most crops. Between 1939 and 1953 the proportion of the cultivated area increased from 15.43 per cent of the total to 17.71 per cent for cereals, and especially spectacular was the increase in potato production from some 16 hectares in 1939 to about 45 hectares in 1953, including the ploughing for this purpose of the field behind Jersey Cottage, probably the first crop to be grown there for a very long time, if ever.[17] There was a corresponding increase in the numbers of livestock: the number of dairy cattle went up from 1,581 to 2,295 over the period and, although the number of sheep decreased during the war, the numbers grew again afterwards to reach levels higher than in 1939.[18] As might be expected there was a growth, if only a temporary one, in the size of the labour force by more than 60 per cent, including, as we shall see, the introduction of members of the Women's Land Army.[19]

Since the war, agriculture in Mark Beech has been relatively prosperous; it certainly was from the 1950s to the 1980s, within the ambit of British subsidy and then the Common Agriculture Policy. In the 1990s, things have become more difficult, and there has been the appearance of fallow as 'set aside'. The biggest changes in Mark Beech have been threefold: first, for 100 years the Falconhurst estate was sub-divided into a number of tenancies and it was farmed, as was very common, in that way. From 1954, as tenancies fell due, the Talbots took the farms one by one into their own direct control and farmed the land via managers, who lived in Horseshoe Green Farm.[20] There were four managers altogether, of whom the most able and successful of the early ones was David Jones, who came from Wiltshire and was manager from 1970-6, when he went to Carmarthenshire to run a farm of his own. By the 1990s the whole estate was taken under the direct control of the family, and Charles

Talbot now farms it himself with professional help and advice, particularly from Mr. Barry Eyre.[21] A dairy herd of 280 Friesian cattle has been established and the milking of this herd and the provision of silage, etc. for it has become the major activity on the estate, although during the winter some of the grassland is let for sheep grazing.[22] The ending of the tenant farms and the advancing pace of further mechanisation has led to a further sharp fall in the number of agricultural workers, and at the time of writing the whole farm is worked by the equivalent of five and a half people, some of them contract workers rather than employees.[23] One or two other people work the land outside the Falconhurst estate, but the sum total of agricultural employment hardly reaches double figures! The remainder of the land in Mark Beech is grazing land, gardens, woods and 'set aside'. Consequently, whereas as late as 1975 all the cottages in Cow Lane, except one, were occupied by farm workers or pensioners from the estate, now only two are so tenanted. The rest are let as holiday homes or to tenants who have no involvement with agriculture, and this has had a marked influence on the character of the community. With the consolidation of the estate and the reduction in the need for farms and other properties to be let to tenants or employees some of the houses, such as Old Buckhurst and Wickens, have been sold and barns and oasts at Old Buckhurst, Pyle Gate and Wickens have been converted for sale as houses.

The second big change in recent times has been the alterations in the landscape. Today more than 80 per cent of the cultivated land is grassland and most crops have simply disappeared on any scale. Hops have gone altogether, as have potatoes on a commercial basis and most cereals. In the surrounding area new crops such as oil seed rape have appeared in abundance, but in Mark Beech the only crop planted in 1998 was 112 acres of maize.[24]

The third change was the sale in 1983 by 2nd Baron Astor of the Hever estate, including the castle, and his departure to live in Scotland. Even in the Astors' time, the castle and its grounds had been developed as a tourist attraction to become one of the most popular of its kind in England. It was sold to Broadland Estates, a leisure company who have increased the tourism to the place over the last 15 years very considerably. The Guthrie family, majority shareholders in the company, live in the castle.[25] William Waldorf Astor had introduced wonderful 16th-century English and German furniture to the house, but all the contents were sold at the same time as the estate, and new things of interest have replaced them. The farms of the estate were sold mainly to their sitting tenants, who thereby obtained their freeholds at bargain prices, although several took on burdensome mortgages in order to do so. Thus, both the Falconhurst and the Hever estates, which together encompass most of Mark Beech, the first south and the second north of the road through the village, have ceased to be divided up into tenant farms, but the former is now united and farmed by its owners and the latter is farmed by its former tenants as owner-occupiers. A major local event while the Astors were at Hever Castle was the annual visit to the castle at the first weekend in November of Queen Elizabeth II and the Duke of Edinburgh. It is said that Queen Elizabeth, the Queen Mother, was a regular visitor before the Second World War to Rickwoods; certainly members of the Bowes-Lyon family lived in Edenbridge and Crockham Hill, so it is feasible that they had friends at Rickwoods and visited them there. King George VI and Queen Elizabeth attended a ball at Hever Castle on 18 May 1938, soon after their Coronation.[26]

The Talbot family continued and continues to play a prominent part in the life of the village. The head of the family from 1910 until his death in 1938 was Sir George J. Talbot,

K.C. (1861-1938). As well as a landowner, he
was a lawyer and became K.C. in 1907, was
knighted in 1923, and became a High Court
judge in 1925. Like his father before him he
took a keen interest in his estate and in the
life of the village of which it was a major
part.[27] Sir George never possessed a car and
when he required one he would hire it with
chauffeur from Harrods.[28] Another distinguished member of Sir George's generation
was his sister Dame Meriel Lucy Talbot D.B.E.
(1866-1956), already noted in a cricket
context, who in a long life of public work
was a member of the Advisory Committee
for Repatriation of Enemy Aliens, Director
of the Women's Branch, Food Production
Department, Board of Agriculture, Woman
Adviser to the Ministry of Agriculture, a
member of the Royal Commission on the
Police, a member of the BBC General
Advisory Council and Chairman of the BBC
Appeals Advisory Committee.[29] Drawing on
her experience from the First World War, in
1941 Dame Meriel wrote the first chapter of

41   *Dame Meriel Talbot (1866-1956), photographed in 1937.
(Charles Talbot)*

an instruction book, W.E. Shewell-Cooper, *Land Girl: a Manual for Volunteers in the Women's
Land Army* (London, n.d., but 1941).[30] Another of his sisters, Gwendolen, married a judge, Sir
Frank Stephenson, and another, Mary, married Rev. Winfrid Burrows, who was to become
bishop of Chichester; at the time of their marriage they gave the church a red stole. Mrs.
Burrows died young and there is a memorial to her in the church.[31] The family's life was
marked by a tragedy when Sir George's heir, John Bertram, died suddenly in 1922 from food
poisoning at the age of 22. In August some of the family went to stay at the *Lochmaree Hotel*,
Gairloch. One day they went out fishing on the loch with a hamper of food which included
some wild duck-paste sandwiches made by Lazenby and Sons of Bermondsey, 'a well-known
high-class brand of potted meat or paste'. Bertram and several other guests from the hotel ate
these sandwiches and eight of them, including two ghyllies, died from botulism. Bertram
expired on 16 August, but his younger brother, Thomas G. Talbot, Q.C. (1905-91), who
consumed beef sandwiches, suffered no poisoning and in due course inherited the estate. The
jury at a Sheriff's Inquiry held on 6 and 7 September found no negligence on anyone's part
and Bertram was brought home to be buried in Mark Beech churchyard.[32] Tom Talbot served
in the army during the Second World War and lost a leg. Afterwards he became very pre-
occupied with his onerous duties as Counsel to the Chairman of Committees of the House
of Lords, in which capacity he served for a long time. However, he was a member of Cowden
Parish Council for many years and served three periods as Chairman in 1931-9, 1945-7 and
1971-9.[33] On his death he was succeeded by his only son, Charles J. Talbot (b.1947), who is

the fifth generation of his family in nearly 150 years to live at Falconhurst. One of the big events at Falconhurst in Tom Talbot's lifetime was a party held there in 1952 to celebrate the centenary of the house.[34] Charles Talbot is among many things very musical, as are many members of his family, and he has organised and conducted biennially extremely competent and enjoyable, semi-professional productions of opera in the grounds of Falconhurst in early July. In 1994 Mozart's *Cosi Fan Tutte* was performed, in 1996 *The Magic Flute*, and in 1998, Smetana's *The Bartered Bride*. To celebrate his 50th birthday in 1997 his wife, Nicola, produced Britten's *Let's Make an Opera* in the village hall, with her husband conducting, to the general delight of the community and friends. Charles Talbot also plays the organ in church and is the choirmaster. Edells is now occupied by Charles Talbot's sister, Joanna, and her husband, Alan Smith, whence he runs the well-known John Topham picture library. Another sister, Mary, who owns the Old Farm, is a senior official in Reuters news agency. A niece has recently acquired Pyle Gate.

The parish church continued to play an influential role in the village, although possibly in more recent times a diminishing one, as is the case in English life generally in the late 20th century. Only a small minority of the population now attend regularly, but until at least the Second World War Holy Trinity enjoyed a prominent role in local activities, including the frequent attendance of children from the school for special services and Sunday School before Matins.[35] As recently as 1945 the Electoral Roll contained 100 names, but now it has only forty-two.[36] Since 1918, in contrast to Robert Hunt's long tenure of the office, vicars have occupied the position for an average of seven years at a time, the longest incumbency being that of Stanley Hide from 1925 to 1938.[37] Probably the most distinguished of those who were vicars of Mark Beech alone was Bernard John Wigan, one of the co-authors of the Alternative Service of the Church of England, who tried out several alternate versions of this rite on the congregation at Holy Trinity.[38] Following Wigan's departure in 1965 no replacement as vicar was appointed and the Rector of Hever became first priest-in-charge and then, in 1966, vicar of Mark Beech, although this was and is of a united benefice, not a united parish.

The Vicarage cottages had been sold in 1953 and in 1956 the Vicarage was divided in two. In 1968 the Vicarage was sold and although, as we have seen, a site was found for a new Vicarage this has never been built and so the history of Mark Beech as a fully autonomous parish came to an end after only 114 years. The vicar from 1966-73 was John Brenton Collins, who had rowed for Cambridge before the Second World War and had experienced ill-treatment as a prisoner of the Japanese during it. From 1973-78 the vicar was Bishop John Keith Russell, who had been a missionary bishop in Uganda and was made Assistant Bishop of Rochester, but who died tragically from leukaemia after only five years in the parish. Today the incumbent is officially the Rector of Hever, with Four Elms, Mark Beech and Toys Hill, but Mark Beech retains an autonomous Parochial Church Council and the office of Vicar of Mark Beech has never been abolished and remains merely in abeyance.

Throughout the period the usual activities of the church continued. One of the highlights of the church's year was the annual garden fête in the summer, which was designed to raise funds and which shared its takings with the village hall from the 1950s.[39] Next was the annual Foundation Day service, held around 14 December, to which distinguished preachers were usually invited. Then, of course, there were the Easter and Christmas festivities. The annual garden fête has now been abandoned and a bazaar has been held instead since the 1970s in November. The church continued to be improved, repaired and beautified. The spire had to be reshingled in 1937 and, again, in 1987. Eight of the nave windows had to be taken out in 1926 on account of weathering,[40] and in 1965 one of those in the chancel was removed at the behest of the vicar.[41] All these windows seem to have been lost and are replaced with plain glass. On the other hand, an entirely new stained-glass window was installed in the rose window in the upper part of the western end of the nave in 1987 by Mr. and Mrs. Eric Finden Hall to a design by Keith and Judy Hill of Staplehurst, Kent, to celebrate the escape of their grand-daughter, Lucy, from drowning and the many weddings held in the church over the years.[42] The chancel ceiling was painted in 1958 by Angela, Countess of Antrim (c.1905-84), in memory of Meriel Lucy Talbot (1866-1936) and Agnes Baines, née Talbot (1863-1930).[43] Around the walls of the nave are line drawings of the Twelve Stations of the Cross by Edgar George Norfield, F.R.S.A. (1885-1977), an artist who was a major contributor to *Punch* and is buried in the churchyard. He lived at Rookery Cottage, which has been occupied since 1964 by Mr. Cecil Paynter, Master of the Vintners' Company in 1993-4. On the left-hand side of the chancel there is a painted statue of the Virgin and Child by an unknown wood carver, which was provided by the Stephenson brothers in memory of their mother, Gwendolen.[44] Yet the most interesting feature of the church may be said to be the many carved memorials, mainly to members of the Talbot family. The most distinguished examples are probably the most recent: a memorial stone in French limestone on an interior wall to Thomas G. Talbot and his wife, Cynthia, née Guest (1908-94), and, outside, a fine stone from the Forest of Dean on their grave, both these beautiful objects being the work of David Kindersley (1915-95), a pupil of Eric Gill.[45] In 1970 the churchyard had to be expanded and a piece of additional land for this purpose was acquired from the Talbots from Church Field. During 1997 the parish was enlivened by the presence of an Australian priest, Rev. Dr. Tom Frame, formerly an officer in the Royal Australian Navy, and his family, on a year's sabbatical.

As we have seen, Holy Trinity's ambience and ritual fits into the Catholic end of the spectrum within Anglicanism, although not of the 'highest' variety. There is a tabernacle and perpetual light, Reservation of the Host, a large number of candles on the altar and a satellite altar placed so that the priest can stand and face the congregation in the westward position. One of the most interesting events in the life of this church came in 1953 when the then bishop of Rochester, David Chavasse (1884-1962), who had lost a leg in a pre-war accident,[46] most unusually attended the Annual General Meeting of the Parochial Church Council accompanied by the Archdeacon. It is clear that he disapproved of Reservation, or he may have received complaints from someone and felt that he had to be seen to do something, and his initial tactic was to call for a repositioning of the tabernacle and the perpetual light. Bishop Chavasse was certainly of an Evangelical disposition. He gave the council a 25-minute lecture on the theology of Reservation and called for changes to be made. The council were reluctant to comply, but also to disobey the bishop and a vote to carry out changes was carried by six votes to one with five abstentions. However a year later nothing had happened and it was decided to establish a sub-committee of two people, including Tom Talbot, to deliberate and report back. The Tabernacle was moved from the altar to a point beside it in the chancel, but nothing more seems to have been done in this matter and it

42   The Village Hall, 1998. (Paul Houlton)

disappeared into the sands of time, Bishop Chavasse retiring in 1960.[47] Yet the sharing of a priest with Hever, where the ritual tradition was distinctly Evangelical, led from the mid-1960s to the modification of the ritual at Mark Beech. Prior to this services had been accompanied by incense, acolytes, altar boys, a sanctuary bell and the tolling of the main bell at the moment of Consecration during the Eucharist.[48] All these practices have now ceased.

Another most important institution in the village has been the village hall. Before the First World War there was a Mark Beech Village Club, which possessed a hut, sited somewhere near Buckhurst, and seems to have been a place of relaxation, particularly for the male members of the community.[49] It had a billiard table and a collection of books, but after the war a project was devised to move the club hut to a new position in Cow Lane.[50] Such a plan would have been costly and it triggered a demand in the village for a proper parish or village hall. So a meeting for all interested people was summoned in March 1922, at which a committee consisting of Guy Ewing (Chairman), Lord Antrim and the vicar (Co-Secretaries), Mr. Woolcombe, who was a solicitor, and Captain Lawford Stone, who lived at High Buckhurst (Treasurers), Mr. Cannon and Mr. Pocock was appointed, and an anonymous gift of £200 to start the project was announced.[51] At a further meeting on Friday 29 May it was revealed that a site had been found for a hall almost opposite the church, which had been kindly provided by Richard Edwin Raxworthy, a London builder who was constructing Fairholme, and that Mr. Woolcombe would transact the conveyance for free. It was agreed that the hall would be vested in three trustees, but would be run on a day-to-day basis by a committee and this remains the situation today. The original trustees were Lord Antrim, Guy Ewing and John Bertram Talbot (who, though the youngest, was to be dead within three months).[52] At the time of writing the trustees are Charles J. Talbot, Michael E. Roberts, who lives at Buckhurst Cottage, a part of the old High Buckhurst, and Hon. Robin Denison-Pender, who is also Chairman of Committee. Mr. Denison-Pender lives at Jessups and was High Sheriff of Kent in 1993-4. The Statutes of Indenture do, however, permit the appointment by the

Executive Committee of up to seven trustees.[53] John Adkin is the Secretary and the author
is Treasurer, having succeeded Mr. John R. Green, who lives at Buckhurst, in 1996.

By November 1922 the Building Sub-Committee could announce that they had
accumulated more than £356, but that at least another £350 would be required.[54] In January
10 tenders for building the hall were received and work commenced in May 1923, a gift
of £100 having been received from G.J. Talbot in February.[55] The hall was completed by
early June and was opened by Hon. Mrs. G.J. Talbot at 7 p.m. on Wednesday 13 June 1923.[56]
The project had cost over £700, including £75 for the land and nearly £43 for moving
the old club hut.[57] At the hall's opening there was still a deficiency of about £250, and on
29 and 30 June there was an exhibition of Guy Ewing's collection of local antiquities, which
raised £15 towards it, and a fête was organised on 18 July to raise more.[58] Guy Ewing, who
has been mentioned several times, was an enthusiastic local historian. He was an auctioneer,
land agent and surveyor, with offices in Mayfair, Tonbridge, Tunbridge Wells and Edenbridge.[59]
He lived for over 30 years first at Cole Allen and, then, at Claydene, and served as Chairman
of Cowden Parish Council from 1912 until his death in 1929. In 1924 he became County
Councillor for the area, and in 1926 he published a history of Cowden which is still cited
in histories of Kent, but which contains only two pages on Mark Beech and those exclusively
on the church.[60] On his death, Guy Ewing was buried in Mark Beech churchyard and was
succeeded as County Councillor for the area by Mrs. Mabel Deed of Bessels Green from
1928 to 1931, by Mr. John E. Skinner of Penshurst from 1931 to 1949, and then by Major
John Warde from Squerryes Court, Westerham.[61] Today the County Councillor for the area
is Mr. Peter Lake, who lives at Walter's Green.

The hall was of brick construction and consisted of a rectangular room, about 48 ft.
by 23 ft., with a stage at one end and a steel trussed roof. Behind and parallel was the old
club hut, which was to provide a kitchen and lavatories, and behind that a grassed space
about the size of a tennis court. This hall has become the principal focus for village life
over the last 75 years. In it were and are held dinners, dances, discos, meetings, lectures,
religious services, theatricals, aerobics, fashion shows, wine tastings, antique fares, bazaars,
bridge days, receptions and entertainments of all kinds. One notable such event was a
concert given in aid of the Cowden and District Nursing Association on 14 January 1933,
at which the performers included Joyce Grenfell, who stayed the night at Falconhurst.[62]
From 1930 to 1965 many theatrical productions of a variety of types, from Shakespeare to
comedy routines, were organised both by the Holland family, who lived at Saxby's, and by
Mark Beech W.I. The majority of these efforts were held in Saxby's Barn or in other places
such as Cowden Village Hall and elsewhere, but a few were put on in the village hall.
Picking a few examples, we find in Mark Beech Village Hall a variety concert in July 1951,
a comedy called *Merry Mock Morris* in January 1952, an historical drama, *The Bronte Sisters*,
in February 1957, and *Little Red Riding Hood* in November 1960.[63] During the Second
World War it served as an important recreational facility for the many service personnel in
the district. This was a time of great trial for the villagers too as there seemed little social
activity and in the early stages of the war the evacuee girls from London found life
frequently irksome. To mitigate boredom an imaginative and fantastical Christmas entertainment or pantomime was organised in the hall in December 1939 with the Westminster girls
(see below) as participants. This play was produced, before she and her husband went to

Canada for much of the war, by Mrs. Gwen Mott, who had written it herself when she had previously been in India. It was called *The Blue Djin of Mars* and still sticks vividly in the memories of those who were present.[64] Meanwhile, the hall has become the headquarters of the Mark Beech branch of the Women's Institute, which was started in about 1931, unsuccessful attempts having been made twice during the 1920s and '30s to start a Mothers' Union,[65] and is the venue for such annual events as Harvest Supper, the Church Bazaar and the Village Christmas Dinner and Party. The Royal British Legion frequently hold dinners and an Alpha course is conducted here too. Another visitor in more recent times has been the lyricist, Sir Tim Rice, and a memorable event in the hall was an evening's entertainment, sponsored by the Edenbridge and District Arts Trust, given by Julian Slade and two of the cast from the revival of *Salad Days* on 15 February 1998. Between the two world wars on Empire Day (24 May) there was dancing round the maypole in Falconhurst Park, somewhere near the cricket ground.[66]

Mark Beech Village Hall took much wear over the years, did not have very adequate foundations and is built on clay soil. This is an area notorious for subsidence and has been identified as such by the insurance companies. The old club hut was destroyed by fire in 1954 and had to be replaced by another one, acquired from the army.[67] Moreover, the walls suffered from constant cracking, which was filled in but rapidly reappeared, and the hall was, no doubt, seriously affected by the bomb which fell nearby during the Second World War. Hever Parish Council had already given the hall £250 in 1977 towards the costs of structural repairs,[68] but matters had got so bad by the 1990s that the committee had to consider pulling the hall down and rebuilding it, if sufficient funds could be raised. There seemed little hope of the village raising the necessary monies from their own resources, as maybe as much as £100,000 was going to be needed.

The hall is situated in the part of the village which is in the civil parish of Hever, which also includes the larger settlements of Hever and Four Elms. Financial assistance had been or was being provided to the halls in those places, and in the 1980s the parish council had bought playing fields in Hever with public funds, so the committee decided to approach the parish council and also the district and county councils for help. The response from all quarters was friendly and helpful: the issue was first brought before the parish council on 7 March 1994, when it was reported that a structural engineer was making a feasibility study for the district council.[69] A special meeting of the parish council, entirely devoted to Mark Beech Village Hall, was called on 7 November 1994 when, *inter alia*, a scheme to demolish and rebuild the hall at an estimated cost of £70,000 was discussed. (The hall committee had already considered and trimmed a scheme costing nearly £90,000.)[70] By means of fund-raising events and interest-free loans from villagers the hall committee had already raised £17,000, which was the minimum necessary to qualify for council assistance. At a meeting of the Building Sub-Committee on 6 July 1995 it was proposed that the parish council should agree to give Mark Beech Village Hall £7,000 or 10 per cent of the contract price and this was endorsed by the full council on 10 July.[71] The matter then passed to the district council, whose relevant sub-committee agreed to provide Sevenoaks's share of the project in September.[72] There had been near unanimous support from the parish council for the scheme; the only dissenter was the Chairman, Dennis Clark, who lived next door to the hall, on the grounds that he could not support such levels of

43   Members of the Theobald Family at Stridewood, c.1925. Notice the countryside in the background, which has remained unchanged from c.1750 to the present. (Mrs. Joanna Smith)

expenditure from the rates, and at a meeting of the council on 18 September 1995 he resigned his chairmanship.[73]

During much of the winter of 1995-6 the hall was closed while rebuilding took place. The successful contractor was local builder Robert N. Theobald, who lived on the other side of the hall, at Wyshe Farm, to Mr. Clark. The architect was Robert H.B. King (1918-96), who gave his services free. Bob King, as he was known to all, was a truly local man. His mother, who was said to be very pretty,[74] had been married out of Pyle Gate Farm to Rev. H. King, the Presbyterian minister at Marsh Green. After attending Judd School, Tonbridge, he started his architectural training, but this was interrupted by the outbreak of war, Bob's enlistment in the 7th Battalion, Royal West Kent Regiment, his capture at Ambert in northern France on 18 May 1940, and five years' imprisonment. He was marched across Europe to Stalag XX in north-west Poland and in 1945 was marched back as far as Germany. After the war he worked for the Church Commissioners, Bromley Council, and then on his own account. Except for a brief period in London, he lived all his life at Marsh Green, Edenbridge, Hever and, for the last six years, at Rose Cottage in Cow Lane, and at various times he served on both Edenbridge and Hever Parish Councils. In his younger days he was an active member of Falconhurst Cricket Club. He did build a few entire houses, but his very great skill was to make additions and alterations to existing houses, particularly older ones, which always blended harmoniously with the original while solving the clients' practical needs; as was said at his funeral in Hever church in September 1996, there can hardly be an older house for many miles around that did not receive his loving attention over the years.[75] His splendidly refurbished hall, with the foundations underpinned, and a new small hall, lavatories, kitchen and entrance, was opened by the Lord Lieutenant of Kent, Lord Kingsdown, on 18 April 1996 in the presence of many local dignitaries, including the Chairmen of Hever Parish and Sevenoaks District Councils and the Chief Constable of Kent, David Phillips, and it is hoped in the village that this hall will serve the community for at least another 75 years.

The third important village institution was the school, which continued to flourish in the inter-war years. In July 1922 the school was inspected and considered to be very satisfactory.[76] In 1924 Miss Jennings completed 25 years as headmistress, and on her retirement in the same year she was replaced by Miss Edith T. Weth.[77] Miss Weth was succeeded in 1931 by Miss Anne K. Morley. Miss Morley died in 1939 and was followed by Miss Sybil Brown. In the 92 years of its existence the school had eight headteachers, two men and six women, one of them married. Four of these teachers, the Misses Jennings, Weth, Morley and Brown, are still remembered in the village today. The school did, however, have financial difficulties; in the summer holidays of 1927 the school playground, which was on the site of what is now Roughitts, had to be repaired and the managers appealed to the villagers for contributions.[78] By 1939 the school was in danger of closure because money which it did not have was required for essential repairs.[79] The outbreak of war saved the school temporarily, and indeed the school was provided with electric light. In September 1939, the girls of Westminster Church Senior School were evacuated to Mark Beech and Hever and the Mark Beech children attended school in the morning and made way for the younger Westminster girls in the afternoon, the older ones going to Hever.[80] But in the summer of 1945, as the war came to an end, the school was informed by Kent County Education Committee that it would close at the end of term and the children be transferred to Hever School.[81] So the school closed for ever and Miss Brown went to teach at Hever. After her retirement, she continued to live in Mark Beech and only died in 1990, aged 99,[82] although it has been suggested by some that she still haunts the old school, which has long been converted to a house in which she herself once lived.

Nevertheless, formal education in Mark Beech did not cease entirely: in 1940 the Riccardi-Cubitts found themselves trapped in Italy at their house at Bordighera in Piedmont and were unable to return to England until the end of the war.[83] They were Catholics and they lent Eden Hall to the Papal Nuncio as a rural retreat, but in 1943 the house was made over to a teaching order of Catholic nuns, the Sisters of St Andrew, as a school and as a sanctuary from the bombing of London.[84] This Order had been established in Tournai in Flanders in the early 13th century. After many vicissitudes they founded, in the late 19th century, a convent and school in Streatham, south London. At the outbreak of war the sisters were evacuated to Worthing, then to Haslemere, then to Liphook and, finally, to Eden Hall, where they have remained ever since.[85] Ghent and Tournai had once been in the same diocese and thus a direct connection between Flanders and Mark Beech was re-established after more than 500 years. Though a connection with Belgium remains, the sisters, with considerable lay help, have conducted autonomously a school for about 110 children, Catholic and non-Catholic, for 55 years. Having originally registered an intention to do so with Messrs Knight, Frank & Rutley in 1939, in 1945 the Riccardi-Cubitts sold the house, which came into the possession of the Order on 10 December,[86] although it is reported by some that the eldest son was not entirely happy with the disposal of the house. Many of the old Mapletreuse farm buildings have now been pulled down and replaced by accommodation more suitable for a school. Since 1968 the nuns have also run a purpose-built residential home for 40 elderly people to one side of the house, with which Kent Social Services have always been involved.

In addition to the school at St Andrew's, since 1965 Mrs. Ann Roberts has run a nursery school for up to 24 children; initially this was in a house in Spode Lane, Cowden, but since 1972 it has been in Mark Beech Village Hall, and over the years it has catered for many of the children in the area.[87]

44 *Falconhurst versus Ashurst, 14 June 1998 with Falconhurst fielding. Compare the unchanging scene with the women's match, 109 years earlier, illustration 37, p.82.*

Falconhurst Cricket Club continued and continues to flourish. In the inter-war period it was transformed from an estate club to a village club. Between the wars two of the outstanding players for the club were Albert Turk, who kept the post office, and John Pocock, the estate carpenter. There was also Wally Cook. Until the 1950s it remained a local club, with most of its players living and working in the district, Ian Lewis being the only member in 1947 to work in London.[88] However, over time it has had increasingly to recruit from a wider catchment, although most of the players retain some connection with the village, living here as children and teenagers, for example, even if they now live and work elsewhere during the week. Falconhurst was never a successful club in the sense that it usually won the majority of its matches; it was the love of playing the game in a beautiful setting which inspired many of its members, though the keenest matches were always against local rivals such as Stonewall Park, Ashurst, Cowden, Chiddingstone, Four Elms, Crockham Hill and Fordcombe. One or two famous cricketers occasionally played for the club, including, between the wars, a Lyttelton cousin of the Talbots, John Cavendish Lyttelton, 8th Viscount Cobham, who was a good cricketer and President of the M.C.C. in 1935. In more recent times, appearances have been made by Ben Brocklehurst, who captained Somerset, and Richard Hutton, who had played for Yorkshire and England. Matthew Fleming, the current Kent and England cricketer, whose family live at Stonewall Park, played for the club of that name as a teenager and it is almost certain that he played against Falconhurst. People still recall Reg Goddard from Horseshoe Green Farm, as a good club cricketer who bowled medium pace and, being a large and strong man ('just like John Ridd in *Lorna Doone*' is one memory), was said to be the only one who could pull the roller both up and down the slight incline on the pitch single-handed and drive great sixes not just out of the ground but over the trees which surrounded it. Probably the most successful period for the club was the early 1960s, under the captaincy of Bill Stephenson, when most seasons the team usually won twice as many matches as it lost, due as much as anything to the presence of two fast opening bowlers, Maurice Sinfield and Colin Denham Davies, who were considered to form the best attack in the club's history and who were also good bats. In 1989 and 1990 Falconhurst reached the Kent final of the National Village Knock-out Cup, but were beaten on both occasions. Other good players in the last 50 years have included Alf Jeffrey, Jack Franklin, James Carnegie, Denver Carr, Stephen Leppard, David Seymour, Charles and James

Lewis and Andrew Paynter. Up to at least the 1950s the highlight of the club's season occurred over the August Bank Holiday, when the club would play a President's XI made up of good imported players on the Saturday, and a Women's XI on the Monday, and a festival atmosphere prevailed. From the late '70s to the early '90s the club went through hard times when it was often difficult to raise teams, especially with the introduction of Sunday games in addition to those on Saturdays, but thanks to the perseverance and enthusiasm of captains and players such as Ken Patterson, Ian King and William and Simon Bellamy, the club not only survived but seems to be secure again. Another big feature of the club's calendar is the Annual Dinner, to which some distinguished cricketer-speakers have been invited, including Frank Woolley, Colin Cowdrey, Godfrey Evans, Lord Cobham, Bill Edrich and Peter Hern.[89] At some date either just before or after the First World War Stanley Baldwin and the Liberal M.P. Freeman Freeman-Thomas (1866-1941), who became Governor of Victoria, of Madras, of Bengal and, finally, Viceroy of India as Lord Willingdon, and was King George V's tennis partner, umpired at Falconhurst on more than one occasion.

Few people know that Mark Beech almost found itself on the periphery of the first airport for London. During the First World War an area at Charcott, about four miles north-east of Mark Beech, was developed as an airfield for the Royal Flying Corps and was taken over by the Royal Air Force on that service's foundation in 1918. Hedges were removed and a grass runway aerodrome was created. The Officers' Mess was the large structure to the south of Chiddingstone Causeway church which has recently been converted into expensive housing units known as Knotley Hall, having spent 40 years as a remand school. The R.A.F. station remained at Charcott through the 1920s, but in the next decade it was considered seriously, along with Croydon, as the site for London Airport. Croydon was chosen and, the R.A.F. having abandoned it, the aerodrome became a private flying club. This venture was unsuccessful and the airfield was closed, only to be reopened by the R.A.F. in 1939. It was used during the war as an emergency landing strip for aircraft such as Spitfires which could not get back to airfields such as Biggin Hill or Kenley or the many others in the area, and as a place to which planes could be dispersed when major bases were under attack. After 1945 it was closed and the land returned to its former owners. Nevertheless, some of the installations, such as fuel points, are still intact.[90]

We have observed above the beginnings of the arrival in Mark Beech of services such as piped running water, sewerage, electricity and telephones. Both electricity and the telephone were installed at Falconhurst before 1914,[91] but they did not become general in Mark Beech until the Second World War. In 1954 a large concrete cistern was built on the top of Mark Beech Hill and the village began to receive piped water from a public supply.[92] This reservoir was fed by gravity right across the Eden valley from a bore and another cistern on the top of Crockham Hill, which is nearly 200 feet higher than Mark Beech Hill. Although these facilities are still in use, Mark Beech is now supplied with pumped water from Bough Beech reservoir which was opened in the Eden valley in 1978.[93] As we have seen, electricity arrived at the school only in 1939 and the church was not connected until 1949.[94] Similarly, most private houses got their supply in the immediate pre- or post-war periods. A small sewerage works was constructed in the field below the church in 1978,[95] but only the properties around the crossroads are connected to it. The district council has a scheme to install mains drainage for most of the village, which it is hoped will be started in the summer of 1999.

45   Hever Station at the opening of the Hurst Green-Eridge railway, 30 June 1888. The people in the truck include members of the Baggallay and Charrington families. (Community of St Andrew)

46   Cowden Railway Station, 1998. The canopy, footbridge, signal box and second track have all been removed. Compare this photograph with Hever Station, above. (Paul Houlton)

Also worthy of mention is the construction by the Ordnance Survey of a permanent base for a surveying theodolyte on the south-west corner of Mark Beech Hill in 1938 as this is a trigonometric point. A walk to the top of the hill will reveal this feature, which is no longer in use as cartography is done now by means of satellites.

For much of this century the medical requirements of the village have been met by a partnership of general practitioners in Edenbridge. One partner, Dr. Brian Milner, who has been here for more than 30 years, and one retired partner, Dr. John Shaw, currently live in the village. Behind them stand three hospitals: Edenbridge and District Memorial Hospital, which was built by public subscription after the First World War to replace an existing hospital but is now essentially a geriatric and convalescent unit with minor accident and operating facilities; and two hospitals in Tunbridge Wells, Pembury and the Kent and Sussex.

The railway continued to play an important role in the area. A few people now commuted to London and it is said that 17 people were employed at Cowden station in the 1920s, including a station master in a gaudy uniform and top hat.[95] Here was a fully operational station, with passenger trains between London and the south coast, goods sidings and a working signal box, which was originally to the north of the 'up' platform, but which was moved to the centre of the 'down' platform, close to the booking hall, as an economy measure in the 1920s. During the Second World War the railway was part of the essential transport system of the nation and prior to the Normandy landings trains loaded with military material were hidden in Mark Beech Tunnel by day and only moved at night to prevent the possibility of observation by German reconnaisance.[97] One witness remembers a German plane trying to bomb the northern entrance of the tunnel, though this was probably not in 1944.[98] Since 1945, however, the railway through Mark Beech has been continually run down. The goods yard was closed in 1960,[99] electrification has failed to materialise, and in 1969 an attempt was made to close the line on the grounds that it was losing very large sums of money. Whatever the truth of that, a public campaign of opposition was mounted and British Rail's case was undermined when one of its key witnesses admitted to the public enquiry held in the town hall at Tunbridge Wells that the real reason for wishing to close the line was that the Ministry of Transport, as it then was, intended to build a relief road in Lewes which would entail the destruction of a railway viaduct.[100] The tribunal's recommendation, therefore, was that the line should only be closed between Uckfield and Lewes. This was put into effect, which means that for nearly 30 years it has been impossible to get directly by train from Cowden to Lewes, Brighton, Eastbourne, Newhaven, etc. Since then the service has deteriorated: the signal box has been closed; the booking office has been shut and the station is now unmanned; there are only a few through trains to or from London at the morning and evening peaks, and the last train down the line today leaves London at 8.26 p.m., thus making the line unusable for theatre visits, etc. to one of the world's major cities, less than 30 miles distant. The most disastrous decision was to make a section of the track from Hever to Ashurst single track and this was effected in the early 1990s. The 'up' platform quickly became overgrown with saplings and has an unkempt appearance. The reason was said to be the instability of the embankment to the south of the station and the fact that it was cheaper to run one track down the centre, which for the time being at least would be safe, than to rebuild the embankment, although there were obviously also long-term maintenance savings by doing it. A direct consequence was the dreadful Cowden train smash of 15 October 1994, when two trains collided head-on in the single-track section just south of Cowden station, and five people were killed, three crew and two passengers.[101] Electronic signalling had been introduced, but drivers had no means of communicating with the controllers, and it is said that observers in the control box at Oxted could see there was going to be a serious incident but could do nothing to prevent it. Drivers have now been provided with radio-telephones.

The story regarding bus services through the village is similar. As recently as 1970 there were 13 buses a day in both directions through Mark Beech, on a circular route which took in Edenbridge and Tunbridge Wells, including some buses on Sundays, but today there are only three buses a day between Edenbridge and Cowden or Holtye. This tale of reduced train and bus services and of shop closures is a practical demonstration of the way that in late 20th-century England the car has taken over as the main means of getting to work, of pursuing leisure and of going to the supermarkets of nearby towns to do much of the shopping. This is further demonstrated by the fact that minor roads, like the ones through Mark Beech, which even a generation ago were relatively traffic-free, are now busy all the time, not only in the rush hours. The ancient road from Cowden Pound to Tyehurst through Mark Beech, though an unclassified road, is part of the shortest route from Edenbridge to Tunbridge Wells and the amount of traffic shows that many people use it. Two attempts in recent years on the part of the Parish Council to get the authorities to impose a 30 or 40 m.p.h. speed limit through the village have failed.

At one time there were a number of shops and a post office in Mark Beech, the latter having existed from the mid-19th century. There were shops at various times at Jessups, Dyehurst and Horseshoe Green, where there was also a blacksmith and a bakery, and at Horseshoe Cottage. The post office was first at Jessups, but from 1913 onwards until it closed in 1991 was in Cow Lane. This was a serious matter as at about the same time the post offices in Cowden and Chiddingstone Hoath also closed. A recent attempt to run a shop at the *Kentish Horse* has failed after only six months. The one facility that has survived, however, is Horseshoe Green Garage, the heir to the blacksmith. Between the wars it was operated by George Dann, who also ran a taxi service from Cowden station. The garage was run for many years by Donald Hepworth, and since 1988 by Chris Gillet. It was originally in the blacksmith's shop beside the *Victoria Arms*, now Victoria House, but a large new building was erected behind in 1968 and an extension in 1982.

47 *Cottages in Cow Lane, with* Kentish Horse *and the church, 1998. (Paul Houlton)*

As in the past, national events, especially those connected with the monarchy, have continued to be marked. For the Festival of Britain in 1951 a brick bus shelter opposite the *Kentish Horse* was built by Cowden Parish Council, although it was not constructed until 1952.[102] The site is in Hever but the council had some spare money from its Festival fund. A wooden bench with a carved inscription was placed in this shelter as the result of a public subscription. For the Queen's Jubilee in 1977 a fête was organised, which included trips in a hot air balloon, the launching of small balloons to wherever the wind would take them and the gift of special mugs to all the children of the village. For the marriage of the Prince of Wales and Lady Diana Spencer the crossroads was closed to cars by a special legal procedure and an open air dance was held. This event was spoilt by an evening of wind and rain.

National politics continued to impinge on the community. Universal male suffrage was assured by the Fourth Reform Act of 1918 and women over the age of 30 were also given the vote. Women received equal treatment in 1928. Mark Beech was transferred to the Sevenoaks parliamentary constituency in 1918, but was put back with Tonbridge in 1997. The area continued to be represented by Conservative M.P.s, apart from Major R.A.S. Williams, who held Sevenoaks for the Liberals in 1923-4. The Conservative M.P.s from 1918 were Sir T.J. Bennet, 1918-23, Capt. H.W. Styles, 1924-29, Sir Edward Hilton-Young, 1929-35, Col. C.E. Ponsonby, 1935-50, (Sir) John Rodgers, 1950-79, and G.M. Wolfson, 1979-97.[103] Having been transferred to the constituency of Tonbridge and Malling, Mark Beech's M.P. since 1997 has been Sir John Stanley. On the district council, Mark Beech was usually represented by Independent or, more recently, by Conservative councillors. Under the Local Government Act of 1972, Sevenoaks Rural District Council was abolished and merged with the Urban District Council and part of Dartford to form a new Sevenoaks District Council. Mark Beech was initially divided between a ward comprising Edenbridge and Cowden, with five councillors, inevitably from Edenbridge, and another, with one councillor, comprising Chiddingstone and Hever. In 1977 the felicitous idea was concocted to create a ward which revived the name Somerden and which comprised Cowden, Hever and Chiddingstone. From 1975 to 1984 Mark Beech was represented by a Liberal, Graham Phillips, who lived at Weller's Town, and might have continued to be so for many years, but he moved away to Tunbridge Wells.[104] Under a boundary review in 1987, the boundaries between Hever and Cowden were altered to incorporate the whole of central Mark Beech in Hever. The *Kentish Horse*, the church, Old Farm, the Old Vicarage and other properties, but not Falconhurst, are now in the civil parish of Hever. The traditional boundary between Cowden and Hever, from which Mark Beech takes its name, was erased and a thousand years of history came to an end.[105] Furthermore, at the time of writing there are new proposals that the boundary between these two parishes should now be fixed down the centre of Stick Hill instead of being a parallel line through fields about two hundred yards to the east of the road (*see* pages 54-5 above). Naturally, throughout this period the parish councils continued to operate on an entirely non-party political basis. Mark Beech seems to have received more attention from Hever Parish Council within the past generation, doubtless because a number of the councillors lived in the village, including, in the early 1990s the Chairman and two councillors out of five (since in 1950 Hever had been divided into two wards, Hever and Four Elms, Mark Beech being in the former).[106] A noteworthy feature of this period was that David Woollett, who lives at How Green, served as Chairman of Hever Parish Council for 26 years from 1961 to 1987.

   Almost our final look at Mark Beech must be some consideration of the village during the Second World War, an era which is still, of course, within the memories of the living. This war was different from any other, not only because there were fewer doubts as to the morality of the cause and the material and human resources of the nation were mobilised more intensively than ever before, but because of the use of air power for the first time and the serious possibility of invasion for the first time for centuries. These factors were especially important for Mark Beech because Kent and Sussex lay on the direct line between German airfields and cities like London, and in the event of invasion it would have been the first area to receive foreign invaders. In terms of the tons of bombs dropped it was, of course, the large industrial cities and ports of Britain which suffered most, but a surprisingly large number of bombs and other pests fell from the sky on these two predominantly rural counties. The Centre for Kent Studies preserves maps created by the Civil Defence authorities, which were published in the *Kent Messenger* in 1945 and record most of the bombs, both high explosive and incendiary, the crashed aircraft, enemy and friendly, and later the V1's or flying bombs, which fell on the county between 1939 and 1945.[107] It looks like the face of a human with a very, very bad case of measles, and the area around Mark Beech was not spared. German aircraft would frequently bomb or strafe small villages or isolated farms at random, and there was a special danger of returning aircraft jettisoning loads that they were not going to take home. It is recalled that a German aircraft circling three times was a particular warning sign because that seemed to indicate a target was about to be bombed. At Chiddingstone there was at least one example of workers in the hop fields being machine-gunned by Stukas, and in July 1940, as they cycled to school somewhere near Buckhurst Farm, three of the Westminster girls, Joan Robinson, Doreen Steen and Jean Fraser, were machine-gunned by a German aircraft but survived unharmed by diving into a ditch. To this day, Joan Robinson, now Mrs. Goddard, remembers the bullets pinging along the road close to her and the plane so low that she could see the pilot's face. She thinks the pilot may have tried to kill these 12-year-old schoolchildren because on his first run over them they shook their fists at the Nazi plane.[108]

   During the Battle of Britain most German bombers attacked across east and north Kent, but older people speak of how they witnessed waves of bombers over Mark Beech and the fights between British and German aircraft in the skies immediately overhead. There were dangers from the shrapnel descending from above which could kill people and animals and smash roof tiles. Bits of shell were often still hot on reaching the ground, as another eyewitness, who tried to pick up a piece, recalls.[109] One incident well-remembered in Mark Beech was when British and German fighters fought over the Uckfield Lane/ Wilderness Farm area and the British aircraft was shot down; as the pilot descended on his parachute the German fired at him and on reaching the ground he was dead. Another British fighter appeared immediately and hit the German, who plunged to earth, trailing black smoke, somewhere to the north, much to the satisfaction of the onlookers.[110] Another event which is well remembered, though it was not an example of danger, was when a Sunderland flying boat which was running out of fuel just managed to land on the lake at Hever without crashing on the end. Having got down successfully, however, it could not take off again because of the increased weight, and it had to be dismantled and taken away on lorries.

During the war the Sevenoaks Rural District area suffered 62 civilian deaths from enemy action and a further 70 were seriously injured. It was the recipient of 3,259 H.E. bombs, about 53,500 incendiary bombs, and 137 V1's. Eighty-six properties were totally destroyed and another 169 severely damaged.[111] Bombs fell in all parts of Hever, Cowden, Chiddingstone, Penshurst and Mark Beech. Most did little damage, although a bomb killed six people at Smarts Hill on 27 October 1940, and another bomb fell on the Mark Beech school playground (when nobody was there) on 7 February 1941, but though it was less than 100 yards from the church did not even break any of the windows. A dance was being held at the Village Hall, and it is still recalled that the walls of the hall buckled before the lights went out.[112] Ten H.E. bombs landed near Buckhurst Farm on 5 December 1940, but did no damage.[113] Another hit a barn near Edells on 21 January 1944.[114] On 30 August 1940 a German Messerschmitt 109 crashed between Gilridge and Leighton Manor. First on the scene was Bert Everest, then aged 32, who was working in the fields nearby. The pilot was unharmed, but many years later Bert said that, as he approached, he was scared the pilot would threaten him with a pistol. In fact he found the German shaking like a jelly, either from shock or from fear of what might happen to him, so that he surrendered immediately and waited in a docile fashion until a local policeman, probably a Special Constable, arrived and took him away.[115] A Messerschmitt 110 came down somewhere near Pyle Gate/Harnett's Farm on 5 September 1940, but the two-man crew were killed, and it is also said that the body of a high-ranking Luftwaffe officer was found in a ditch near Jessups, presumably propelled from an aircraft which crashed some distance away.[116] An oral tradition in the village claims that in March 1941 bombs totally destroyed Tyehurst Farm and killed all the occupants, refugees, it is said, from London, who thought that Mark Beech was a safer place to be. However, there is no record of this event in the Civil Defence registers, and although there can be no doubt that there was a house on the site before 1939 the truth is that the house crumbled through neglect and was used by the Astor estate as a source of materials.[117] The remains of the house can still be seen beside the footpath from Mark Beech to Chiddingstone, surrounded by rhododendrons and other plants that have gone wild, and looking rather incongruous in this situation.

Another house vacated and dismantled was the pair of cottages at Stridewood, on the border of Mark Beech and Chiddingstone, which was owned by the Meade-Waldos.[118] Some of the bricks from these properties were re-used to build the cricket pavilion at Stonewall Park. Fortunately nobody in Mark Beech was killed by enemy action and property damage was relatively slight: a bungalow at Gilridge was gutted entirely by an incendiary device in 1944.[119] When the bombardment by V1s started on 13 June 1944 many fell short of their target, London, on account of either technical malfunction or of being hit by British anti-aircraft guns or fighter aircraft, and in the first three months 137 of these weapons fell on the Sevenoaks Rural District, including several around Mark Beech.[120] One such bomb hit Penshurst on 21 August, and two of them fell in succeeding weeks in the fields south of Horseshoe Green. Four 'doodlebugs' fell in the parish of Cowden, six in Hever and eight in Chiddingstone, including one which destroyed the outbuildings at Larkins Farm.[121] The school at Eden Hall broke up early on 11 July so that the children could go to safer places because during the last 24 days of term at least 28 V1s were counted passing overhead, and others were heard but not seen.[122] When the Germans started to fire V2 rockets at south-east England in September 1944 several landed in the area, including one at Penshurst on 5 November, one at Ide Hill on 11 November, one at Southborough on 13 November, one at Chiddingstone on 1 February 1945, and another at Penshurst on 4 March.[123] One hundred and thirty rockets fell on the historic county of Kent, including 17 in the Sevenoaks R.D.C. area and another at Tonbridge.[124]

British defences consisted not only of fighter aircraft, but of a range of measures including searchlights, anti-aircraft guns and barrage balloons. During the Battle of Britain and the Blitz a great line of guns was positioned just north of Mark Beech on an alignment from Dorking to Rochester, and dozens of balloons were tethered along the North Downs. Following the start of the Germans' V1 bombardment, 2,000 balloons were aligned from Limpsfield to Cobham and 1,000 guns just to the south of the balloons.[125] At Mark Beech itself, a number of guns were sited just south of Horseshoe Green Farm, one was placed at the bottom of the field between Cherry Tree Cottage and the Bakery, below Broomyfield, and behind, on Hoppers Bank, was a Home Guard post.[126] A searchlight was positioned near the bottom of Stick Hill. The *Queens Arms* became the night-time headquarters of both the A.R.P. and of the Special Constables.[127] At least nine men seem to have been enrolled as Special Constables, far fewer than in the first war, and they included Lewis Dale, Walter Penfold and Tom Ridley.[128]

The Germans planned to invade south-east England in September 1940 if command of either the air or the sea could be obtained, and the prevention of the former was the principal British objective in the Battle of Britain. Pill boxes were built in the Eden valley and several can still be seen. If the enemy had got ashore and advanced on London in pursuit of their first military objective, which was to take a line from Gravesend to Guildford, Mark Beech would have come under German control. The line of the Medway and the Eden was designated as that at which a last stand would have been made before the capital. Edenbridge was declared to be a Nodal Point, and whatever troops were present, and this could theoretically have included the recently formed Local Defence Volunteers, later the Home Guard, would have been ordered to blow the bridge and hold the north bank of the river for three days until other troops arrived. In effect, the British Commander, General Ironside, planned to use the two rivers as anti-tank ditches. The plans for the civilian population were exactly the opposite to those of the First World War in that it was to be encouraged to stay put and, above all, not to obstruct the roads for military traffic.[129]

It was these factors, among others, which brought more soldiers to the area than during the first war. Troops were once again stationed on Ashdown Forest and in Stangrove Park, Edenbridge, but also between Charcott and Weald and in Mark Beech itself.[130] At one stage of the war, large numbers of tanks were stationed down the track from Pyle Gate and in the woods around the Hole, and we have already noted the hiding of trains in Mark Beech Tunnel and the use of the village hall for recreation, although at one point during the war the village hall was used to paint camouflage material.[131] These troops, according to recollection, were predominantly British; no Americans, for example, seem to have appeared around Mark Beech, but there were a few Poles and soldiers from other Continental allies billeted at Crippenden.[132] A Canadian unit was encamped near the *Queens Arms* at one point in the war, and there were Canadians at Hartfield, Hammerwood and at Chiddingstone;[133] the exact date is uncertain, but it was probably at one of three times: two Canadian divisions were already stationed in England from June 1940 and the 2nd Division was deployed between Guildford and Westerham to help repel a German invasion; Canadian troops departed from Newhaven in summer 1943, prior to the Dieppe Raid; Canadian units were among those that were part of the decoy army in Kent in summer 1944, though they may have been further east.[134] Incidentally, as part of the attempts to make the Germans believe the invasion was coming in the Pas de Calais, the Mark Beech Home Guard were deployed in April-June 1944 to patrol the section of railway line between Bough Beech and Penshurst giving the impression that this line was of special importance.[135] It is probable that Canadian troops were in the vicinity on at least the first and third occasions, and Sister Teresa of St Andrew's Convent, who was a school-girl at the time, remembers large numbers of Canadians passing along the road in 1944.[136] Some of the Polish soldiers scandalised the local population, it is said, because when off duty they wore white lipstick and got more excessively drunk than others.[137]

In the memories of those participants and observers still alive the Home Guard unit in Mark Beech was a source of constant merriment. The Local Defence Volunteers, as the organisation was known originally, was launched on 15 May 1940 and became the Home Guard in July after being referred to as such in a speech by Winston Churchill.[138] (Churchill, of course, had connections with the area as his home was at Chartwell, about four and a half miles north of Mark Beech, and before that he had lived at Lullenden, just out of Cowden to the west and about three miles from Mark Beech.)[139] The Home Guard was organised on a county basis, although Kent was divided in two, as so often in its history, west and east. Relevant to Mark Beech was the 20th (Sevenoaks) Battalion, Kent Home Guard, from which a company was formed at Edenbridge and a further sub-unit at Mark Beech. Home Guard battalions were associated with their county regiments, and therefore the Mark Beech Company was allowed to wear the badge of the Royal West Kent Regiment.[140] They always assembled outside the *Kentish Horse* under the command of Captain Streatfield and his deputy, Reg Goddard, and were dismissed there too, although it is said that usually members were inside the pub before being formally dismissed![141] There were about 15 members of the company and they included, as well as Streatfield and Goddard, Jack Beddy, John and Wally Leppard (until the latter went in the army), Alf Voyce, Wally Cook, George Brooks and Jack and Roy Baker.[142] Their duties seem to have been enforcing the blackout with the A.R.P., searching for enemies dropping by parachute, guarding crashed aircraft and some buildings, preparing for invasion and, it would seem, indulging in jollity and practical jokes. On one occasion there was a report of a German aviator downed in the woods below Falconhurst and the Home Guard was deployed to capture this dangerous enemy; after scouring the woods and calling upon the miscreant to surrender on pain of being shot it was discovered that the escapee was a horse, which had got out of one of Billy White's fields![143] The Home Guard had a hut on Hopper's Bank, which they proceeded to burn down by leaving the stove alight and stoked up when they departed one morning.[144] As we have seen, the Home Guard might have been included amongst those who would, if necessary, have been ordered to defend the line of the Eden, although for some time they did not have proper uniforms nor much weaponry.

The final incomers, apart from soldiers and refugees, were the Women's Land Army. In the Second World War all young adult women as well as men were required to register for deployment in some form of national service. Some were drafted into the women's branches of the armed services and some were steered into factories engaged in war work, while others were recruited into the Land Army.[145] These young woman were put onto the farms to undertake agricultural labour, and so girls from cities who had no previous experience of rural life or of farm work frequently found themselves lifting potatoes, driving tractors and doing all the other farming activities. The Women's Land Army had in fact been formed on 1 June 1939 in anticipation of war so that there were already 1,000 volunteers waiting by early September. In Kent there were 262 Land Girls by the end of 1939, and 475 by December 1940; they reached a maximum strength of 4,169 in July 1943.[146] At least 35 women were lodged at a hostel at Marlpit Hill, Edenbridge, and others were housed at Hever Grange. Some stayed on the farms where they were working. At least a dozen young woman seemed to have worked around Mark Beech and in at least three cases ended up marrying local men.[147]

A 'casualty' of the Second World War might be said to have been Falconhurst. Dry rot was found in the house in 1943 and in the circumstances of war and, indeed, its immediate aftermath it was not possible for the Talbot family to take all the steps probably necessary to preserve it. Consequently the infestation spread almost out of control. Plans were drawn up to rebuild the house, which now required very extensive attention. These plans proved to be too expensive, so eventually, in 1960-1, all Brandon's original mansion was dismantled. Any loss was tragic, but the destruction involved the disappearance of a very fine library with all its wood panelling. The home now occupied by the Talbots is the extension to Falconhurst, created by Coleridge in 1913, along with a few walls of the old house, including the main doorway with the family's arms carved above it, in an almost gothic scene.[148]

A big talking point in the village was the presence for nearly two months in 1970 of a drilling rig, operated by Conoco, in the field between Buckhurst Farm and Jessups. No oil in commercial quantities was found, but a geologist subsequently stated that it was more likely to be found on land around Wilderness Farm. Nothing more has happened since that time, although at the time of writing preparations are being made to drill for gas near Pyle Gate.

The most traumatic event, however, in the recent history of Mark Beech was the hurricane in autumn 1987. It occurred on the night of 15-16 October and the winds, which may have touched speeds of nearly 120 m.p.h., reached their peak at about two or three in the morning and had disappeared by daybreak. In the middle of the night the air was brown with sand and salt and days later the leaves on the windward side of trees were scorched. Some people slept through it all, but many villagers lay in bed listening to the wind howling like a banshee, tiles clattering off the roof, and all sorts of thumps, bangs and crashes going on outside, wondering all the time what would happen next. Doctor's wife Mrs. Linda Milner, who lived at Bannisters Barn and had midwifery training from many years past, bravely went out to deliver a baby at Saxbys, the mother being quite unable to be transported to hospital in Tunbridge Wells on account of the blocked roads. Given the wooded character of the landscape and maximum resistance offered by the trees which still had their leaves on, the damage was very extensive. The wind seemed to wriggle around like a snake or flooding river so that paths of destruction were easily visible through undamaged areas. Trees were down all over the place, and for some hours after daylight all roads out of the village were blocked. If this hurricane had occurred during the day, when children were going to school and adults were at work or going about their normal affairs, there would undoubtedly have been many fatalities. In some places, such as the wood on the north-west corner of Mark Beech Hill, trees can still be seen lying on the ground 12 years later. Electricity was cut off for more than two weeks, so that in households without emergency generators, pumps and boilers on central heating systems were out of action and, with no gas in the village, only those households with Agas and similar stoves or with solid fuel boilers could cook or heat water; nor could radios or televisions without batteries be used. The telephone became intermittent for several days; sometimes it worked faintly, sometimes it did not work at all. The train service was halted for many days. The general clearing up went on for months. There was also some property damage, Jersey Cottage, for example, losing about a third of its roof, as did Broomyfield, and Eden Hall numberless tiles and many trees.[149]

As it approaches a new century, Mark Beech seems in many respects unchanged over the last 30 years, and probably much longer. We have noted several times that for a place so close to one of the largest and most thriving cities in the world, Mark Beech remains a remarkable oasis of rural beauty and considerable tranquillity with little increase in population. The combination of an inability to build new houses, a decline in agricultural employment, a decrease in family size and the reduction of multi-occupancy has meant that the population is now only 298, an increase of only 21 per cent since the middle of the 19th century.[150] This figure is made up of 260 adults and 38 children under eighteen.[151] Whereas in 1891 the children under 14 constituted more than a third of the population, today, differently defined, they constitute only 12.75 per cent. The population includes 47 nuns, old people and others living at Eden Hall (or 15.3 per cent of the population); in 1891, when it was a private house, there were 11 people there (4.4 per cent).[152] Mark Beech's population is lower today than it was in 1921, in 1931, at the outbreak of war in 1939 and, indeed, in 1871. This must be very rare for any settlement in the south-east of England during this period.

As the Millennium approaches plans are afoot to celebrate it in Mark Beech. It is intended to hold a dance in the village hall with a marquee on the garden behind on the night of 31 December 1999/1 January 2000. It is possible that a specially designed stone seat, with suitable inscription, will be erected on the triangle of land in front of the church and next to the pub. Every inhabitant is to be photographed outside their front door in the last few weeks of 1999 and the children of the village are going to compile a profile of the village and its residents in 1999 and be given a specially commissioned commemorative mug. Finally, this study has been inspired, partially at least, by the Millennium in order to provide an appraisal of a High Weald village over what is, indeed, more than 2,000 years of its history.

Appendix A[1]
Some Houses in Mark Beech

THERE ARE no structures in Mark Beech older than the later Middle Ages; although the date of Wickens is unknown and it might be older, Wickens is not strictly in Mark Beech. This is true of most English villages unless they contain a Roman villa, an Anglo-Saxon or Norman church, an early medieval castle or manor house. Bramsells and Old Buckhurst, and possibly others, are on sites which have been occupied since the Norman Conquest or earlier, although the present houses are much younger. Two of the oldest houses in the area are Hever Castle and Hever Brocas, two manors whose land extended to Mark Beech. The first entirely brick or stone building, the second Edells, did not appear until about 1840. Before the 19th century all buildings in Mark Beech were certainly timber-framed; the usual practice was to put a timber plate on a brick or stone base and build a timber frame upwards, with a clay tile roof on top. The timbers were interfilled with lath and plaster but, as this was not very weatherproof, after a period of time the timbers on the ground floor would be interfilled with brick. A special architectural feature of this region of west Kent, north Sussex and east Surrey was that the upper stories were tile-hung with clay tiles, usually at a later date, and many new houses in the area are still constructed in this way even where the ground floor is exposed brick. Until about 1550 few houses had chimneys, and in hall houses a wood fire would be lit on the floor and the smoke escaped through a hole in the roof or a vent at the top of a gable. There are no thatched houses in Mark Beech, although there is one in Hever. To date 10 houses, the church and a barn have been listed. When the Talbots arrived in the middle of the 19th century the only structures in the centre of Mark Beech were, probably, the *Kentish Horse* (part of), Old Farm, Bramsells and the barn at Falconhurst. A few houses have disappeared since 1850, such as the original Curd's and Brook farmhouses, two cottages at Horseshoe Green, Stridewood, a cottage between Bramsells and Buckhurst, a cottage opposite the *Queens Arms* and, of course, Pound House, which was not strictly in Mark Beech. Being on clay soil houses in Mark Beech are somewhat prone to subsidence, especially in the drier summers that we seem to have experienced in recent times, and houses which have had to be dealt with in this respect include Bannisters Barn, Jessups and Summerhill. The situation is confused by there being two Buckhurst Cottages and, until recently, two Buckhurst Farms. If we include Wickens and Wilderness Farm there are 13 listed buildings in Mark Beech, namely Brook Farmhouse, Cole Allen, Heathen Street Cottage, Hole Cottage, Holy Trinity Church, Horseshoe Cottage, Horseshoe Green farmhouse, Old Buckhurst (listed as Buckhurst farmhouse), Old Farm, Pyle Gate, Pyle Gate Barn, Wickens and Wilderness Farm. Characteristics of some of the houses in Mark Beech are as follows:

Ashtrees: Entirely wooden house erected during First World War, 100 yards east of crossroads, to house manager of poultry farm. Verandah in front. Formerly called the Brown House.

Bannister's Barn: Named after the Bannister family, who owned the land on which it is situated. Converted in 1948 from agricultural building which existed at least as early as mid-19th century (see 1869 Ordnance Survey map). Originally single storey, but central section rebuilt as two stories in 1967 by R.H. King (see page 101). Unusual in that it has two single-storey wings and a two-storey centre. On south side of road 200 yards east of Mark Beech crossroads. Recent internal alterations. Large garden behind.

Barn Platt: Originally stables on High Buckhurst farm. Converted to house in late 1940s. Origin of name unknown. Adjacent to Jersey Cottage.

Beeches and Birches: Two semi-detached bungalows with verandahs on front built in Uckfield Lane *c*.1920-2 for retired colonial policeman, Henry Woodhams.

Bowlinglands: Timber-framed house on west side of Stick Hill. Possibly 17th-century. Formerly public house known as the *Bricklayers Arms*, popularly as the 'Barking Donkey'. Closed 1910 and converted to house. Not listed. The Manor of Cowden Lewisham Court Papers contain documents on the pub for the years 1841-60 (CKS: U1000/7/T17).

Bramsells: Probably the oldest continuously occupied site in Mark Beech as it is mentioned in Domesday Book, the only one in the village to be so. The present house is a timber-framed, tile-hung, early 17th-century structure, but with substantial 20th-century additions, in appropriate style. In the civil parish of Hever, on the north side of the old road, about 500 yards west of the crossroads. Listed.

Brook Farm: At top of Blowers Hill on north side. Second house of this name, original being near present site of Cowden station. Timber-framed 17th-century house, much altered in 19th century. Listed.

Broomyfield: On the top of Hoppers Bank, with magnificent views to the south and west. Of uncertain age, but has some timber framing and is certainly pre-1750, though with modern additions.

Buckhurst Cottage: The western half of High Buckhurst, which was divided in 1951. The last house in Mark Beech proper going out towards Chiddingstone Hoath. In civil parish of Hever. For further details see High Buckhurst.

Buckhurst Cottage: Another of the village's older buildings. Small 17th-century timber-framed cottage. Brick-faced. Recent additions, in style, on back. Adjacent to Buckhurst Farm. Listed (smallest property to be so).

Buckhurst Farm: Possibly a very old inhabited site (see page 29). First mentioned in 1216, but this reference is probably to Old Buckhurst. Present house half-timbered and tile-hung. Built in 1790s with small modern addition. Has two wells. A barn behind is undoubtedly older.

Cherry Tree Cottage: Two Victorian farm labourer's cottages, just east of Horseshoe Green, united as one property in 1970s by R.H. King (*see* page 101).

Cole Allen: Large timber-framed house from 17th century, much altered in 18th and 20th centuries. Near top of Stick Hill. Listed. The home of Guy Ewing, London estate agent, historian of Cowden, and County Councillor. He went to live at Claydene and is buried in Mark Beech churchyard.

Cowden Station: At bottom of Blowers Hill. Built in 1888 for L.B.S.C.R., with stationmaster's house. Polychromatic brickwork. Some cast-iron pillars, etc. Iron and wood bridge between platforms and the canopies and cast-iron frames on both platforms removed in 1992. Signal box removed 1987. Single-track operations. 'Up' platform overgrown. Unmanned and now in a very sorry state.

Edells: Originally a timber-framed farmhouse, which was raised in late 1830s. First brick house in Mark Beech, constructed 1839-40 (but see *Queens Arms*). Very considerably altered and added to in 1873 by Joseph Clark. The Vicarage, 1852-1905 (see page 73).

Eden Hall (St Andrew's): Originally known as Mapletreuse (sometimes called Mapletroughs, Maplebroughs, Mapletrees or Maple Trows). Timber-framed farmhouse. Large brick extension built on front by Sir Richard Baggallay, 1877-8. Given to Thomas Cubitt on his marriage in 1893 and renamed by him. The Baggallays went to live in Moat Farm, Cowden, and Ernest Baggallay later became Chairman of the Parish Council. Set well back on west side of Stick Hill. Now St Andrew's Convent, a school and residential home for elderly. Military hospital in the First World War. Much of original destroyed in early 1960s.

Elylands: 16th-century, timber-framed, tile-hung house on east side of Stick Hill. Fine example of its type. Listed.

Fairholme: In civil parish of Hever, on south side of road, about 300 yards west of crossroads. Built almost over Mark Beech railway tunnel. Architect unknown. Notable features are the Kent Arms in stained glass in front door panel and very large windows. Large brick house built in 1921-2 by London builder, R.E. Raxworthy, who also gave land for Village Hall (see also Rookery Cottage and Summerhill).

Falconhurst: Large Victorian mansion designed by David Brandon in the Jacobean style in 1852 for John Chetwyn Talbot and added to by John D. Coleridge in 1913. Brandon's part demolished on account of dry rot in 1960-1. Mentioned in Pevsner. Still occupied by Talbot family. Interesting barn at entrance older than house. Within the curtilage are Falconhurst Farm, Falconhurst Lodge and the Small House, all built in 1850s. Interesting garden.

Gilridge: Site of a very old house, but present structure a very extensive rebuilding of about 1860.

Heathen Street Cottage: Early to mid-17th-century timber-framed cottage. Formerly known as Mapletreuse Cottage and Eden Hall Cottage. Listed. Up Heathen Street or Lane, just west of Stick Hill and south of St Andrew's Convent. Origin of name obscure (see James, A., *Heathen Street*, 1991, pp. 1-2).

High Buckhurst: The half of High Buckhurst which has retained original name. Originally four cottages, known as Woodside, built in late 1880s/early 1890s by Horace Banister Collins. Totally reconstructed *c.*1899-1900, incorporating some of old structure, while occupied by Stephen Streatfield, tenant of A.H. Denny. In 1930s and '40s the whole house constituted the small *Mark Beech Hotel* (see also Buckhurst Cottage, above). Sometimes referred to in documents as Mark Beech Farm (see Old Farm).

Hole Cottage: Vies with Old Buckhurst as the oldest house in Mark Beech. Timber-framed, with later brick and tile-hanging. Probably built *c.*1480. Originally part of a house at least three times bigger. Most of it pulled down in 1830s. Suffered war damage in 1943. Part of Falconhurst estate, but tenanted by the Landmark Trust as a holiday cottage. Down in woods, near Cowden station, below Pyle Gate. Listed. (Known to the author's children as the 'Witch's Cottage' or the 'Rumpelstiltskin's Cottage'.)

Holy Trinity Church: Built in 1852 in Old English style, at a cost of *c.*£1,400. Architect: David Brandon. On crossroads. Listed. Mentioned in Pevsner. Large beech tree in churchyard. High Church ritual (see pages 61-2, 97-8 for more details).

Horseshoe Cottage: On south side of road from Horseshoe Green to Cowden station. A 17th-century, heavily beamed cottage created from two smaller ones. One half formerly a shop, as can be seen from style of window. Listed.

Horseshoe Green Farm: Formerly known as Coleman's Farm. Very fine timber-framed, tile-hung farmhouse. The core is a late medieval hall house which vies with the Hole, Old Buckhurst and Wickens as the oldest in the village. Contains some very good interior panelling. Listed.

Jersey Cottage: Former Jersey cowman's cottage, hence name. Built in 1906, but possibly with older antecedents. Additions made in 1949, 1973 and 1984, the last by R.H. King (see page 101). Central core half-timbered. Partially tile-hung. Originally part of High Buckhurst Farm.

Jessups: One of the finest looking houses in the village. Brick house built *c.*1870, in a style which makes it look older. Undoubtedly on site of pre-existing house. Twentieth-century additions. Said to have been two cottages. Once known as Willets. A pig farm in former times. Formerly shop and post office. Another fine garden.

Kentish Horse: The main public house in village. On crossroads. Became inn in late 1830s. Building of uncertain age. Much altered, particularly in 20th century. Visibly consists of three parts. Northern part, on front, at least 18th-century, but possibly older. Once owned by the Burfoots. Formerly a Whitbread pub but now a Free House. Had Mark Beech AA sign affixed to it in 1930s. Once two cottages? Briefly also known as the *Kentish Arms*.

Lambert Cottage: Formerly known as Alcocks. On Hartfield road between Pyle Gate and The Pound. Within Falconhurst Estate, but sold in 1894. Once owned by a Rector of Cowden (Harvey). Has a very deep well.

Lower Buckhurst: Formerly pigeon-loft to High Buckhurst Farm. Converted to house and expanded in late 1940s. Next to Jersey Cottage.

New House: Built down fields from Buckhurst Farm in 1993, now the farmhouse. Modernised Weald style. One of very few new houses built since 1955. Architect: Leslie Humphreys.

Newtye Farm or Cottages: Really in Chiddingstone at far end of Newtye Hurst. Both names are on old maps and documents. Almost certainly an old timber-framed structure. Said by some to have been destroyed by enemy action in 1940-1, but no documentary evidence. 'Died' of neglect and used by Astor estate for its materials.

Nightingales: 1930s house in Uckfield Lane. Augmented in 1996.

Oak Tree House: Large Tudor-style house in Uckfield Lane, built in 1993 on site of old shack. One of few new houses. Architect: Glyn Doughty Design.

The Old Bakehouse: Victorian brick structure, built *c.*1860. As its name says, it is the old bakery. About 100 yards east of Horseshoe Green. Converted to a dwelling in 1959-60, but augmented twice in 1980 and 1987.

Old Buckhurst: Probably the oldest extant house in Mark Beech (but see Wickens). First mentioned in 1216, but almost certainly on much older site (see Buckhurst above and p.29). Last house in parish on road to Chiddingstone Hoath. Late 16th-century hall house. Formerly known as Buckhurst Farm or Low Buckhurst. Listed. Presently occupied by direct descendant of W.E. Gladstone. Has old barn behind it converted to dwelling in 1990. Has one of several fine gardens in village, created by present occupants, open to public on occasional basis in summer.

Old Farm: Oldest house in the centre of village, in Cow Lane. Formerly known as Mark Beech Farm and as Killick's. Small timber-framed 17th-century house, with 'cat-slide' roof. Listed. Once owned by the Burfoots.

Old Vicarage: Lutyens/Weald-style vicarage built by John D. Coleridge in 1905. Of very large dimensions. Divided in two in 1958 and sold into private ownership in 1968 (see page 96).

Pyle Gate (Pilegate): Large timber-framed 17th-century house on Hartfield Road. Listed. May have been site of Roman bloomery in second and third centuries. Has a listed 17th-century barn. Barn, oast and outbuildings converted to dwellings 1997-8.

Queens Arms: Brick public house at top of Stick Hill at Pound crossroads. Vies with Edells as the oldest brick building in village, probably built in 1840-1. Mother and daughter (Maynard) have been licensees for 70 years. Owned by Whitbread. Probably prime site for future development.

Rickwoods: Large Victorian mansion, built on prime site in 1899 down Wickens Lane by corset manufacturer, Mr. Nutter. One of the most splendid properties in Mark Beech. Once occupied by Brigadier Bagnold of 'Desert Rat' fame (see Bagnold, R.A., *Libyan Sands*, London, 1935). There is a separate Rickwoods Farm, recently renovated (see also Wickens). Very large garden.

Riding Light: Pre-fab with brick skin. Just to west of Buckhurst Cottage and Farm. Built *c.*1953-4.

Rookery Cottage: Brick cottage built in Uckfield Lane in 1936 for retired head of convent, 100 yards north of crossroads, by Raxworthy, who also built Summerhill and Hawthorns further down Uckfield Lane. Originally called Holy Cross Cottage. Once the home of artist Edgar Norfield. Augmented in mid-1960s.

Roughitts: Brick and white-washed house built in 1952 at crossroads on site of former school playground. Occupied by Leppard family ever since.

Spring Grove: Modern house in Wealden style between crossroads and village hall. One of the few houses erected in Mark Beech since 1955. Built 1976. Architect: D.S. Hine.

Summerhill: Brick and rendered house near top of Uckfield Lane, built *c.*1925 by Raxworthy. Occupied for many years by Francis Mott, Canadian-born psychologist. Major additions, 1997, these the last commission of Bob King; completed by Julian Black. 'Not named after A.S. Neill's famous school of the same name' (Mrs. Gwen Mott, 18/1/98).

Victoria House: Formerly *Victoria Arms* public house at Horseshoe Green, closed during First World War. Mid-19th-century structure. Adjacent to blacksmith and later garage. Neighbouring houses, Horseshoe Cottages, built 1860-1900.

Village Hall: Plain brick building, with slate roof, just west of crossroads, almost opposite church. Built in early 1920s and much refurbished in mid-1990s.

Vine Cottage: House at Gilridge, which is just in Mark Beech. A 19th-century farm building, converted to house not later than 1920s. For a brief period was garage to Gilridge before conversion. Has old roof timbers, which may be reused from older building. So called because there was there once an old and large vine.

Wickens: Possibly the oldest house in the area, though technically a few feet outside the parish. Large timber-framed farmhouse from late 15th century, but the core probably older. Confusingly once known as Rickwoods (Farm), so there have been three different houses on different sites with this name (see Rickwoods). Known in 19th century as Gainsford's Farm. Listed.

Wilderness Farm: Strictly in Hever, but has Mark Beech postal address. Down Wilderness Lane. Small timber-framed yeoman's house, probably of 17th century. Occupied by the Leppard family since First World War. Once owned by Streatfields, then by Astors. Listed.

Wood Cottage: Modern brick and tile-hung house down Uckfield Lane. Built in 1990 to replace former wooden Colt House, hence name.

Woodside: Typical inter-war brick house of substance. Built in early 1920s. Last house in Mark Beech down Uckfield Lane. Stands back from road. Occupied for many years by novelist and former aviator, David Beaty, who once held the record for the longest flight of a champagne cork, achieved in this garden! (*Guinness Book of Records*)

Wyshe Farm: Mid-1930s brick house built between Fairholme and the Village Hall.

Other houses not dealt with individually in this appendix include School House, School Cottages, Mark Beech Cottages, Post Office Cottages, Horseshoe Green Cottages, Grove Cottages and a number of houses in Uckfield and Cow Lanes.

Appendix B(i)
Vicars of Mark Beech,
1852-1999

1852-1904	Robert Shapland Hunt
1904-1912	William Starey
1912-1913	Hugh Howard Williams
1913-1920	Arthur Lumley Temple
1921-1924	Arthur Stephen Withers Moore
1925-1938	Stanley Hide
1939-1950	Albert Edward Cornibear
1950-1959	Lewis William Rye Hollowood
1959-1965	Bernard John Wigan
1966-1973	John Brenton Collins
1973-1978	Bishop John Keith Russell
1979-1990	Derek Chapman
1990-1994	Brian Dudley Simmons
1995-	Paul Jonathan Plumley

Appendix B(ii)
Headteachers, Mark Beech School,
1852-1945

1852-1870	John King
1870-1881	William Weighel Kibblewight
1881-1890	Mrs. Emma Sarah Fox
1890-1899	Miss Jane Scott
1899-1924	Miss Mary Jennings
1924-1931	Miss Edith Weth
1931-1939	Miss Anne K. Morley
1939-1945	Miss Sybil Brown

References

Abbreviations employed in the References and Bibliography

Arch. Cant.:	*Archaeologia Cantiana*
Birch:	*Cartularium Saxonicum*, ed. Birch, W. de G., 3 vols., London, 1885-93
BM Add MS:	British Museum Additional Manuscript
CKS:	Centre for Kentish Studies, Maidstone
Detsicas:	Detsicas, A.P., *The Cantiaci*, Gloucester, 1987
DNB:	*Dictionary of National Biography*
EHR:	*English Historical Review*
Everitt:	Everitt, A.M., *Continuity and Colonization: the evolution of Kentish settlement*, Leicester, 1986
Ewing:	Ewing, G., *Cowden: the Records of a Wealden Parish*, Tunbridge Wells, 1926
Hasted:	Hasted, E., *History and Topographical Survey of Kent*, 2nd edn., 12 vols., London, 1797-1801
Kemble:	*Codex Diplomaticus Aevi Saxonici*, ed., Kemble, J.M., 6 vols., London, 1839-48
PRO:	Public Record Office, Kew
SAC:	Sussex Archaeological Collections
Somers-Cocks:	Somers-Cocks, H.L. and Boyson, V.F., *Edenbridge*, Edenbridge, 1912
SuAC:	Surrey Archaeological Collections
TRHS:	Transactions of the Royal Historical Society
Witney (1):	Witney, K.P., *The Jutish Forest*, London, 1978
Witney (2):	Witney, K.P., *The Kingdom of Kent*, Chichester, 1986
VCH:	*Victoria County History*

Chapter I: The Setting

1. Witney (1), pp.5-13; P. Brandon and B. Short, *The South East from A.D. 1000*, pp.4-12.
2. For the Eden, Kent Water and the Upper Medway see R.H. Goodsall, *The Medway and its Tributaries*, pp.24-37. In this study all mileages cited are 'as the crow flies'.
3. *Ibid.*, pp.24-5.
4. At the 1991 Census the population was recorded as 7,581.
5. S.W. Wooldridge and F. Goldring, *The Weald*, chaps. 2, 3 and 8; G.H. Garrard, *A Survey of the Agriculture of Kent*, pp.21ff; J.L.M. Gulley, 'The Wealden Landscape in the early 17th century and its antecedents', Ph.D. Thesis, p.45; J.T. White, *The South-East Down and Weald: Kent, Surrey and Sussex*, pp.21-4.
6. Everitt, p.53.
7. G. Markham, *The Inrichment of the Weald of Kent*, p.2.
8. D. Defoe, cited in 'Visitors Notes, Hole Cottage', by Landmark Trust, p.3.
9. W. Marshall, *The Rural Economy of the Southern Counties comprising Kent, Surrey, Sussex and the Isle of White*, pp.343-4.
10. T.D.W. Dearn, *An Historical, Topographical and Descriptive Account of the Weald of Kent*, p.71.
11. G. Buckland, 'On the Farming of Kent', pp.281-2, cf. Hasted, III, p.203; J. Boys, *A General View of the Agriculture of the County of Kent*, p.71.
12. White, *op. cit.*, p.85; Witney (1), p.5; Everitt, pp.25-30; J.L. Bolton, *The Medieval English Economy, 1150-1500*, p.10.
13. P. Wormald, 'Sir Geoffrey Elton's *English*: A View from the Early Middle Ages', p.321.
14. G. Ward, 'The Manor of Lewisham and Its Wealden "Dens" ', p.113.
15. I cannot find this in Bede, but it is cited in Everitt, p.23, and in C. Rayner, *Sevenoaks Past*, p.5.
16. Gulley, *op. cit.*, p.394.
17. Everitt, p.32.
18. F.W. Jessup, *History of Kent*, pp.16, 29; Witney (2), pp.20, 68; Everitt, pp.24-5; Brandon and Short, *op. cit.*, p.13.
19. White, *op. cit.*, p.38; Everitt, p.25.

20. White, *op. cit.,* pp.36-43; Witney (1), pp.16-17; Everitt, p.26.
21. See below n.22 and chap. 3.
22. J. Bosworth and T.N. Noller, *An Anglo-Saxon Dictionary,* p.674.
23. W. Lambarde, *A Perambulation of Kent;* W. Camden, *Britannia: Kent;* J. Philipot, 'The Visitation of Kent taken in the Years 1619-21'; R. Kilburne, *A Topography or Survey of the County of Kent;* Sir Edward Bysshe, 'A Visitation of the County of Kent, 1663-68'; J. Harris, *The History of Kent;* T. Philipot, *Vilare Cantianum; or Kent Surveyed and Illustrated;* Hasted, III; E.W. Brayley, *The Beauties of England, Wales and Scotland;* Dearn, *op. cit.;* W.H. Ireland, *A New and Complete History of the County of Kent;* C. Greenwood, *The County of Kent.*
24. Markham, *op. cit.;* Boys, *op. cit.;* J. Banister, *A Synopsis of Husbandry, being Cursory Observations in the Several Branches of Rural Economy;* Marshall, *op. cit.;* Buckland, *op. cit.*
25. *The Journeys of Celia Fiennes,* (c.1685-1703), ed. C. Morris; D. Defoe, *A Tour thro' the Whole Island of Great Britain,* 1724-26, ed. G.D.H. Cole; V.J.B Torr, 'A Tour Through Kent in 1733', pp.267-80; A. Young, *A Six Weeks Tour of the Southern Counties of England,* 'A Fortnight's Tour in Kent and Essex'; W. Cobbett, *Rural Rides.*
26. W.E. Buckland, *The Parish Registers and Records of the Diocese of Rochester,* p.94; R. Homan, *The Victorian Churches of Kent,* p.75.
27. Sir Stephen Glynne, *Notes on the Churches of Kent;* L.L. Duncan, *The Parish Churches of West Kent;* C.H. Fielding, *The Records of Rochester;* F. Grayling, *County Churches: Kent.* Others which make no mention of Mark Beech include: H.R.P. Boorman and V.J. Torr, *Kent Churches, 1954;* J.A. Syms, *Kent County Churches;* J.E.Vigar, *Exploring Kent Churches;* J.A. Syms, *Kent County Churches Continued;* J.A. Syms, *Kent County Churches Concluded;* J.E. Vigar, *Kent Churches.*
28. J.B. Johnston, *The Place-Names of England and Wales,* p.361; E. McClure, *British Place-Names,* pp.207ff.
29. J.K. Wallenberg, *Kentish Place-Names; The Place-Names of Kent.*
30. R. Furley, *A History of the Weald of Kent.*
31. R. Church, *Kent,* p.78, M. Crouch, *Kent,* p.135, and A. Bignell, *The Kent Village Book,* p.138 contain very brief references to Mark Beech, but G. Cling, *Kent,* J.C. Cox, *Rambles in Kent,* A. Beckett, *The Wonderful Weald,* D.C. Maynard, *Old Inns of Kent,* A. Oswald, *Country Houses of Kent,* S. Kaye-Smith, *The Weald of Kent and Sussex,* A. Bignell, *Kent Villages,* T.A. Bushell, *Kent,* R. Darby, *Journey Through the Weald,* and B. Cox, *English Inn and Tavern Names* have nothing, whilst always discussing Chiddingstone, Cowden and Hever.
32. S. Bagshaw, *A History, Gazetteer and Directory of the County of Kent,* pp.703-4; *Kelly's Directory of Kent, 1855,* p.499, *1878,* p.1550; R.W. Blencowe, 'Cowden and Its Neighbours', p.117.
33. J. Eastman, *Historic Hever: the Church,* p.14; Buckland, *op. cit.,* Ewing, pp.142-3; J.C. Cox, *Kent,* p.201. [Cox is a revised edition of Cling, *op. cit.*]
34. See *inter alia* n.31 above.
35. CKS, Maps 17/35; Hasted, III, map between pp.158-9.
36. CKS, CTR/99b.
37. *A Bibliography of Kent and Supplement.*
38. CKS: Talbot Papers, J.C. Talbot's sketch map for a parish, U1612/P18.
39. CKS: Talbot Papers, map of area, U1612/P19.
40. See Chapters 2 and 3 below.
41. W.E. Buckland, *op. cit.,* pp.281-2.

Chapter II: Celts and Romans

1. For this chapter I am particularly indebted to Detsicas, *passim,* but see also: S.S. Frere, *Britannia: a History of Roman Britain;* P. Salway, *Roman and Anglo-Saxon Britain;* P. Drewett, D. Rudling and M. Gardiner, *The South East to A.D. 1000,* chap. 6; M. Millett, *The Romanisation of Britain;* N. Higham, *Rome, Britain and the Anglo-Saxons,* chaps. 1 and 2.
2. Tunbridge Wells Museum, Accession Nos. 85/324 (1-98), 85/325 (1-8); J.H. Money, 'Excavations at High Rocks, Tunbridge Wells, 1954-56: Appendix F, Sandstone Outcrops in the Weald', p.221.
3. For details of this fort see Royal Commission on the Historical Monuments of England (hereafter RCHME), Unique Identifier 407284, 12 February 1997; C.R. Smith, *Collectanea Antiqua: Notices of Ancient Remains,* pp.71-2; G. Payne, 'Report on Finds in Kent'; E.A. Downman, Plan of Dry Hill, 1903, Kingston Museum, S(913) No. 3666(9); S.E. Winbolt and I.D. Margary, 'Dry Hill Camp, Lingfield'; I.D. Margary, 'Notes on Dry Hill Camp, Lingfield'; C.F. Tebbutt, 'Notes on Dry Hill Camp, Lingfield'; P.J. Gray, 'Dry Hill and Its Origins'; J. Forde-Johnstone, *Hillforts of the Iron Age in England and Wales,* pp.19-20; D. Field and P. Nicolaysen, 'Surrey Earthworks'; D.G. Bird, 'Dry Hill Camp, Lingfield'; Drewett *et al.,* *op. cit.,* pp.145-61.
4. Letter to author from East Surrey Water Co., 29 January 1997.
5. Forde-Johnstone, *op. cit.,* p.23; Drewett *et al.,* *op. cit.,* pp.117-77.
6. Tebbutt, *op. cit.,* p.119; Witney (1), p.17; Gray, *op. cit.,* p.56.
7. E. Straker, *Wealden Iron,* pp.28, 224, 231; Winbolt and Margary, *op. cit.,* p.80; H.G. Schubert, *History of the British Iron and Steel Industry,* p.36; Witney (1), pp.17, 20.
8. F.W. Jessup, *Kent History Illustrated,* p.6; White, *op. cit.,* pp.17, 34.
9. Forde-Johnstone, *op. cit.,* pp.19-20.
10. Detsicas, pp.1-2.
11. Jessup, *op. cit.,* p.14, *A History of Kent,* p.18; Witney (1), pp.21-6, 22 (Map 3), 29, 189-90 (Appendix B); Detsicas, p.2.
12. I.D. Margary, 'An Early Trans-Wealden Trackway'.
13. CKS: Streatfield Papers, U908/P3.

14. Gray, *op. cit.*, pp.53-6.
15. P. Jones and N. Pennick, *A History of Pagan Europe*, pp.79-110; B. Cunliffe, *The Ancient Celts*, pp.183-210.
16. Jessup, *Kent History Illustrated*, p.16; Witney (2), p.12; Brandon and Short, *op. cit.*, p.80.
17. Strabo, *Geography*, ed. G. Aujac, IV, 3, 3 and IV, 5, 1; Diodorus Siculus, *History*, ed. C.H. Oldfather (ed.), V, 21, 3; Detsicas, pp.6-7, 201; N.P. Brooks, 'The Creation and Early Structure of the Kingdom of Kent', p.55.
18. Julius Caesar, *The Conquest of Gaul*, pp.110-1.
19. B. Cunliffe, *Iron Age Communities in Britain*, pp.75-84; Detsicas, pp.6-8.
20. Detsicas, pp.7-8.
21. Detsicas, pp.10, 39-59, 83-4, 96.
22. Jessup, *op. cit.*, p.18; Detsicas, p.107.
23. Detsicas, pp.9-10; Everitt, chaps. 3 and 4 *passim*.
24. Detsicas, pp.155-6, 171-7.
25. I.D. Margary, 'A New Roman Road to the Coast: I, The Road from Edenbridge to Maresfield through Ashdown Forest', 'Roman Roads in West Kent', 'Roman Communications between Kent and the East Sussex Ironworks', *Roman Ways in the Weald*, pp.59-62, *Roman Roads in Britain*, pp.124-64; H. Cleere, 'The Roman Iron Industry in the Weald and Its Connexion with the Classis Britannica'; Detsicas, pp.33-8; B.K. Herbert, 'The London to Lewes Roman Road'.
26. G. Ward, *Sevenoaks Essays*, p.254; Winbolt and Margary, *op. cit.*, p.80; Goodsall, *op. cit.*, pp.25-6; Witney (2), p.137.
27. Witney (1), pp.189-90; Detsicas, p.33.
28. *VCH: Kent, III*, p.153; Detsicas, pp.140, 145.
29. British Museum Deposit Register 13; RCHME, 407287, p.3; Payne, *op. cit.*, p.34; Winbolt and Margary, *op. cit.*, p.92; Margary, 'New Roman Road', I., p.37.
30. RCHME, 407287, p.1; Winbolt and Margary, *op. cit.*, p.92.
31. R. Jenkins, 'A Romano-Gaulish Statuette from Cowden, Kent', but see also Ewing, pp.15-16.
32. J.C. Cox, *op. cit.*, p.203; G.J. Copley, *An Archaeology of South-East England*, pp.139, 278. It would seem that Johnston introduced this error in the rev. 5th edn. of 1927 as there is no mention of a Roman camp or an intaglio ring in earlier editions of Cox's book published in 1903, 1915, 1920 and 1923.
33. Cox, *op. cit.*, p.214.
34. Marl is a natural mix of clay and carbonated lime, which is found in abundance in the Weald and which was used as fertilizer until the 19th century: Gulley, *op. cit.*, p.143; Brandon and Short, *op. cit.*, pp.65-7, 172.
35. M.C. Delany, *The Historical Geography of the Wealden Iron Industry*, pp.46-7; Straker, *op. cit.*, p.231; E. Straker and I.D. Margary, 'Ironworks and Communications in the Weald in Roman Times'; Schubert, *op. cit.*, pp.178ff., 194-7; Cleere, *op. cit.*, p.173; Detsicas, pp.171-7; H. Cleere and D. Crossley, *The Iron Industry of the Weald*, *passim*, but especially chap. 4 and Gazetteer, pp.288-393.
36. Interview with Mr. Stephen Bagnold, who lived at Rickwoods as a child and adolescent, 25 November 1997.
37. Caesar, *op. cit.*, V, 12, cited in Detsicas, p.155.
38. Witney (2), p.13; Detsicas, pp.33-153.

Chapter III: The Jutes

1. For this chapter I am especially indebted to Witney (1), Witney (2) and Everitt.
2. Detsicas, pp.25-31.
3. Salway, *op. cit.*, pp.386-7, 417-18, 460, 467; Higham, *op. cit.*, pp.48-9.
4. Witney (2), p.40.
5. Witney (2), p.12. Legend has it that Hengest was accompanied by Horsa, his brother (or father or son), but whereas Hengest is considered an historical person Horsa is now not: G. Ward, 'Hengest', pp.77-97; Witney (2), pp.42-3; J.N.L. Myres, *The English Settlements*, p.109; Brooks, *op. cit.*, pp.57-8; R. Eales, *An Introduction to the Kent Domesday*, p.7; Higham, *op. cit.*, pp.1-16. There must, however, remain doubts about the authenticity of Hengest also.
6. Witney (2), pp.41, 116.
7. Brooks, *op. cit.*, 57-8; Eales, *op. cit.*, pp.7-8.
8. Witney (2), pp.41-4.
9. Witney (2), pp.32-43, 73-4; Eales, *op. cit.*, p.7.
10. Witney (2), p.74.
11. Bede, *A History of the English Church and People*, pp.55-6; Witney (2), pp.15, 75-6, 138.
12. Witney (2), pp.29, 78-9, but see also J.E.A. Jolliffe, *Pre-Feudal England: the Jutes*, *passim*; C.F.C. Hawkes, 'The Jutes of Kent', pp.91-111; Myres, *op. cit.*, pp.113-27.
13. Witney (2), p.16.
14. Witney (2), p.21; Higham, *op. cit.*, pp.153ff.
15. White, *op. cit.*, p.86; Witney (2), p.17.
16. Everitt, pp.103-4.
17. Witney (2), p.20.
18. White, *op. cit.*, p.86.
19. Witney (2), p.21.

20. Kemble, No. 986, IV, p.271; Birch, No. 33, I, p.55; *VCH: Surrey, II*, pp.55-64; D. Whitelock (ed.), *English Historical Documents*, I, *c*.500-1042, 2nd edn., Doc. 54, pp.479-80; Witney (2), pp.90, 144.

21. Witney (2), p.146.

22. C.J. Arnold, *An Archaeology of the Early Anglo-Saxon Kingdoms*, pp.146-7.

23. Witney (2), p.116.

24. Witney (2), pp.57, 73, 89-90, 146.

25. Witney (2), pp.163-5.

26. E.B. Fryde, D.E. Greenway, S. Porter and I. Roy (eds.), *Handbook of British Chronology*, 3rd edn., pp.15, 25-6.

27. Brooks, *op. cit.*, p.71.

28. Jessup, *op. cit.*, pp.51-2; Witney (2), pp.60-1; Eales, *op. cit.*, p.12. However in the summer of 1997 what may be the foundations of Cnut's (1016-35) palace were found at Chelsea: *The Times*, 19 August 1997, p.5. Obviously this is much later than the Jutish and early English kings (and is not in Kent, anyway).

29. Jessup, *History of Kent*, p.36; Witney (2), p.129.

30. Witney (1), p.57; Witney (2), pp.29, 52.

31. Witney (1), pp.39-40, 90.

32. Witney (2), p.54.

33. W. Illingworth (ed.), *Rotuli Hundredorum*, I, p.233; Witney (1), p.32.

34. H.W. Knocker, 'The Valley of Holmesdale: Its Evolution and Development', 'The Evolution of Holmesdale: 2, the Village Communities', 'The Evolution of Holmesdale: 3, the Manor of Sundrish'; Witney (2), p.12. C. Rayner, *Sevenoaks Past, with the Villages of Holmesdale* does not include the Mark Beech area.

35. Witney (1), p.5; Witney (2), p.65; Eales, *op. cit.*, p.26. As early as the mid-19th century it was pointed out that gavelkind was possibly not quite as widespread in Kent as sometimes assumed, although lawyers always had to be prepared for it, e.g. C.I. Elton, *The Tenures of Kent*; *passim*.

36. Talbot Papers, CKS U1612/Z107 p.30. There was another example in 1792 regarding Haysland, near Horseshoe Green: *ibid*, p.49.

37. Witney (2), p.24; Everitt, *passim*.

38. Witney (1), p.32; Witney (2), p.55.

39. Eales, *op. cit.*, p.12.

40. Witney (1), p.56.

41. Witney (1), p.33; Witney (2), p.55.

42. Witney (1), pp.201-2, 224-7.

43. F.R.H. Du Boulay, 'Denns, Droving and Dangers', p.78; Witney (1), pp.68, 78-9, 102; Witney (2), p.79.

44. Witney (2), pp.68-9.

45. Everitt, *passim*.

46. Witney (2), pp.68-9.

47. K. Cameron, *English Place-Names*, p.70; Witney (1), pp.37-8; Witney (2), pp.57-8.

48. Ward, 'The Manor of Lewisham', p.112; Everitt, pp.35-9, 122, 155-6.

49. P. Morgan (ed.), *Domesday Book: Kent*, pp.12d, 13a; Witney (1), pp.60, 98; Witney (2), p.162.

50. Witney (1), p.73; Witney (2), p.136. Cowden was also known as Amboldisherst: Wallenberg, *Place-Names of Kent*, p.337; Witney (1), p.289 f. 73.

51. Witney (1), pp.58, 68.

52. Witney (1), p.66; Witney (2), p.193.

53. Witney (1), pp.127-53; Everitt, *passim*.

54. Witney (1), pp.38, 220-1.

55. Witney (1), p.40.

56. Witney (1), pp.53, 133, fig. 13.

57. Witney (1), pp.78-82.

58. Witney (1), p.94; P.H. Sawyer, *From Roman Britain to Norman England*, p.137; G.R.J. Jones, 'Multiple Estates and Early Settlement', pp.20-9; C. Taylor, *Village and Farmstead*, p.182; Brandon and Short, *op. cit.*, p.35.

59. For settlement patterns from the etymology of place-names see G.R.J. Jones, 'Settlement Patterns in Anglo-Saxon England'; J.M. Dodgson, 'Place-Names from *ham*, distinguished from *hamm* Names, in relation to the settlement of Kent, Surrey and Sussex'; Witney (2), pp.82-6, 239-41; Everitt, pp.103ff.; Myres, *op. cit.*, pp.29-44; M. Gelling, *Signposts to the Past: Place-Names and the History of England*, pp.106-29; Higham, *op. cit.*, pp.189-209.

60. Witney (2), pp.84-6.

61. Witney (2), pp.85-6.

62. *Arch. Cant.*, XX (1893), pp.xlix-l.

63. Johnston, *op. cit.*, p.361; A.H. Smith (ed.), *English Place-Name Elements*, II, p.37; McClure, *op. cit.*, pp.207ff.

64. See chap. 1, n.21.

65. Kemble, No. 72, I, pp.84-5; Birch, No. 141, I, pp.206-7; Witney (1), p.272; K.P. Witney, 'The Woodland Economy of Kent, 1066-1348', p.24.

66. Kemble, No. 204, I, pp.257-8; Birch, No. 346, I, pp.483-4; Witney (1), pp.19-20, 220; P.H. Sawyer, *Anglo-Saxon Charters: an Annotated List and Bibliography*, No. 175, p.115.

67. Witney (1), p.187.
68. Witney (1), p.219.
69. Kemble, No. 287, II, pp.71-2; Birch, No. 506, II, pp.113-5; Sawyer, *op. cit.*, No. 331, pp.152-3.
70. Everitt, pp.144-5.
71. Witney (2), p.112; P.H. Blair, *An Introduction to Anglo-Saxon England*, pp.120-4; G.R. Owen, *Rites and Religions of the Anglo-Saxons*, *passim*; D. Wilson, *Anglo-Saxon Paganism*, pp.44-66; Jones and Pennick, *op. cit.*, pp.126-31.
72. Bede, *op. cit.*, p.108; H. Mayr-Harting, *The Coming of Christianity to Anglo-Saxon England*, pp.30-9; C. Thomas, *Christianity in Roman Britain to A.D. 500*, pp.347-55; Jessup, *Kent History Illustrated*, pp.19-21; Witney (2), p.125.
73. Bede, *op. cit.*, pp.199-202; 'Poenitentiale Theodori', Book Two, I, printed in *Councils and Ecclesiastical Documents relating to Great Britain and Ireland*, ed. A.W. Haddan and W. Stubbs, III, pp.173-203; Witney (2), p.125.
74. C.J. Godfrey, *The Church in Anglo-Saxon England*, p.310; for the evolution of the parish in Kent see J.M. Kemble, *The Saxons of England*, II, pp.418ff; Furley, *op. cit.*, I, pp.198, 401, II, p.707; W. Page, 'Some Remarks on the Churches of the Domesday Survey', pp.61-102; *VCH: Kent, II (1926)*, pp.1-24; R.H. Hodgkin, *A History of the Anglo-Saxons*, II, pp.424-7; G.W.O. Addleshaw, 'The Beginnings of the Parochial System', 'The Development of the Parochial System from Charlemagne (768-814) to Urban II (1088-89)'; M. Deanesley, *The Pre-Conquest Church in England*, pp.191ff.; Godfrey, *op. cit.*, pp.310-7; D.J.V. Fisher, *The Anglo-Saxon Age*, pp.100-1, 106, 295, 957-75; Jessup, *History of Kent*, p.32; Blair, *op. cit.*, p.157; Sawyer, *From Roman Britain to Norman England*, pp.136-8, 245-6; F. Barlow, *The English Church, 1000-1066*, pp.183-208, 221-2, *The English Church, 1066-1154*, pp.51-3; D.C. Douglas and G.W. Greenaway (eds.), *English Historical Documents, II, 1066-1154*, pp.651-2; Witney (2), p.176; Everitt, pp.182-205; J. Blair (ed.), *Minsters and Parish Churches: the Local Church in Transition*, pp.1-20.
75. Addleshaw, 'Beginnings', p.317.
76. Witney (1), p.144.
77. T. Hearn (ed.), *Textus Roffensis*, pp.229-30; *Domesday Monachron* in *VCH: Kent, III*, pp.253-69; G. Ward, 'The List of Saxon Churches in the *Textus Roffensis*', 'The List of Saxon Churches in the *Domesday Monachron* and the *White Book of St Augustine's*'; H.C. Darby and E.M.J. Campbell, *The Domesday Geography of South-East England*, pp.495-9; Brandon and Short, *op. cit.*, p.35.
78. Ward, 'Roffensis', pp.56-7.
79. Brandon and Short, *op. cit.*, pp.44-6.
80. Everitt, p.265.
81. Everitt, p.281.
82. Illingworth, *op. cit.*, I, p.233; Furley, *op. cit.*, II, p.707; H.R. Loyn, 'The Hundred in England in the Tenth and Early Eleventh Centuries', pp.1-15.
83. 918 (Countess of Flanders); 964 (King Edgar); 1015 (King Ethelred II); 1016 (Edward the Confessor); 1044 (Edward the Confessor). Full references will be given as these charters are analysed below.
84. O. von Opperman, *Die alteren Urkunden des Klosters Blandinium*, *passim*, but see also C. Johnson, review of Opperman, *EHR*, XLIII (1928), pp.615-7.
85. Sawyer, *Anglo-Saxon Charters*.
86. Kemble, No. 518, II, pp.410-2; A. van Lokeren (ed.), *Chartes et Documents de l'Abbaye de Saint Pierre au Mont Blandin à Gand*, I, p.40; C. Johnson (ed.), *Registrum Hamonis Hethe: Diocesis Roffensis*, ed. C. Johnson, pp.32-3; Opperman, *op. cit.*, pp.101-4; A.R. Martin, 'The Alien Priory of Lewisham', p.104; J. Dhondt, 'La Donation d'Elftrude à Saint-Pierre de Gand', pp.122-9; Sawyer, *op. cit.*, No. 728, p.236.
87. *DNB*, VI, pp.224-5; D. Knowles, *The Monastic Order in England*, pp.39-40; N.P. Brooks, 'The Career of St Dunstan', pp.16-21.
88. Sir Frank M. Stenton, *Anglo-Saxon England*, p.340; J. Miller, 'The Priory at Lewisham', Thesis for Diploma in Local History, pp.6-7.
89. Dhondt, *op. cit.*, pp.122-9, 143-7; Martin, *op. cit.*, p.104; Sawyer, *op. cit.*, p.236.
90. *DNB*, I, p.161; A.P. Smith, *King Alfred the Great*, pp.222-4.
91. P. Grierson, 'The Relations between England and Flanders before the Norman Conquest', p.85.
92. Grierson, *op. cit.*, p.87, n.2; Witney (1), p.40; Miller, *op. cit.*, pp.9-11.
93. J.H. Round (ed.), *Calendar of Documents preserved in France illustrative of the History of Great Britain and Ireland*, I, 918-1206, No. 1372, p.500; *Liber Traditionum: Sancti Petri Blandiniensis*, ed. A. Fayen, pp.52-3; Hasted, I, p.237; E. Varenbergh, *Histoire des relations diplomatiques entre le Comté de Flandre et l'Angleterre au moyen age*, p.40; *VCH: Kent, II*, p.238.
94. J. de Saint-Genois, 'Précis analytique: Des documents historiques concernant les relations de l'ancien comté de Flandre avec l'Angleterre, conservés aux archives de la Flandre Orientale', p.241 (where it is misdated); Sawyer, *op. cit.*, No. 728, p.236.
95. Sawyer, *ibid*.
96. J.E.G. de Montmorency, 'Early and Medieval Records of Greenwich', p.15.
97. C. Vanden-Haute, 'Notes sur quelques chartes de l'Abbaye de Saint-Pierre à Gand', pp.411-4.
98. Opperman, *op. cit.*, I, pp.283-93.
99. Miller, *op. cit.*, p.9.
100. Dhondt, *op. cit.*, pp.120-2.
101. Miller, *op. cit.*, pp.6-7.
102. Fryde *et al.*, *op. cit.*, p.27.
103. L.L. Duncan, *A History of the Borough of Lewisham*, p.19; Wallenberg, *op. cit.*, p.7.
104. Grierson, *op. cit.*, p.86.
105. J. de Saint-Genois, 'Note sur le sejour du roi Edouarde-le-Confesseur à l'Abbaye Saint-Pierre à Gand, en 1006, et sur le biens possedés par cette abbaye en Angleterre', pp.257-9; Lokeren, *op. cit.*, I, No. 896, pp.392-423; Miller, *op. cit.*, pp.8-10.

106. Montmorency, *op. cit.*, p.16.
107. Saint-Genois, *op. cit.*, pp.257-9; F. Barlow, 'Edward the Confessor's Early Life, Character and Attitudes', p.231; F. Barlow, *Edward the Confessor*, pp.36-7.
108. Saint-Genois, *op. cit.*, pp.257-9, 'Précis analytique', pp.242-3.
109. Sawyer, *op. cit.*, No. 1002, p.299.
110. Wallenberg, *Kentish Place-Names*, 324-5; Dhondt, *op. cit.*, pp.130-1, 147-59.
111. W.H. Stevenson, 'Trinoda Necessitas', p.702, f. 61.
112. F.E. Harmer, *Anglo-Saxon Writs*, p.82; T.J. Oleson, *The Witenagemot in the Reign of Edward the Confessor*, p.150.
113. P. Chaplais, 'The Original Charters of Herbert and Gervase, Abbots of Westminster, 1121-57', in P.M. Barnes and C.F. Slade (eds.), *A Medieval Miscellany for Doris Mary Stenton*, pp.92-3; Miller, *op. cit.*, p.12.
114. P. Morgan (ed.), *Domesday Book: Kent*, pp.12d, 13a; Hasted, I, p.507.
115. Ewing, pp.19-20, 46-58; G. Ward, 'The Manor of Lewisham', pp.112-7; Witney (1), pp.220-1.
116. Kemble, No. 771, IV, pp.80-4.
117. Round, *op. cit.*, No. 1375, pp.502-3; H.W.C. Davis, (ed.), *Regestra Regum Anglo-Normannorum, 1066-1154, I, Regestra Willelmi Conquestoris et Willelmi Rufi, 1066-1100*, No. 141, pp.37-8; C. Johnson (ed.), *Registrum Hamonis Hethe: Diocesis Roffensis*, pp.28-31.
118. T.D. Hardy (ed.), *Rotuli Chartarum*, I, Part 1, p.184; Johnson, *op. cit.*, I, pp.35-6.
119. Illingworth, *op. cit.*, I, p.233; Lokeren, *op. cit.*, I, No. 896, p.417; L.L. Duncan's Transcripts of Lewisham Manor Court Rolls, 181/45; CKS: Talbot Papers U1215, pp.39, 43; CKS: Tithe Awards (Cowden), 1841, CTR 99A, p.9; Ward, *op. cit.*, p.114. Other examples could be cited, but the point is made.
120. Ward, *op. cit.*, p.115.
121. Ewing, pp.19-20, 57-8; Ward, *op. cit.*, p.114; Witney (1), p.221.
122. Ward, *op. cit.*, pp.113-14.
123. Wallenberg, *op. cit.*, pp.207-16, 299-301; Witney (2), p.120.
124. Other spellings of Shernden include Sharden, Sardenne, Scharanden, Sharnden: Somers-Cocks, *op. cit.*, p.68, n.9.
125. Witney (1), pp.225-6. There is also a Sandfields Farm in Hever, near the railway station.
126. Knocker, 'Holmesdale 3', *passim*; F.R.H. Du Boulay, *The Lordship of Canterbury*, pp.39-43, 374-5; Witney (1), pp.201, 225-6.
127. Knocker, 'Valley of Holmesdale', p.172; Ward, *op. cit.*, pp.115-7.
128. CKS (Sevenoaks), The Manor of Lewisham: Cowden (Knocker Collection), U1000/M7/2; Gordon Ward Notebooks, Cowden III, pp.24-6.
129. Witney (1), p 160, 219, 296 n.35.
130. CKS (Sevenoaks), The Manor of Penshurst Halimote (Knocker Collection) U1000/M19, M21, M29; Ewing, pp.70-2.
131. Ewing, p.71.
132. CKS, Talbot Papers, U1612/Z107, pp.14-15.
133. CKS (Sevenoaks), U1000/9/M18; Ewing, p.56.
134. Pound House appears in the 1841 Tithe Award and in the Census up to 1881, when it was occupied by the Longley family, who also ran the *Queens Arms*: CKS: Tithe Award, 1841, CTR/99A & B; Census, 1841-81.
135. Everitt, pp.144-6.
136. Wallenberg, *Place-Names of Kent*, p.83; Everitt, p.145.

Chapter IV: The Norman Conquest and Beyond

1.   J. Gillingham, '1066 and All That Elton', TRHS, 6th Ser., VII (1997), pp.329-30. There are a number of editions of the letters of Henry VIII to Anne Boleyn, see bibliographies in E.W. Ives, *Anne Boleyn*, and R.M. Warnicke, *The Rise and Fall of Anne Boleyn*.
2.   F. Baring, 'The Conqueror's Footsteps in Domesday', p.19, n.13; R.A. Brown, *The Normans and the Norman Conquest*, pp.154-7; Brandon and Short, *op. cit.*, pp.26-31; R.H. George, 'The Contribution of Flanders to the Conquest of England', pp.81-99.
3.   Brandon and Short, *op. cit.*, p.29; For the new Anglo-Norman ruling élite, see J.A. Green, *The Aristocracy of Norman England*, *passim*.
4.   R. Mortimer, 'The Beginnings of the Honour of Clare', pp.119-41; R. Mortimer, 'Land and Service: the Tenants of the Honour of Clare', pp.177-98; J.C. Ward, 'The Lowy of Tonbridge and the Lands of the Clare Family, 1066-1217', 'Fashions in Monastic Endowment: the Foundations of the Clare Family, 1066-1314', 'Royal Services and Reward: the Clare Family and the Crown, 1066-1154'; Green, *op. cit.*, pp.55-6
5.   W.V. Dumbreck, 'The Lowy of Tonbridge'; Witney (1), pp.101-2, 121-3, 143-4, Map 17 p.165, 167-9.
6.   Dumbreck, *op. cit.*, p.136-7.
7.   *VCH: Kent*, III, p.41; Darby and Campbell, *op. cit.*, p.387; Witney (1), pp.218-9.
8.   Ewing, pp.58-67; Witney (1), pp.218-9.
9.   *Supra* pp.40-1.
10. J. Greenstreet, 'Abstracts of the Kent Fines Levied in the Reign of Edward II', *Arch. Cant.*, XI (1877), No. 87, p.327; Ewing, p.13.
11. E.W. Brayley, *A Topographical History of Surrey*, IV, p.203; *VCH: Surrey*, IV, pp.330-2.
12. Inquisitions Post-Mortem, V, 8 Edward II [1315]: for Cowden Church see p.344.
13. N.H. MacMichael, 'Filston in Shoreham: a Note on the Place-Name', p.134; Du Boulay, *op. cit.*, pp.86, 348-9, 360-1, Appendix; Witney (1), p.225.
14. Kemble, II, No. 518, pp.410-2; J. Newton, *Chiddingstone: an Historical Exploration*, p.34.
15. Darby and Campbell, *op. cit.*, p.513; Jessup, *History of Kent*, p.45.
16. H.C. Darby, *Domesday England*, pp.90-1.

17. *VCH: Kent, III*, p.208.

18. *Ibid*. *VCH: Surrey, I*, p.311.

19. *VCH: Surrey, I*, Surrey Domesday, p.31; Darby and Campbell, *op. cit.*, p.368; J. Glover, *The Place Names of Kent*, p.38. For Battle Abbey and its holdings in this area see E. Searle, *Lordship and Community: Battle Abbey and Its Banlieu, 1066-1538, passim*; Malden claimed that the site of Bramsells was irrecoverable: H.E. Malden, 'Domesday Survey of Surrey', p.464. Limpsfield and Bramsells certainly seem to have become detached from the abbey by the Reformation: *Valor Ecclesiasticus*, I, p.153.

20. Wallenberg, *op. cit.*, pp.81-3. For Rickwoods see n.80 below.

21. CKS (Sevenoaks), Gordon Ward Notebooks, Chiddingstone (Streatfield) II, p.34. The next mention of Mark Beech seems to be in 1596 when Henry Streatfield settled four parcels of land at Mark Beech on his son, Richard: CKS, Streatfield Papers, U908/T253.

22. CKS (Sevenoaks), Gordon Ward Notebooks, Cowden I, pp.9, 19, Cowden III, p.25; Ewing, 19; Witney (1), p.221.

23. *Supra*, p.40.

24. CKS (Sevenoaks), Gordon Ward Notebooks, Chiddingstone I, p.124; Chiddingstone II, p.24, Cowden I, p.6, Cowden III, pp.22-3, 24-6, Hever I, pp.12, 15, 29; Streatfield Papers: Rough Draft of Estate Maps by Humphrey Giles, 1742, The Lord's Land Farm in Cowden, CKS/U908/T12; CKS: Tithe Award, 1847, CTR/99b [Lord's Land, Field No. 252]; *The Concise Oxford Dictionary*, 8th edn., ed. Allen, R.E., Oxford, 1990, p.276.

25. CKS: Tithe Maps and Award, CTR/99A and B; CKS (Sevenoaks), Gordon Ward Notebooks, Cowden III, pp.22-3, Chiddingstone II, p.24; Ewing, p.238.

26. Details in nn.30-40, below.

27. Opperman, *op. cit.*, I, pp.283-93.

28. Saint-Genois, *op. cit.*, pp.246-8; Lokeren, *op. cit.*; I, p.104; Round, *op. cit.*, I, No. 1375, pp.502-3; Davis, *op. cit.*, No. 141, pp.27-8; Johnson, *op. cit.*, pp.28-31; Martin, *op. cit.*, pp.105-6.

29. C. Hardwick (ed.), *Historia Monasterii S. Augustini Cantuariensis*, ed. pp.408-9; Johnson, *op. cit.*, I, pp.34-5; Martin, *op. cit.*, p.127.

30. *Supra*, n. 27.

31. Saint-Genois, *op. cit.*, p.245; Lokeren, *op. cit.*, I, p.106; Round, *op. cit.*, No. 1376, p.503; *op. cit.*, Davis, *op. cit.*, I, No. 323, p.84; Martin, *op. cit.*, p.126; Miller, *op. cit.*, p.14.

32. Round, *op. cit.*, No. 1377, pp.503-4; C. Johnson, H.A. Cronne and H.W.C. Davis (eds.), *Regestra Henrici Primi, 1100-35*, No. 730, pp.1103-5; Martin, *op. cit.*, p.126.

33. Saint-Genois, *op. cit.*, p.252; Lokeren, *op. cit.*, No. 181, p.115; Johnson *et al.*, *op. cit.*, No. 1109, pp.90-1 [This document is considered most suspect].

34. C. Johnson (ed.), *Registrum Hamonis Hethe*, I, p.34; *Regestra Henrici Primi*, No. 1148, p.136.

35. Lokeren, *op. cit.*, No. 215, pp.132-3; Round, *op. cit.*, No. 1379, p.504; C. Johnson and H.A. Cronne (eds.), *Regestra Regis Stephani ac Mathildis Imperatricis ac Ganfridi et Henrici, Ducum Normannorum*, No. 340, p.129; Martin, *op. cit.*, p.127.

36. *Supra*, n.28.

37. Hardy, *op. cit.*, I, Part 1, p.184; *Registrum Hamonis Hethe*, pp.35-6; Martin, *op. cit.*, p.127. [8 February 1209].

38. Sir W. Dugdale, *Monasticon Anglicanum*, eds. J. Caley, H. Ellis and B. Bandriel, VI, Part 2, p.998; Calendar of Charter Rolls, I, Henry III, 1226-57, p.91; Martin, *op. cit.*, p.127. [Westminster, 14 February 1229].

39. Lokeren, *op. cit.*, I, No. 1065, p.679; Martin, *op. cit.*, p.127.

40. Calendar of Patent Rolls, Edward III, 1374-77, London, 1916, p.18; Martin, *op. cit.*, p.127.

41. Eugenius III; Alexander III; Honorius III, twice; Innocent IV: full references given below.

42. Saint-Genois, *op. cit.*, Nos. 18-19, pp.255-7; Lokeren, *op. cit.*, I, Nos. 167-9, pp.110-1; Round, *op. cit.*, Nos. 1381-2, p.505; Martin, *op. cit.*, pp.107-8; Miller, *op. cit.*, pp.28-29.

43. Lokeren, *op. cit.*, No. 215, pp.132-3, No. 235, pp.141-2, No. 261, p.154, No. 355, pp.194-6, No. 486, p.254; Johnson, *op. cit.*, I, pp.36-7; Martin, *op. cit.*, p.107.

44. Martin, *op. cit.*, pp.109-10. [16 March 1226 and November 1226].

45. Martin, *op. cit.*, p.110.

46. *VCH: Kent, II*, p.238; J. Nichols, *Some Account of the Alien Priories and of Such Lands as they are known to have possessed in England and Wales*, II, p.137; D. Knowles, *The Religious Houses of Medieval England*, p.127; D. Knowles and R.N. Hadcock, *Medieval Religious Houses*, p.86.

47. Martin, *op. cit.*, pp.106-7, 120; Miller, *op. cit.*, pp.23-4.

48. Miller, *op. cit.*, p.25.

49. Martin, *op. cit.*, p.106.

50. Lokeren, *op. cit.*, I, No. 896, pp.392-423.

51. *Ibid.*, II, No. 1147, pp.47-8, No. 1343, pp.53-5, No. 1503, pp.90-3.

52. Martin, *op. cit.*, pp.111-5; M.M. Morgan, 'The Suppression of the Alien Priories', p.208; Miller, *op. cit.*, pp.29-36.

53. *Supra*, n. 39.

54. British Museum Add MS 6164, f. 416; PRO/E106/101/1: Extents, writs and inquisitions relating to possessions of Alien Priories including Greenwich, 43 Edward III [1370]; Miller, *op. cit.*, pp.17-21.

55. PRO/E106/11/16: Petition relating to possessions of Alien Priories, including Greenwich; PRO/E106/11/32: Receipts from Alien Priories, including Greenwich.

56. Lokeren, *op. cit.*, No. 1439, pp.129-32; Miller, *op. cit.*, p.22.

57. Rotuli Parliamentorum, III, p.499; Miller, *op. cit.*, pp.35-6.

58. Martin, *op. cit.*, p.109.

59. Powicke, Sir M., *The Thirteenth Century, 1216-1307*, pp.376-7.
60. *Supra*, n.21.
61. Philipott, *op. cit.*, p.217.
62. L.F. Salzman, 'Some Sussex Domesday Tenants', p.174.
63. *Ibid.*, p.178; A. Tomkinson, 'Retainer at the Tournament of Dunstable, 1309', p.75; N.E. Saul, *Scenes from Provincial Life: Knightly Families in Sussex, 1280-1400*, p.33.
64. W.D. Cooper, 'Proofs of Age of Sussex Families', pp.25-6; L.F. Salzman, 'Some Sussex Domesday Tenants: II, the Family of Dene', p.170; C.J. Phillips, *A History of the Sackville Family*, passim. Until more can be found about Agnes we do not know if she was Malemains' first wife or whether she had children by him. Given her probable age neither looks likely. An ancestor, also Nicholas Malemains, and his heirs, who held land in Northamptonshire, was Henry I's champion against the French: *VCH: Northants, III*, pp. 181-2; A.L. Poole, *From Domesday to Magna Carta, 1087-1216*, p.124.
65. Inquisitions Post-Mortem, III, No. 316, p.198, VI, No. 95, p.65. No further clue is to be found in L.C. Loyd, *The Origins of Some Anglo-Norman Families*.
66. See Patent Rolls, Henry III, 1232-47, pp.469, 499, 503; 1247-58, p.42; Close Rolls, Henry III, 1237-42, p.388; 1247-51, p.217; L.F. Salzman, *An Abstract of The Feet of Fines relating to the County of Sussex*, I, No. 504, p.137, II, Nos. 523, 815, 893, pp.4, 86, 108.
67. Salzman, 'Sussex Tenants', p.174; N.E. Saul, *op. cit.*, p.2.
68. Salzman, *op. cit.*, p.166.
69. *Ibid.*, p.174; *VCH: Northamptonshire, II*, pp.109-14; M.J. Franklin (ed.), *The Cartulary of Daventry Priory*, No. 693 (2 January 1226), p.226.
70. *VCH: Sussex, II*, pp.77-80; G.M. Cooper, 'Some Account of Michelham Priory in Aldington', pp.134-5; L.F. Salzmann, *The History of the Parish of Hailsham, the Abbey of Otham and the Priory of Michelham*, pp.198-9, 'Sussex Tenants', p.174.
71. *VCH: Sussex, II*, p.77; Cooper, *op. cit.*, p.135; Salzman, *Parish of Hailsham*, p.203; Salzman, *op. cit.*, p.174; Ewing, pp.48-9.
72. I.J. Churchill, R. Griffin and F.W. Hardman (ed.), *Calendar of the Kent Feet of Fines*, p.317 [1 June 1261].
73. Calendar of Charter Rolls, III, Edward I & II, 1300-26, pp.433-4.
74. *Supra*, n.39.
75. Calendar of Patent Rolls, IV, 1408-13, p.424.
76. Ewing, pp.48, 75.
77. *Ibid.*, p.49. Sandherste/Sandfields Farm is about 250 yards from Kent Water, but no documents after 1081 link it with Cowden Lewisham. Maybe it became detached by sub-infeudation at quite an early date.
78. Witney (1), p.222; Ordnance Survey TQ 44/54 at 494405.
79. Lokeren, *op. cit.*, No. 896, I, pp.392-423, No. 1147, II, pp.47-8, No. 1343, II, pp.53-5 [24 December 1343]; British Museum, ADD MS 6164, f. 416, No. 1403, II, pp.90-3 [3 November 1376]; Miller, *op.cit.*, pp.20-2.
80. Somers-Cocks, p.72.
81. Ewing, p.61.
82. CKS (Sevenoaks), The Manor of Lewisham: Cowden, U1000/7/M11/1; Ewing, p.51.
83. L.L. Duncan's Transcripts of Lewisham Manor Court Rolls, 181/45, 181/47, 181/49, 181/60.
84. *Ibid.*, 181/48. It seems that in the 15th century, if not earlier, Esscore was held in part by the Manor of Chiddingstone Burghersh. This may have been a longstanding situation, or may indicate encroachment as a result of the events of 1414-15, or Chiddingstone Burghersh may now have held regularly of Lewisham. The earliest extant record of this dates from 1420 when Laurence Riccard (hence Rickwoods) held a croft and garden, and thereafter this land is always referred to as Ashour Garden (Gordon Ward Notebooks, Cowden, IV, p.4). That Mrs. Joan Cole of Cowden was admitted in 1440 to hold for life two crofts of land at Asschore in the Manor of Chiddingstone Burghersh was very kindly drawn to my attention by Mr Lionel Cole of Hawkhurst. It should, however, be noted that there is another Ashour at Penshurst/Bidborough.
85. Rotuli Parliamentorum, III, p.499; Miller, *op. cit.*, pp.35-6. There was another alien priory at Wythyham, founded by a count of Mortain, which did suffer in 1413: *VCH, Sussex, II*, pp.123-4.
86. Rotuli Parliamentorum, IV, p.22; E.C. Lodge and G.A. Thornton (eds.), *English Constitutional Documents, 1307-1485*, pp.318-9; Morgan, *op. cit.*, p.209; J.R. Roskell, *The Commons and Their Speakers in English Parliaments, 1376-1523*, p.158; Miller, *op. cit.*, p.36.
87. Dugdale, *op. cit.*, VI, Pt. 1, p.31; Calendar of Patent Rolls, V, 1341-1417, pp.479-80 [1 April 1415]; J. Nichols, *op. cit.*, II, p.137; *VCH: Surrey, II*, pp.89-94; E.M. Thompson, *The Carthusian Order in England*, p.239; J. Cato, 'Religious Change under Henry V', pp.110-1.
88. Lokeren, *op. cit.*, No. 1656, II, p.192; Thompson, *op. cit.*, p.244.
89. J.A. Tremlow (ed.), *Calendar of Entries in the Papal Registers relating to Great Britain and Ireland: Papal Letters*, vol. X, 1447-55, pp.237-8 [10 December 1455]; Thompson, *op. cit.*, p.245.
90. Gulley, *op. cit.*, pp.390, 400, 421, 427, 434; Witney (1), pp.182-3; Brandon and Short, *op. cit.*, pp.49-51.
91. Gulley, *op. cit.*, p.398; White, *op. cit.*, p.102; Everitt, p.54.
92. Gulley, *op. cit.*, p.390; Everitt, p.33.
93. R.E. Glasscock, 'The Distribution of Lay Wealth in Kent, Surrey and Sussex in the early Fourteenth Century', p.63; Everitt, p.22.
94. Witney (1), pp.154-71.
95. Witney (1), pp.168, 216, 219, 296 n. 35.
96. Hardwick, *op. cit.*, pp.408-9; Witney (1), pp.86, 154, 198, 219-20.
97. Witney (1), p.171.
98. Du Boulay, *op. cit.*, pp.360-1; Witney (1), pp.168-9, 216, 219, 289 n. 65.
99. Hasted, III, pp.190-2; Ireland, *op. cit.*, III, pp.390-2.
100. Calendar of Patent Rolls: Richard II, 1381-85, p.326 [3 November 1383]; S. Pearson, *The Medieval Houses of Kent*, p.128.

101. Hasted, III, p.192; Ireland, *op. cit.,* III, p.392; Warnicke, *op. cit.,* p.8.

102. Ewing, p.238.

103. 6 inch Ordnance Survey Map, 1869.

104. J. Eastman, *op. cit.,* pp.5, 11; Ewing, pp.13-14. At Hever there seems to be no break in the periods either 1533-58 or 1642-60, but after the Restoration John Petter was ejected in 1662: Eastman, *op. cit.,* p.11.

105. Hasted, III, pp.203-10; Ireland, *op. cit.,* pp.398-403; Ewing, pp.12-14; Wallenberg, *The Place-Names of Kent*, p.81; White, *op. cit.,* p.100; Witney (1), pp.65, 140; Eastman, *op. cit.,* p.2; Furley, *op. cit.,* II, p.407; *VCH: Kent,* II, p.160; Glover, *op. cit.,* p.132; B.R. More, 'The Parish of Hever'; D.G. Higgs, 'The Manor of Hever Brocas and the Brocas Family'.

106. *VCH: Kent,* II, p.160; Anon, 'Charters of Cumbwell Priory, Part 1', p.209.

107. Anon, *Simple Guide to Hever Church*, p.3.

108. Ewing, p.13.

109. Conversations with Dr. Ward, plus Ward, 'Fashions in Monastic Endowment', *passim.*

110. Ewing, p.13.

111. M. McKisack, *The Fourteenth Century, 1307-99*, pp.203-9, 384-498; E.F. Jacob, *The Fifteenth Century, 1399-1485, passim.*

112. R.A.L. Smith, *Canterbury Cathedral Priory: a Study in Monastic Administration*, pp.125-6; Witney (1), p.161.

113. M. McKisack, *The Fourteenth Century*, pp.313, 331-2, 347-8; Witney (1), p.181.

114. Witney (1), p.300, n.141. Frienden is not included in M. Beresford, *The Lost Villages of England*, nor in M. Beresford and J.G. Hurst (eds.), *Deserted Medieval Villages.*

115. P. Ziegler, *The Black Death*, p.167.

116. R. Horrox (ed.), *The Black Death*, p.71.

117. *Ibid.,* pp.71-2.

118. McKisack, *op. cit.,* pp.297-9, 306-8; Horrox, *op. cit.,* p.72.

119. *VCH: Sussex,* II, p.14; F.A. Gasquet, *The Black Death*, p.115; P. Ziegler, *op. cit.,* p.167.

120. N.P. Brooks, 'The Organization and Achievement of the Peasants of Kent and Essex in 1381', pp.247-70. See also W.E. Flaherty, 'The Great Rebellion in Kent of 1381', and McKisack, *op. cit.,* pp.407-19.

121. Sir J. Dunlop, *The Pleasant Town of Sevenoaks*, pp.75-7.

122. W.D. Cooper, 'Jack Cade's Followers in Kent'. See also W.D. Cooper, 'The Participation of Sussex in Cade's Rising'.

123. Cooper, 'Jack Cade's Followers', pp.247-71.

124. Newton, *op. cit.,* p.55.

125. R.A. Griffiths, *The Reign of Henry VI: The Exercise of Royal Authority, 1422-61*, pp.610-65. For 1471 see C.F. Richmond, 'Fauconberg's Kentish Rising of May, 1471'.

126. I.M.W. Harvey, *Jack Cade's Rebellion of 1450*, p.157.

127. R. Virgoe, 'Some Ancient Indictments in the King's Bench referring to Kent, 1450-52' in F.R.H. Du Boulay (ed.), *Documents Illustrative of Medieval Kent*, pp.254-5.

128. For this point in general see J.G. Bellamy, *Crime and Public Order in England in the Later Middle Ages, passim.*

Chapter V: From Henry VIII to Queen Victoria

1. *Valor Ecclesiasticus*, I, p.353, II, pp.53, 62; Salzman, *Parish of Hailsham*, p.246.

2. *VCH: Surrey*, II, p.92; H. Colvin (ed.), *History of the King's Works*, IV, 1485-1660 (Part II), pp.96-123.

3. Hasted, III, pp.192-3; Ireland, *op. cit.,* III, pp.392-3.

4. Colvin, *op. cit.,* IV (i), pp.219-20.

5. Calendar of State Papers, Spain, III, Part II, Henry VIII, 1527-29, p.846.

6. Church, *op. cit.,* p.59.

7. Ewing, pp.49-50.

8. Hasted, III, pp.204-5; Ireland, *op. cit.,* III, pp.399-400; Ewing, pp.49-50.

9. Hasted, III, pp.193-4; Ireland, *op. cit.,* III, p.393.

10. Hasted, III, pp.194-5, 204-5; Ireland, *op. cit.,* 393-4, 400; Ewing, p.50.

11. *Ibid.,* pp.51-4.

12. *Ibid.,* pp.51-4.

13. CKS (Sevenoaks), Manor of Lewisham in Cowden, U1000/7/M9/1.

14. CKS (Sevenoaks), Manor of Lewisham in Cowden, U1000/7/M7/1.

15. CKS (Sevenoaks), Manor of Lewisham in Cowden, U1000/7/M11/1; Somers-Cocks, pp.69-74; Ewing, pp.48-50, 58-62.

16. CKS: Talbot Papers, U1612/Z107, pp.24-7; Land Tax Records, 1780-1832, Q/RPL/89-93; Tithe Maps and Awards, 1841, CTR/99A & B; interview with Mrs. Jane Gladstone (present owner), 5 January 1997, and photocopy of deed of 19 November 1847 provided by her.

17. CKS: Talbot Papers, U1612/Z107, pp.32-4; Land Tax Records; Tithe Maps and Awards.

18. N.M. Jacoby, *A Journey Through Medicine, passim.*

19. CKS: Talbot Papers, pp.5-8; Land Tax Records; Tithe Maps and Awards, 1841, CTR/99A & B.

20. *Ibid.*; Greenwood, *op. cit.,* p.116.

21. CKS: Talbot Papers, pp.7-8; CKS (Sevenoaks), Manor of Lewisham in Cowden, U1000/7/M9/2, 3; Land Tax Records; Tithe Maps and Awards; Ewing, p.57.

22. Talbot Papers, pp.34-8; Land Tax Records; Tithe Maps and Awards.

23. Talbot Papers, pp.38, 44-6; Land Tax Records; Tithe Maps and Awards.
24. Talbot Papers, pp.39-43; Land Tax Records; Tithe Maps and Awards.
25. Talbot Papers, pp.27-9; Land Tax Records; Tithe Maps and Awards.
26. Talbot Papers, pp.10-11, 50-1; Land Tax Records; Tithe Maps and Awards.
27. CKS: Civil Defence Log, July-December 1943, C/Ad/1/9
28. 'Visitors Notes, Hole Cottage', p.4.
29. Talbot Papers, pp.10-11; CKS (Sevenoaks), Manor of Penshurst Halimote, U1000/9/M21, pp.47-8; Land Tax Records; Tithe Maps and Awards; Ewing, pp.71-2.
30. Talbot Papers, pp.10-11; Land Tax Records; Tithe Maps and Awards.
31. Talbot Papers, pp.9-10; Land Tax Records; Tithe Maps and Awards.
32. Talbot Papers, pp.21-3 [sold 1918]; Land Tax Records; Tithe Maps and Awards.
33. Talbot Papers, pp.9-16; Land Tax Records; Tithe Maps and Awards.
34. Talbot Papers, pp.16-8; Land Tax Records; Tithe Maps and Awards.
35. Talbot Papers, pp.18-20; Land Tax Records; Tithe Maps and Awards.
36. Talbot Papers, pp.29-32; Streatfield Papers, U908; Land Tax Records; Tithe Maps and Awards.
37. CKS: Woodgate Papers, U1050, passim; Ewing, pp.29-30; Newton, op. cit., pp.57-8.
38. Hasted, III, pp.190-7, Ireland, op. cit., III, pp.394-5, R.J.P. Kain, 'The Land of Kent in the Middle of the Nineteenth Century', Ph.D. Thesis, p.367, Figure 9:4. Professor Kain says 996 acres, but this must refer to Hever Cobham only; when Hever Brocas was sold in 1919 that alone comprised over 1,000 acres.
39. CKS: Streatfield Papers, U908/T186.
40. Anon., Hever Castle, p.12.
41. CKS: Streatfield Papers, U908/T10, T147, T155, T156.
42. J. Banister, op. cit.; Institute of Historical Research, Poll Books: Kent, 1754, 1790, 1806; West Kent, 1835, 1847, 1852, 1857, 1859, 1865, 1867.
43. Ewing, passim.
44. Gulley, op. cit., p.80. See also n.65 below.
45. M. Zell, 'Population and Family Structure in the Sixteenth-Century Weald'.
46. CKS: Streatfield Papers, U908/P66.
47. Garrard, op. cit., p.31.
48. Gulley, op. cit., p.242.
49. Ibid., pp.252, 259.
50. Ibid., pp.295-6. For other general descriptions of High Weald agriculture in the period 1500-1750 see E. Kerridge, The Agricultural Revolution, pp.132-3; H.P.R. Finberg and J. Thirsk (eds.), The Agrarian History of England and Wales, IV, 1500-1640, pp.57-9; Vi, 1640-1750, pp.270-6.
51. B.M. Short, 'Agriculture in the High Weald of Kent and Sussex, 1850-1953', Ph.D. Thesis, p.82.
52. B. Harwood, The High Weald in Old Photographs, p.113, The High Weald in Old Photographs: a Second Selection, p.152.
53. Gulley, op. cit., pp.268, 351.
54. Ibid., p.268; D.W. Harvey, 'Locational Change in the Kentish Hop Industry'; Short, op. cit., p.76.
55. Ibid., p.75.
56. PRO/IR18/3641: Tithe Files, Hever.
57. CKS: Tithe Award, 1847, CTR/99b, Cowden, Field No. 775; Talbot Papers, p.46; Short, op. cit., p.79, fig. 2:8; Brandon and Short, op. cit., pp.324-5.
58. Short, op. cit., pp.76, 77, fig. 2:2.
59. Kain, op. cit., p.148, Table 5:1; p.151, Table 5:3; Short, op. cit., p.68, Table 2:4.
60. Kain, op. cit., p.335, Table 8:1.
61. Short, op. cit., p.69, Table 2:5.
62. PRO/IR18/3641: Tithe Files, Hever, Commissioner Browne's Report; Kain, op. cit., p.255, Table 6:9.
63. PRO/IR18/3565: Tithe Files, Chiddingstone, Commissioner Matthews's Report.
64. PRO/IR18/3579: Tithe Files, Cowden, Commissioner Woolley's Report.
65. PRO/IR18/3641: Tithe Files, Hever, Commissioner Browne's Report.
66. Short, op. cit., p.86, Table 2:10, p.108, Table 2:14.
67. D.C. Coleman, 'The Economy of Kent under the Later Stuarts', Ph.D. Thesis, pp.57-63; A.R.H. Baker, 'The Field Systems of Kent', Ph.D. Thesis, 'Some Fields and Farms in Medieval Kent'. In the 1840s farmers were grubbing out hedges to make fields bigger: Finberg and Thirsk (eds.), The Agrarian History of England and Wales, VI, 1750-1850, p.286.
68. CKS: Talbot Papers, pp.39-40.
69. CKS: Streatfield Papers, U908/T204, 219.
70. Tenancy agreement of 18 January 1918 between Col. Sir Henry Streatfield and John Sherwood, in possession of Mrs. Walter Leppard, Edenbridge.
71. Tenancy agreement of 22 April 1930 between Col. Sir Henry Streatfield and Mrs. Emily Sherwood and George Leppard, in possession of Mrs. Walter Leppard, Edenbridge. On 29 September 1949 Mrs. Sherwood ceased to be a joint tenant and was replaced by Lionel Montagu Leppard. Meanwhile the landlord had become Col. J.J. Astor.
72. Brandon and Short, op. cit., pp.170, 187-8. For the Wealden iron industry during this period see Ewing, pp.84-113; Cleere and Crossley,

op. cit., chaps. 6-9.

73. Ewing, pp.94, 100.

74. *Supra*, p.27.

75. Interview with Robert H. King, who as a boy cycled from Marsh Green to Edenbridge station, past Whitmore's Tannery, to go to school in Tonbridge, 24 April 1994.

76. A. Armstrong (ed.), *The Economy of Kent, 1640-1914*, p.119.

77. Ewing, p.147; E. Turner, 'Ancient Parochial Account Book of Cowden'; Gulley, *op. cit.*, p.204; Brandon and Short, *op. cit.*, pp.170-1, 186; Armstrong, *op. cit.*, pp.87-8, 90-5.

78. Observation to author by Prof. Audrey-Anne Michie, Historic Homes Consultant, North Carolina Museum, 2 January 1998.

79. Turner, *op. cit.*, p.117.

80. B. Keith-Lucas, 'Kentish Turnpikes', p.366, *Parish Affairs: the Government of Kent under George III*, pp. 64, 84, 99, 102.

81. Ewing, p.230.

82. Ewing, pp.74, 144.

83. C.W. Chalklin, *Seventeenth Century Kent*; P. Clark, *English Provincial Society from the Reformation to the Revolution: Religion, Politics and Society in Kent, 1500-1640*, p.321.

84. CKS: Sevenoaks Union Papers, Letter Books, 1836-39, ACb.1, I, pp.65, 85-6, 149, 153; II, p.44; N. Yates, R. Hume and P. Hastings (eds.) *Religion and Society in Kent, 1640-1914*, pp.123, 139-41, 155; Ewing, p.206; Newton, *op. cit.*, pp.38-41; Rayner, *op. cit.*, pp.48, 116.

85. Yates *et al.*, *op. cit.*, pp.140, 171-3; M.E. Rose, *The Relief of Poverty, 1834-1914*, pp.34-9; A. Brundage, *The Making of the New Poor Law*, *passim*.

86. Dr. Mark Ballard, Kent Archivist, 12 September 1997.

87. B.W. Hill, *British Parliamentary Parties, 1742-1832*, pp.163-231.

88. J.R. Vincent, *Pollbooks: How the Victorians Voted*, pp.1-33.

89. Institute of Historical Research: Poll Books, Kent, 1754, 1790, 1802; West Kent, 1835, 1847.

90. *Ibid.*, 1835.

91. *Ibid.*, West Kent, 1847.

92. J. Cave-Brown, *Knights of the Shire of Kent, 1275-1831*; Sir Lewis Namier and J. Brooke, *The History of Parliament: the House of Commons, 1754-90*, pp.312-3; R.G. Thorne, *The History of Parliament: the House of Commons, 1790-1820*, pp.214-5; J.R. Vincent and M. Stenton (eds.), *McCalmont's Parliamentary Poll Book: British Election Results, 1832-1918*, pp.150-1.

93. Institute of Historical Research: Poll Books, West Kent 1835, 1852.

94. Vincent and Stenton, *op. cit.*, pp.150-1.

95. L.L. Duncan, 'The Renunciation of the Papal Authority by the Clergy of West Kent, 1534', pp.299, 307.

96. Eastman, *op. cit.*, p.6; Ewing. pp.73-4, 120-1.

97. J.S. Cockburn (ed.), *Calendar of Assize Records: Kent Indictments, Charles I*, pp.56, 64, 83, 93, 142, 157, 186, 219, 225-6, 335, 339, 355-6, 386, 416, 428, 444, 460, 518. This family was variously described as Pytion, Physion, Phevion, Fiffen, Fivion, Phythion, Feven, Feveon, Phithien, Phifion, Phivion and Phithion.

98. A.M. Everitt, *The County Committee of Kent in the Civil War*, p.21.

99. Somers-Cocks, pp.89-90; Everitt, *op. cit.*, p.21, *The Community of Kent and the Great Rebellion, 1640-60*, pp.206-7.

100. Somers-Cocks, pp.77, 89. Surprisingly, S.R. Gardiner, *History of the Great Civil War, 1642-49*, has nothing on Kent in 1642-3.

101. Everitt, *County Committee*, p.21.

102. Everitt, *Community of Kent*, pp.111-2.

103. *Ibid.*, pp.190-2.

104. *Ibid.*, pp.195-201.

105. *Ibid.*, pp.202-5.

106. *Ibid.*, pp.212ff.

107. *Ibid.*, p.305.

108. *Ibid.*, p.309.

109. J.L. and B. Hammond, *The Village Labourer, 1760-1832*, 4th edn., pp.240ff; M. Dutt, 'The Agricultural Labourers' Revolt of 1830 in Kent, Surrey and Sussex', Ph.D. Thesis, *passim*; E.J. Hobsbawm and G. Rudé, *Captain Swing*, pp.3-68; Brandon and Short, *op. cit.*, p.234.

110. Hammond, *op. cit.*, *passim*; Hobsbawm and Rudé, *op. cit.*, *passim*.

111. Hammond, *op. cit.*, *passim*; Hobsbawm and Rudé, *op. cit.*, *passim*.

112. *Ibid.*, p.170.

113. *The Times*, 17 September 1830, p.3.

Chapter VI: The Arrival of the Talbots, the Church and the Railway

1. *The Times*, 16 April 1849, p.3

2. CKS: Talbot Papers, Biographical Card; R.L. Arrowsmith (ed.), *Charterhouse Register, 1769-1872*, p.364; J. Foster (ed.), *Alumni Oxoniensis, 1715-1866*, IV, p.1385; F. Boase, (ed.), *Modern English Biography*, III, p.871; *Burke's Peerage*, 1959, p.2057.

3. E.S. Talbot, *Memories of Early Life*, p.2.

4. E.S. Talbot, *op. cit.*, p.3; Lady G. Stephenson, *Edward Stuart Talbot, 1844-1934*, pp.1-2.

5. *The Times*, 28 April 1847, p.13.

6. CKS: Talbot Papers, U1612/Z107, pp.3-21.

7.   Talbot Papers, pp.21-51.

8.   A. Felstead, J. Franklin and L. Pinfield, *Directory of British Architects, 1834-1900*, p.122.

9.   M. Girouard, *The Victorian Country House*, pp.18, 53-4, 405, 436; Homan, *op. cit.*, p.106.

10. Talbot Papers, p.9.

11. Sheffield City Archives: Wharncliffe Muniments, J.C. Talbot to Lady Wharncliffe, 21 August 1851, Wh.M, 563-49, cited by kind permission of the Earl of Wharncliffe and of the Sheffield City Archivist.

12. Felstead *et al.*, *op. cit.*, p.192.

13. Interview with Charles J. Talbot, 24 February 1997.

14. J. Newman, *West Kent and the Weald*, p.415.

15. Talbot, *op. cit.*, p.22; Lady Stephenson, *op. cit.*, p.5.

16. *Ibid.*, pp.3-4.

17. Letter from Mr. Simon Bailey, Oxford University Archives, Bodleian Library, Oxford, 18 February 1997.

18. W.E. Gladstone, *Diaries, III: 1840-48*, pp.433-4 [13 February 1845].

19. P. Butler, *Gladstone: Church, State and Tractarianism*, pp.131-59. See also P.J. Jagger, *Gladstone: the Making of a Christian Politician*, and D.W. Bebbington, *William Ewart Gladstone: Faith and Politics in Victorian Britain*; M.J. Lynch, 'Was Gladstone a Tractarian? W.E. Gladstone and the Oxford Movement, 1833-45', pp.364-89; T.L. Crosby, *The Two Mr. Gladstones*, pp.44-5.

20. *DNB, 1931-10*, pp.811-5; T. Darington Jones, *Kent: At the Opening of the Twentieth Century, with Contemporary Biographies by W.T. Pike*, p.123; A. Mansfield, *Edward Stuart Talbot and Charles Gore*, pp.1-30; N. Yates, 'The Oxford Movement and Anglican Ritualism', p.36; H.C.G. Matthew, *Gladstone, 1875-98*, p.12. It is interesting that none of the large number of publications on the Oxford Movement, even those specifically on Kent, include Holy Trinity, Mark Beech, etc. as part of that tendency: e.g., N. Yates, *Kent and the Oxford Movement*, 'Bells and Smells: London, Brighton and South Coast Religion Reconsidered', 'The Impact of the Oxford Movement', in Yates *et al.* (ed.), *Religion and Society in Kent, 1640-1914*, pp.67-75.

21. W.E. Gladstone to Mrs. Gladstone, 17 January 1870, in A.T. Bassett (ed.), *Gladstone to His Wife*, p.175.

22. CKS: Talbot Papers, U1612/Q1.

23. J.G. Talbot, *Markbeech, 1852-1902*, pp.11-12; E.S. Talbot, *op. cit.*, pp.9-10; Ewing, pp.142-3; *DNB*, XIX, pp.168-70.

24. M. Harrison, *Victorian Stained Glass*, p.83; P. Cowen, *A Guide to Stained Glass in Britain*, pp.58-9.

25. J. G. Talbot, *op. cit.*, p.1.

26. Interview with Mrs. Joanna Smith, née Talbot, 18 April 1997.

27. Interview with Mr. Cecil Paynter, former Churchwarden, 2 January 1997.

28. E.S. Talbot, *op. cit.*, p.21.

29. Fielding, *op. cit.*, pp.68-9. He was probably Thomas Bowdler (1782-1856), the nephew of Thomas Bowdler (1754-1825), the well-known expurgator of Shakespeare. Bowdler junior was an incumbent at Sydenham and founder and secretary of the Church Building Society. Ironically he was very hostile to the Tractarians: *DNB*, II, p.954.

30. Gladstone, *Diaries, IV: 1848-54*, pp.429-30 [21-26 May 1852]; B. Askwith, *The Lytteltons: A Family Chronicle of the Nineteenth Century*, pp.125-6.

31. Sir J. Stephenson, *My Life: a Memoir for My Children*, p.21, kindly shown to the author by Sir John's brother.

32. Sheffield City Archives: Wharncliffe Muniments, J.C. Talbot to Lady Wharncliffe, Calais, 4 October 1851, Wh.M, 563-50; J.C. Talbot to Lady Wharncliffe, Florence, 25 October 1851, Wh.M, 563-51; J.C. Talbot to Lady Wharncliffe, Rome, 14 November 1851, Wh.M, 563-52; E.S. Talbot, *op. cit.*, pp.16-9.

33. J.G. Talbot, *op. cit.*, pp.20-1; C.W. Boase (ed.), *Registrum Collegii Exoniensis*, II, p.168; *Crockford's Clerical Directory*, p.689; Arrowsmith, *op. cit.*, p.203; Foster, *op. cit.*, II, p.716.

34. E.S. Talbot, *op. cit.*, pp.5-6.

35. *Ibid.*, p.19.

36. A. Lebey, *Les Trois Coups d' État de Louis-Napoléon Bonaparte*, pp.269-398; I. Guest, *Napoleon III in England*, p.55.

37. *Kelly's Directory of Kent, 1855*, p.432.

38. CKS: Talbot Papers, U1612/Q6; 'Vulliamy: Clockmaker to the King' in B. Loomes, *Watchmakers and Clockmakers of the World*, p.330; G.H. Baillie, C. Ilbert and C. Clutton (eds.), *Britten's Old Clocks and Watches and Their Makers*, p.633.

39. Holy Trinity, Mark Beech, Vestry Minutes, 1915; Interview with Mr. Cecil Paynter, 2 January 1997.

40. J.G. Talbot, *op. cit.*, p.5.

41. CKS: Talbot Papers, U1612/P18&19.

42. Interview with Charles J. Talbot, 24 February 1997.

43. E.S. Talbot, *op. cit.*, p.19.

44. 1861 Census returns, as cited in *VCH: Kent*, III, pp.356-70, *VCH: Sussex*, II, pp.215-28.

45. Hereafter usually written as LBSCR.

46. C.F. Dendy Marshall, *A History of the Southern Railway*, pp.193-231. See also H. Ellis, *The London, Brighton and South Coast Railway*, *passim*; H.P. White, *A Regional History of the Railways of Great Britain: II, Southern England*, pp.91-95, *The Forgotten Railways of the South East of England*, *passim*.

47. Marshall, *op. cit.*, pp.507-10.

48. *Ibid.*, p.221.

49. *Ibid.*, pp.220-1.

50. PRO British Transport Historical Records SSX4/4, p.1: Surrey and Sussex Junction Railway Company [hereafter SSJR], Balance Sheet, 30 August 1866.

51. V. Mitchell and K. Smith, *Branch Lines to Tunbridge Wells*, p.2.

52. For the Waring Brothers see, *inter alia*, H. Pollins, 'Railway Contractors and the Finance of Railway Development in Britain'; W.H.C. Smith, 'Anglo-Portuguese Relations, 1851-61', Ph.D. Thesis, pp.78-99; J.R. Kellet, *The Impact of the Railways on Victorian Cities*, pp.14, 72, 75-7, 201, 433; L. Popplewell, *Bournemouth Railway History: an Exposure of Victorian Engineering Fraud*, pp.56-91.

53. PRO/BTHR/SSX/4/3, pp.25-31, 34-5: SSJR, General Book; SSX4/5 pp.2-7: SSJR Register of Accounts and Cheques; CKS: Meade-Waldo Papers, U2193/T17.

54. PRO/BTHR/SSX/4/5, pp.2-7, Register of Accounts and Cheques; CKS: Meade-Waldo Papers.

55. PRO/BTHR/LBS/1/74, p.87: LBSCR, Minutes of Board, 13 February 1866.

56. PRO/BTHR/LBS/1/74, p.87: Agreement between LBSCR and SSJR, 18 May 1866; LBS 1/74, pp.194-5: LBSCR, Minutes of Board, 29 May 1866.

57. Sir J. Clapham, *An Economic History of Britain: Free Trade and Steel, 1850-86*, pp.375-7; R. Floud and D. McCloskey (eds.), *The Economic History of Britain since 1700, II: 1860-1939*, pp.229-30.

58. T. Coleman, *The Navvies, passim.*

59. *Tunbridge Wells Journal*, 16 August 1866, p.2; 17 August 1866, p.2.

60. *Tunbridge Wells Standard*, 10 August 1866, p.3; *Sevenoaks Express and District Advertiser*, 14 August 1866, p.1.

61. CKS: QSD/W4/5, p.14, Statement by Superintendent Richard Dance, 11 August 1866.

62. *Tunbridge Wells Standard*, 10 August 1866, p.3; 17 August 1866, p.2.

63. CKS: QSD/W4/5, pp.2-3, Statement by John West, 11 August 1866.

64. CKS: Statement by Dance, p.14; QSD/W4/5, pp.6-7, 12, Statements by William Stanbrook and P.C. William Solly; *Tunbridge Wells Standard*, 17 August 1866, p.2.

65. Statement by Dance, p.16.

66. *Tunbridge Wells Standard*, 10 August 1866, p.3.

67   CKS: QSD/W4/6, p.3 (Police statements).

68. Holy Trinity, Mark Beech Burial Register, 12 August 1866: Sarah Ann Brown, aged 2 years 7 months.

69. N. Longmate, *King Cholera: the Biography of a Disease*, p.222.

70. Holy Trinity, Mark Beech Burial Register, 13 and 17 September 1866; Registrar-General for England and Wales, Death Certificates for Michel and Franz Smidth, Register Nos. Sevenoaks, 295/1866 and 296/1866.

71. *Sussex Advertiser*, 8 August 1866, p.2.

72. *Sevenoaks Express and District Advertiser*, 14 August 1866, p.1.

73. *Sussex Advertiser*, 14 August 1866, p.4.

74. For more details of these riots see T. Boyle, 'The Mark Beech Riots, 1866'. See also J. Stevenson, *Popular Disturbances in England, 1832-1939* (forthcoming).

75. PRO/BTHR/LBS/1/74, pp.331-2: LBSCR, Minutes of Board, 21 February 1867.

76. PRO/BTHR/LBS/1/74, p.415: LBSCR, Minutes of Board, 11 July 1867.

77. Mitchell and Smith, *op. cit.*, p.2.

78. *Kelly's Directory of Kent, 1924*, p.494; Interview with Mr. Billy White, 23 November 1969.

Chapter VII: The Evolution of the Village, 1850-1918

1. J.D. Chambers and G.E. Mingay (eds.), *The Agricultural Revolution, 1750-1880*, pp.170-97; E.L. Jones, *The Development of English Agriculture, 1815-73*, pp.17-25; P. Mathias, *The First Industrial Nation*, pp.311-4.

2. *Ibid.*

3. C. Cook and J. Stevenson, *The Longman Handbook of Modern European History*, p.243.

4. Brandon and Short, *op. cit.*, pp.322-30; G.E. Mingay, 'Agriculture', in A. Armstrong (ed.), *The Economy of Kent* pp.69-81.

5. Kain, *op. cit.*, p.192, Table 6:1, p.201, Table 6:2.

6. Short, *op. cit.*, p.107; Brandon and Short, *op. cit.*, p.326.

7. *Ibid.*, p.107.

8. Brandon and Short, *op. cit.*, p.324.

9. Short, *op. cit.*, p.68, Table 2:4.

10. *Ibid.*, pp.76, 79, Table 2:8.

11. *Ibid.*, pp.158ff.

12. Sheffield City Archives: Wharncliffe Muniments, J.C. Talbot to Lady Wharncliffe, 21 August 1851, Wh.M, 563-49.

13. Short, *op. cit.*, pp.82ff, 90, Table 2:11.

14. *Ibid.*, pp.170, 173, Table 3:13.

15. D. W. Harvey, 'Fruit Growing in Kent in the Nineteenth Century', pp.95-108.

16. Short, *op. cit.*, pp.196-7.

17. Brandon and Short, *op. cit.*, pp.323-4.

18. Finberg and Thirsk (eds.), *op. cit.: VIII, 1914-39*, chaps. V-VII; P. E. Dewey, 'Food Policy and Production in the United Kingdom, 1914-18'; T. Wilson, *The Myriad Faces of War: Britain and the Great War, 1914-1918*, pp.537-8; S. Pollard, *The Development of the British Economy, 1914-90*, pp.21-2.

19. Short, *op. cit.*, p.206; *Edenbridge Chronicle*, 12 April 1915, p.2.

20. Short, *op. cit.,* p.207, Table 4:3; Brandon and Short, *op. cit.,* p.329.
21. Short, *op. cit.,* p.217, Table 4:4, p.219, Table 4:7.
22. *Kelly's Directory of Kent, 1915,* p.479, *1918,* p.441, *1922,* p.467; Interview with Mr. Billy White, who came to live in Mark Beech from Buckinghamshire in 1906, 23 November 1969.
23. Short, *op. cit.,* p.222, Table 4:8, p.239, Table 4:15.
24. Armstrong (ed.), *op. cit.,* pp.30-4.
25. *Ibid.*
26. CKS: Census 1861, 1871, 1881, 1891 (Microfilm); *Kelly's Directory of Kent, 1909,* p.478, *1913,* p.493.
27. CKS: Census 1891, Cowden (Microfilm).
28. *Ibid.*
29. See *The Church Magazine,* the magazine of the Rural Deanery of Tonbridge, August 1922 (reporting a fête on 20 July).
30. B.F.L. Clarke, *Church Buildings of the Nineteenth Century: a Study of the Gothic Revival in England,* pp.209-14; D. Yarwood, *The Architecture of England,* 2nd edn., p.466; D. Verey, 'George Frederick Bodley: Climax of the Gothic Revival', in J. Fawcett (ed.) *Seven Victorian Architects,* pp.84-101.
31. *The Times,* 17 December 1902, p.9; Falconhurst Visitors Book, 12-14 December 1893; J.G. Talbot, *op. cit.,* p.6; Lady Gwendolen Stephenson, *Memorandum on the Parish of Mark Beech,* Talbot Papers U1612/Z114, January 1943, p.60.
32. Interview with Mr. Charles J. Talbot, 24 February 1997.
33. CKS: Talbot Papers, U1612/Q18.
34. *Ibid.*
35. CKS: Talbot Papers, U1612/Q13.
36. Lady Stephenson, *op. cit.,* p.60; *DNB, 1922-30,* pp.655-7.
37. Holy Trinity, Mark Beech, Vestry Minutes, 1945.
38. *Ibid.,* 1953; *The Church Magazine,* December 1923.
39. Lady Stephenson, *op. cit.,* p.60.
40. *Ibid.*
41. Yates *et al., op. cit.,* pp.55-6.
42. CKS: Talbot Papers, U1612/Q7; B.F.L. Clarke, *op. cit.,* p.252.
43. Interview with Mr. Alan Smith (present owner/occupier of Edells), 12 October 1997.
44. CKS: Talbot Papers.
45. CKS: Talbot Papers; Ordnance Survey, 6 inch Map, Kent Sheet LIX.3, 1869.
46. CKS: Streatfield Papers, U908; Ordnance Survey, 6 inch Map, Kent Sheet LIX.3, 1869.
47. CKS: Talbot Papers.
48. CKS: Census 1881, Cowden (Microfilm).
49. Interview with Mrs. Margaret Dale, 3 January 1997.
50. Ordnance Survey, 6 inch Map, Kent Sheet LIX.3, 1869, revised 1936-7.
51. Felstead *et. al., op. cit.,* p.19.
52. Talbot Papers, U1612/Q17.
53. Talbot Papers, U1612/Q16.
54. Holy Trinity, Mark Beech, Burial Register, 8 July 1904. (Two of Hunt's unmarried sisters, Jane Ellen and Dorothea Boyra, died in 1894 and 1902.)
55. Gladstone, *Diaries, IV,* p.526, [15 May 1853].
56. Lady F. Cavendish, *The Diary of Lady F. Cavendish,* I, pp.52-7, 90, 170.
57. Sir J. Stephenson, *op. cit.*
58. J.G. Talbot, *op. cit.,* pp.42-7.
59. Lady Stephenson, *op. cit.,* pp.60-1.
60. *Vide* Appendix B(i).
61. Interview with Sister Teresa, St Andrew's Convent, 17 December 1997; J. Venn (ed.), *Biographical History of Gonville and Caius College, 1348-1897,* pp.373, 383-4; J.R. Vincent and M. Stenton (eds.), *Dod's Parliamentary Companion, 1886,* p.164; *Who Was Who, 1928-40,* p.49; copy of abstract of contract between Ernest Baggallay and Charlotte Anne Cubitt, 28 June 1892: St Andrew's Archives, Eden Hall.
62. Biographies of Thomas Cubitt, William Cubitt (1791-1863), Lewis Cubitt, Lewis Cubitt (1835-72), Charlotte Cubitt (1830-1926), Thomas Riccardi-Cubitt, Fede Maria Riccardi (1862-1950): St Andrew's Archives, Eden Hall; *DNB, V,* pp.267-70.
63. Cowden Parish Council Minutes, 4 December 1894, I, p.1; 5 January 1895, I, p.2.
64. Interview with Sister Teresa, Archivist, St Andrew's Convent, 19 December 1997.
65. Biographies of Thomas and Fede Riccardi-Cubitt, St Andrew's Archive, Eden Hall.
66. Ewing, p.28.
67. W.G. Hoskins, 'The Rebuilding of Rural England, 1570-1640', 'The Great Rebuilding', but see also C. Platt, *The Great Rebuilding of Tudor and Stuart England.*
68. Sale Catalogue of 1,000 acres in Chiddingstone, Sundridge, Chevening, Cowden and Hever on 14 May 1909 by Messrs. Langridge and Freeman at Tokenhouse Yard, London, in possession of Mr. Donald Hepworth, Victoria House, Horseshoe Green. Copy at CKS.
69. CKS: Talbot Papers, U1612/Z107, pp.32-47.

70. CKS: Census 1871, Cowden (Microfilm).

71. CKS: Census 1841, 1851, Cowden (Microfilm).

72. *Kelly's Directory of Kent, 1913*, p.493; Sale Catalogue, 1909.

73. *Kelly's Directory of Kent, 1913*, p.493; Interview with Mr. John Skinner, Blackham, 12 March 1997; Sale Invoice, Messrs. Fox and Manwaring, Edenbridge, 5 November 1926 (supplied by Mr. J. Skinner).

74. CKS: Census 1891, Cowden (Microfilm); Interview with Mr. Richard Ballard (formerly Police Constable at Cowden), 12 September 1997; Interview with Miss Elsie Maynard, licensee of *Queens Arms*, whose grandparents were at *Bricklayers Arms*, 20 December 1997.

75. *Ibid*.

76. See nn.78-9 below.

77. Vincent and Stenton, *op. cit.*, p.230; N.E. Johnson (ed.), *The Diary of Gathorne Hardy, later Lord Cranbrook, 1866-92*, pp.364-5 [2 April 1878]. Gathorne Hardy was made Viscount Cranbrook in 1878 and Baron Medway and Earl of Cranbrook in 1892. Cranbrook remained active in the Lords and as he was interested in Church matters and religious education he remained in contact with J.G. Talbot. It was he who had given the cypress seeds to Mark Beech Church, see p.64.

78. R. Harcourt Williams (ed.), *The Salisbury-Balfour Correspondence, 1869-92*, p.120.

79. *Who Was Who, 1897-1916*, p.696; CKS: Kent County Council Year Book, 1921-22.

80. *The Times*, 2 February 1910, p.11, 5 February 1910, p.11; Holy Trinity, Mark Beech, Burial Register, 4 February 1910.

81. Lady Stephenson, *Edward Stuart Talbot*, p.6; G. Battiscombe, *Mrs. Gladstone: the Portrait of a Marriage*, pp.94-5; Askwith, *op. cit.*, pp.125-6; Gladstone, *Diaries, IV*, pp.429-30, 21 May-3 June 1852. (Gladstone and his wife had dined with the Talbots on 2 February, p.392.)

82. Battiscombe, *op. cit.*, pp.32-5; S.G. Checkland, *The Gladstones: a Family Biography, 1764-1851*, p.312; S. Fletcher, *Victorian Girls: Lord Lyttelton's Daughters*, p.3.

83. Gladstone, *Diaries, IV*, pp.526-7, 14-19 May 1853, 8-14 July 1854; *VI*, pp.265-6, 26-9 March 1864, pp.344, 25-7 March 1865.

84. CKS: Census 1861, Cowden (Microfilm); Gladstone, *Diaries, VI*, p.21.

85. Askwith, *op. cit.*, p.145; Fletcher, *op. cit.*, pp.59-60, 142.

86. E.S. Talbot, *op. cit.*, pp.24, 28-9; Lady Stephenson, *op. cit.*, p.7; Fletcher, *op. cit.*, pp.38-42.

87. Gladstone, *Diaries, IX*, 19 April 1876, p.119; Fletcher, *op. cit.*, pp.221-4. The closeness of the three families is exemplified by the fact that on 14 July 1884 Mr. and Mrs. J.G. Talbot and Mr. and Mrs. W.E. Gladstone attended the marriage of Robert Lyttelton at St Margaret's, Westminster (Gladstone was Prime Minister): J.G. Talbot to Neville Lyttelton, 18 July 1884, Sir Neville Lyttelton Papers, Fam/NGL/96, Queen Mary and Westfield College, London, by kind permission of the Archivist. See also Gladstone, *Diaries, XI*, p.174, 14 July 1884.

88. Gladstone, *Diaries, V*, pp.278ff, 16 February 1858; R. Jenkins, *Gladstone*, p.186. For an earlier example of Gladstone being at Great George Street see Gladstone to Mrs. Gladstone, 14 & 18 July 1855, in Bassett, *op. cit.*, p.111.

89. *Who Was Who, 1897-1916*, p.120.

90. Gladstone, *Diaries, IX*, p.134, 17 June 1876; Falconhurst Visitors' Book, 7-10 July 1916, 27 February-3 March 1917; Sir J. Stephenson, *op. cit.*, p.27.

91. L. Masterman (ed.), *Mary Gladstone (Mrs. Drew): Her Diaries and Letters*, London, p.72 (letter of 22 April 1858); in her old age Mary wrote that as a child Mrs. Talbot 'gave me the impression that I was "wanting", i.e. half-witted'; P. Jalland, 'Mr. Gladstone's Daughters', p.101.

92. Sir Neville Lyttelton, *Eighty Years: Soldiering, Politics, Games*, pp.183-4.

93. *The Church Magazine*, January 1899.

94. *Edenbridge Courier*, 4 September 1914, p.2, cited in W. Griffiths, 'Edenbridge During the First Five Months of the Great War', p.37.

95. Askwith, *op. cit.*, p.138.

96. E. Lyttelton, *Alfred Lyttelton: an Account of His Life*, p.69.

97. Falconhurst Visitors' Book, 24-5 July 1875, 18 April 1878, 16 December 1878; Fletcher, *op. cit.*, p.182; Lady Stephenson, 'Memorandum', p.11.

98. Lady Stephenson, *op. cit.*, pp.10ff; Sir J. Stephenson, *op. cit.*, p.129.

99. The framed scorecard of this match may be seen on a wall in the public bar of *The Rock* public house at Chiddingstone Hoath.

100. D.H. Brooksbank, 'Sliding Down the Bannisters of Life', p.32.

101. Lady Stephenson, *op. cit.*, p.11; Sir J. Stephenson, *op. cit.*, p.44.

102. *The Church Magazine*, November 1921 and April 1924.

103. Cowden Parish Council Minutes, I, 5 June 1908, p.37.

104. Ewing, pp.153, 163.

105. *The Church Magazine*, July 1922.

106. *Kelly's Directory of Kent, 1859*, p.435.

107. *Ibid*.; Sir J. Stephenson, *op. cit.*, pp.18, 22.

108. CKS: Talbot Papers, U1612/Q11.

109. CKS: Census, 1881 Cowden (Microfilm); Registrar-General for England and Wales, Birth Certificate for Helen Mary Fox, Register No. Sevenoaks 225/1880.

110. *Kelly's Directory of Kent, 1905*, p.462; Interview with Mrs. Margaret Dale, The Grove, 7 January 1997; Interview with Mrs. John Leppard, 9 December 1997.

111. *Kelly's Directory of Kent, 1924*, p.494.

112. *The Church Magazine*, December 1931.

113. R. Ogley, *Kent: a Chronicle of the Century*, I, *1900-24*, p.81.

114. CKS: Talbot Papers, U1612/Z115, Miss Talbot's Diary of Parish Events, 20 August 1904-31, p.10 [December 1922].
115. Ogley, *op. cit.*, I, pp.29, 34, 49.
116. *DNB, Missing Persons* (1993), pp.27-8.
117. *DNB, 1971-80*, pp.22-4; *Who Was Who, 1981-90*, p.27; Ogley, *op. cit.*, p.177.
118. Ordnance Survey, 6 inch Map, Kent Sheet LIX.3, 1869.
119. Map with Conveyance Deed of 25 March 1911, between the Executors of E.A. Denny and Edmund M. Dean: High Buckhurst Papers, in possession of and by kind permission of Mr. and Mrs. Michael Roberts, Mark Beech.
120. CKS (Sevenoaks): Sevenoaks Union, Pauper Index, W1Z, p.414; Census, 1871, Cowden (Microfilm).
121. Sevenoaks Union, Register of Deaths, 1866-99, W1D, p.46; Census 1881, Hever; Holy Trinity, Mark Beech, Burial Register, 1852-1998, 15 November 1879.
122. Sevenoaks Union, Register of Births, 1866-96, W1E, pp.9, 10.
123. Holy Trinity, Mark Beech, Burial Register, 5 July 1897.
124. CKS (Sevenoaks): Sevenoaks Union, Servants and Apprentices Book, AW1, p.1.
125. Vincent and Stenton, *op. cit.*, pp.150-1.
126. Institute of Historical Research: Poll Book, West Kent, 1868.
127. *DNB, 1912-21*, pp.345-7; H.G. Hutchinson, *The Life of Sir John Lubbock, Lord Avebury*, I, pp.66-86, 94-5, 99-100, 119-20.
128. Institute of Historical Research: Poll Books, West Kent, 1852, 1857, 1859, 1865, 1868.
129. Poll Book, West Kent, 1868.
130. In what were admittedly geographically different constituencies the Liberal share of the vote increased from 42.1 per cent in 1880 in the old West Kent division to 48.2 per cent in 1885 in the new South-West Kent or Tonbridge division. For an analysis of electoral behaviour in the new constituency see H. Pelling, *Social Geography of British Elections, 1885-1910*, pp.68-71. For the Third Reform Act see A. Jones, *The Politics of Reform, 1884, passim*.
131. Vincent and Stenton, *op. cit.*, Part II, pp.123-4.
132. Hever Parish Council Minute Book, I, 16 June 1895, p.16.
133. Cowden Parish Council Minute Book, I, 14 April 1900, p.14; I, 20 August 1900, p.15; I, 4 August 1901, p.16; *Supra*, n.102.
134. Cowden Parish Council Minute Book, II, 25 March 1933, p.50; II, 13 April 1933, p.54; II, 3 August 1933, p.59. There certainly is not one now and nobody in the village can remember one being installed.
135. Interview with Mr. Billy White, 23 November 1969.
136. Hever Parish Council Minute Book, II, pp.123-4.
137. Hever Burial Books.
138. *Edenbridge Courier*, 7 August 1914, p.1.
139. *Edenbridge Courier*, 15 March 1915, p.1.
140. Anon, *Cowden in the Great War*, pp.9-10.
141. CKS: Talbot Papers, U1612/Z115, Miss Talbot's Diary of Parish Events, p.49; *Cowden in the Great War*, p.9.
142. CKS: Belgian Refugees, C/A2/10/42, 23 October, 15 November, 4 December 1914, 1 January 1915.
143. *Edenbridge Courier*, 15 November 1914, p.1. This was known as Fort Pitt: Mrs. Vera Meade, née Cubitt to Albert Edward Harvey, 21 August [1918], St Andrew's Archive, Eden Hall.
144. CKS: Belgian Refugees, C/A2/10/42.
145. *Cowden in the Great War*, p.8.
146. Holy Trinity, Mark Beech Burial Register, 10 May 1916.
147. Biographical sheet on Countess Riccardi-Cubitt, Vera Alicia Maria Cubitt (Mrs. Meade), b. 1894, Theodora Fede Maria, b. 1897, and Monica Yolanda Cubitt, b. 1901. Mrs. Meade was Kent VAD No. 88: St Andrew's Archives, Eden Hall; *Cowden in the Great War*, p.8.
148. Mrs. Meade to Albert Harvey, 21 August [1918], St Andrew's Archive, Eden Hall.
149. *Edenbridge Courier*, 12 April 1918, p.1; Mrs. Meade to Albert Harvey, 15 May [1918], St Andrew's Archives, Eden Hall.
150. Mrs. Meade to Albert Harvey, 15 May [1918], St Andrew's Archives, Eden Hall.
151. CKS: Tonbridge and Tunbridge Wells Relief Committee, C/A2/6/28-1915; *Cowden in the Great War*, pp.7-8.
152. CKS: Tonbridge and Tunbridge Wells Relief Committee, C/A2/6/28.
153. *Cowden in the Great War*, p.5.
154. *The Church Magazine*, July 1922.

Chapter VIII: Modern Mark Beech, 1918-99

1. HMSO: Census Report, Kent, I, p.16; *Whitaker's Almanac*, 1998, p.542; *Kelly's Directory of Kent, 1938*, p.487.
2. J. Stevenson, *British Society, 1914-45*, pp.129-30, 221-42.
3. Cockburn, *op. cit.*, No. 1501, p.317.
4. K. Robbins, *The Eclipse of a Great Power: Modern Britain, 1870-1992*, p.144.
5. *Supra*, p.85.
6. CKS: Meade-Waldo Papers, U2193/E10, Catalogue of Messrs. Knight, Frank & Rutley for sale of 1,015 acres, being part of the Meade-Waldo Hever Estate, 1919, Lots 22 and 36. Here is an example of a landed family selling off large amounts of land after the First World War. (For this phenomenon see F.M.L. Thompson, *English Landed Society in the Nineteenth Century*, pp.328-35; Stevenson, *op. cit.*, pp.331-4.)
7. Robbins, *op. cit.*, pp.223-8.

8. Stevenson, *op. cit.*, pp.231-42; Ogley, *op. cit.*, II, *1925-49*, pp.86, 166.

9. Interview with Mrs. John Leppard (who has lived in Roughitts ever since it was built), 9 December 1997.

10. Interview with Mrs. Marjorie Peters, formerly of Mark Beech, now of Tunbridge Wells, 25 November 1997.

11. Letter from Mr. I.B. Bigwood, Sevenoaks District Council, 28 January 1997.

12. Finberg and Thirsk (eds.), *op. cit.*, *VIII, 1914-39*, chapters X, XIII, XIV, XVIIC.

13. Short, *op. cit.*, p.281, Table 5:4, p.317, Table 5:19.

14. *Ibid.*, p.305, Table 5:14.

15. *Ibid.*, p.319, Table 5:20.

16. R.J. Hammond, *History of the Second World War: Food*, II, pp.3-274; Pollard, *op. cit.*, pp.166-8.

17. Short, *op. cit.*, pp.362-4, Table 6:7, p.375, Table 6:10a; Interview with Mr. Billy White, 23 November 1969.

18. Short, *op. cit.*, pp.352m Table 6:3; p.384 Table 6:12. The only setback to prosperity was an outbreak in August 1957 of foot-and-mouth desease among cattle on several farms in the vicinity, including Greybury, Chatfield and Ockham: Ogley, *op. cit.*, III, 1950-75, p. 60.

19. *Ibid.*, p.358, Table 6:6a.

20. Interview with Mr. Charles J. Talbot, 24 February 1997.

21. *Ibid.*

22. *Ibid.*

23. *Ibid.*

24. *Ibid.*

25. Telephone interview with Miss Pat Humphreys, Hever, formerly Lord Astor's secretary, 7 December 1997.

26. Ogley, *op. cit.*, II, pp.94, 167.

27. *DNB, 1931-40*, pp.845-6.

28. Interview with Mr. A.W. Stephenson, 7 January 1997.

29. *Who Was Who, 1951-60*, p.1065; *The Times*, 16 December 1956, p.11.

30. A copy of this interesting publication was lent to the author by Mrs. John Leppard, who has possessed it since joining the Women's Land Army.

31. J.G. Talbot, *op. cit.*, p.6; *The Church Magazine*, December 1921.

32. *The Times*, 18 August 1922, p.8, 21 August, p.6, 22 August, p.8, 8 September, p.7; Holy Trinity, Mark Beech, Burial Register,

33. *Who's Who, 1992*, p.1817.

34. Interview with Miss Doreen Graves, Mark Beech, former servant at Falconhurst, 10 January 1998.

35. Interview with Mrs. Margaret Dale, 3 January 1997.

36. Information supplied by Mrs. Mary Boyle, Electoral Registration Officer, Holy Trinity, Mark Beech.

37. *Vide* Appendix B(i). One vicar, Arthur Moore, died in office on Christmas Day 1924, three years after arrival: *The Church Magazine*, February 1925.

38. Interview with Mr. C. Paynter, 2 January 1997.

39. Holy Trinity, Mark Beech, Vestry Minutes, 1952.

40. *The Church Magazine*, October 1924.

41. Interview with Mr. C. Paynter, 2 January 1997.

42. Information supplied by Mrs. Jill Linden, churchwarden.

43. Interview with Mrs. Joanna Smith, 18 April 1997.

44. Interview with Mr. A.W. Stephenson, 7 January 1997.

45. Interview with Mr. Charles J. Talbot, 24 February 1997.

46. *DNB, 1961-70*, pp.188-9.

47. Holy Trinity, Mark Beech, Vestry Minutes, 1950 and 1951; Interview with Mr. Michael Holland, 1 April 1998.

48. Interview with Mr. Charles J. Talbot, 24 February 1997.

49. *Kelly's Directory of Kent, 1905*, p.385; *The Church Magazine*, August 1921.

50. *The Church Magazine*, December 1921.

51. *Ibid.*, March 1922.

52. *Ibid.*, June 1922.

53. Mark Beech Village Hall Trust, Statutes of Indenture, in possession of Mr. Charles J. Talbot, Falconhurst.

54. *The Church Magazine*, December 1922.

55. *Ibid.*, January and February 1923.

56. *Ibid.*, July 1923.

57. *Ibid.*, December 1922.

58. *Ibid.*, August 1923.

59. R.H. Sutton, *Historical Notes of Wythyham, Hartfield and Ashdown Forest*, p.cclx.

60. G. Ewing, *Cowden: the Records of a Wealden Parish*, cited many times in this study. Mark Beech is mentioned on pp.142-3, but only in connection with the church. Cowden Parish Council Minute Books, I, 24 July 1912, p.50; I, 5 March 1929, p.289.

61. Holy Trinity, Mark Beech, Burial Register, 1927; CKS: Kent County Year Books, 1928-49.

62. Falconhurst Visitors' Book, 9-12 June 1933; Sir J. Stephenson, *op. cit.*, pp.129-30 (where the date is wrong).

63. Information supplied by Mr. Michael Holland, Holtye.

64. Letters from Mrs. Gwen Mott, formerly of Mark Beech, now of Feckenham, Worcestershire, 12 and 19 January 1998; Telephone interview with Mrs. Joan Goddard, now of Alton, Hampshire, 17 December 1997.

65. *The Church Magazine*, January and October 1927, May and September 1939.

66. Interview with Mr. Alf Voyce, 31 March 1998.

67. Interview with Mr. Ken Dann, 29 August 1997.

68. Hever Parish Council Minutes, III, 11 July 1977, pp.262-3, IV, 30 September 1977, p.2.

69. *Ibid.*, V, 7 March 1994, p.127.

70. *Ibid.*, V, 7 November 1994.

71. *Ibid.*, V, 6 and 10 July 1995, p.149.

72. *Ibid.*, V, p.149.

73. *Ibid.*, IV, 18 September 1995, p.153.

74. Mrs. Meade to Albert Harvey, 6 November [1918], St Andrew's Archives, Eden Hall.

75. L.F. Ellis, *History of the Second World War, United Kingdom Military Series: the War in France and Flanders, 1939-40*, pp.80-1.

76. *The Church Magazine*, July 1922.

77. *Ibid.*, July and August 1924.

78. *Ibid.*, July 1927.

79. *Ibid.*, July and August 1939.

80. *Ibid.*, November 1939; Telephone interview with Mrs. Joan Goddard, who was one of the evacuees, 17 December 1997; letters from Mrs. Gwen Mott, 12 and 19 January 1998; Interview with Mrs. Walter Leppard, 8 January 1998.

81. Holy Trinity, Mark Beech, Vestry Minutes, 1945.

82. Holy Trinity, Mark Beech, Burial Register, 24 April 1990.

83. St Andrew's Archives, Eden Hall.

84. Interview with Sister Teresa, St Andrew's Convent, 19 December 1997; The Community's Diary, 1, 7, 10 and 20 September 1943, St Andrew's Archives, Eden Hall.

85. Interview with Sister Teresa, 19 December 1997.

86. Interview with Sister Teresa, 19 December 1997; The Community's Diary, 10 December 1945.

87. Interview with Mrs. Ann Roberts, Mark Beech, 5 June 1997.

88. A.W. Stephenson, *Some Memories of Falconhurst Cricket*, March 1985 (unpublished typescript in author's possession); Interview with Mr. Ian Lewis, formerly of Mark Beech, now of Fordcombe, 7 January 1998.

89. Interview with Mr. Ian Lewis, 7 January 1998; Interview with Mr. Alf Voyce, 31 March 1998.

90. R.J. Brooks, *Kent Airfields Remembered*, pp.43-56.

91. CKS: Talbot Papers, U1618/Q18.

92. Letter from Mr. I. Adams, Sutton and East Surrey Water plc., 29 January 1997.

93. *Ibid.*

94. Holy Trinity, Mark Beech, Vestry Minutes, 1945.

95. Letter from Mr. M. Cush, Southern Water Services, 13 February 1997.

96. Interview with Mr. Billy White, 23 November 1969.

97. Interview with Mr. Cecil Paynter, 2 January 1997.

98. Mr. Cyril Skinner of Four Elms, as reported by Mr. Mark Mead, 15 March 1998.

99. Mitchell and Smith, *op. cit.*, pp.16, 18.

100. Author's personal recollections.

101. *Edenbridge Courier*, 21 October 1994, pp.1-3.

102. Cowden Parish Council Minutes, III, 3 May 1952, p.103, III, 10 May 1952, 22 August 1952, p.111.

103. *Whitaker's Almanac*, 1919-80.

104. Sevenoaks District Council, Deputy Returning Officer's Reports (kindly supplied by Chief Executive).

105. Hever Parish Council Minute Book, IV, 30 September 1977, p.120; 13 March 1978, p.128; 28 June 1978, p.135; 13 September 1978, p.138; Letter from Mr. I.B. Bigwood, Sevenoaks District Council, 28 January 1997.

106. Hever Parish Council Minutes, III, 24 August 1949, p.110, 23 May 1950, p.123, 25 July 1950, p.126.

107. *Kent Messenger*, 15 September 1944, p.1; *Sevenoaks News*, 21 September, p.1.

108. Interview with Mr. S. Gower, Chiddingstone Hoath, whose mother remembers the incident, 10 January 1998; Telephone interview with Mrs. Joan Goddard, Alton, Hampshire, 17 December 1997.

109. Interview with Miss Elsie Maynard, 10 January 1998. For a contemporary account of the aerial combat over Kent, although a little to the east of Mark Beech, at Sissinghurst, see N. Nicolson (ed.), *The Diaries and Letters of Harold Nicolson, 1939-45*, p.105, 18 August 1940, p.107, 2 September, p.108, 4 September, pp.110-1, 15 September.

110. Interview with Mrs. John Leppard, 9 December 1997; Interview with Mrs. Walter Leppard, 8 January 1998.

111. Bombs, etc. dropped and casualties in Sevenoaks RDC area to be found in, *inter alia*, T.H. O'Brien, *The Official History of the Second World War: Civil Defence*, pp.652-68; A. Rootes, *Front Line County: Kent at War, 1939-45*, pp.203-8; R. Ogley, *Doodlebugs and Rockets: the Battle of the Flying Bomb*, p.134, *Kent at War: The Unconquered County, 1939-45*, pp.218-9, D.G. Collyer, *Buzz Bomb Diary, passim*.

112. CKS: Civil Defence Log, January-June 1944, C/Ad/1/13; Rootes, *op. cit.*, pp.92, 204.

113. Civil Defence Log, July-December 1940, C/Ad/1/6.

114. Civil Defence Log, January-June 1944, C/Ad/1/10.
115. Interview with Mr. W. Everest, 21 May 1973.
116. Interview with Mr. Richard Ballard, 2 April 1998.
117. Interview with Mrs. Walter Leppard, 7 January 1998.
118. *Ibid*.
119. Interview with Mrs. John Leppard, December 1997.
120. *Sevenoaks News*, 21 September 1944, p.1; Ogley, *op. cit*., pp.216-9.
121. Diary of the Community, 16 June 1944, St Andrew's Archives, Eden Hall; H.E. Bates, *Flying Bombs over England* (ed. R. Ogley), p.44; D.G. Collyer, *op. cit*., pp.133-46.
122. Diary of the Community, 11 July 1944, St Andrew's Archives, Eden Hall.
123. Ogley, *op. cit*., p.217.
124. *Ibid*., p.217.
125. Bates, *op. cit*., pp.44-5.
126. Interview with Mrs. John Leppard, 7 December 1997; Interview with Mr. Alf Voyce, 31 March 1998.
127. Interview with Miss Elsie Maynard, 10 January 1998.
128. Interview with Mr. Richard Ballard, 2 April 1998. Mr. Ballard, the Police Constable at Cowden, 1965-89, possesses a photograph of the nine men, but cannot identify all of them.
129. Sir W. S. Churchill, *The Second World War: II, Their Finest Hour*, pp.232-3; R. Wheatley, *Operation Sea Lion: German Plans for the Invasion of England, 1939-42*, pp.40-1; R. Macleod and D. Kelly (eds.), *Ironside Diaries, 1937-40*, pp.371-2, 378-80; K.R. Gulvin, *Kent Home Guard: a History*, p.71; Rootes, *op. cit*., p.195; S. Ward, *War in the Countryside, 1939-45*, p.130.
130. Interview with Mr. Cecil Paynter, 2 January 1997; Interview with Mrs. Margaret Dale, 3 January 1997; Interview with Mrs. John Leppard, 7 December 1997; Interview with Mrs. Elsie Maynard, 10 January 1998.
131. Interview with Mr. Cecil Paynter, 2 January 1997; Interview with Mrs. Margaret Dale, 3 January 1997.
132. Interview with Miss Elsie Maynard, 10 January 1998.
133. *Ibid*.
134. C.P. Stacey, *The Official History of the Canadian Army in the Second World War, I: Six Years of War*, pp.289, 345; *III, The Victory Campaign*, pp.46, 92; J.R.M. Butler, *The History of the Second World War: Grand Strategy, II, September 1939-June 1941*, p.279. The British Commander, General Ironside, inspected Canadian troops in Kent on 6 July 1940: *Ironside Diaries*, p.382.
135. Interview with Mr. Alf Voyce, 31 March 1998.
136. Interview with Sister Teresa, St Andrew's Convent, 19 December 1997.
137. Interview with Miss Elsie Maynard, 10 January 1998.
138. Sir W.S. Churchill, *op. cit*., pp.147-8; Ogley, *op. cit*., pp.30-1, *Kent: A Chronicle of the Century*, II, p.110.
139. M. Gilbert, *Churchill: A Life*, pp.372, 450.
140. C. Graves, *The Home Guard of Britain*, pp.22, 25, 95-6, 224; I. Grant and N. Maddren, *The Countryside at War*, pp.52-66; S. Ward, *op. cit*., pp.127-45; Gulvin, *op. cit*., p.71.
141. Interview with Mrs. John Leppard, 7 December 1997.
142. *Ibid*.; Interview with Mr. Alf Voyce, 31 March 1998.
143. Interview with Mrs. John Leppard, 7 December 1997.
144. *Ibid*.
145. Stevenson, *op. cit*., pp.177, 444-5.
146. V. Sackville-West, *The Women's Land Army*, Appendix I, p.95.
147. Interview with Mrs. John Leppard, 7 December 1997; Interview with Mrs. Walter Leppard, 8 January 1998. (Both these ladies were Londoners in the W.L.A. who married local men.) For the Women's Land Army see Sackville-West, *op. cit*.; Grant and Maddren, *op. cit*., pp.44-7; S. Ward, *op. cit*., pp.34-45; Ogley, *Kent at War*, p.97.
148. Sir J. Stephenson, *op. cit*., p.179; Interview with Mr. Charles J. Talbot, February 1997.
149. Information supplied by author, Mr. Richard Brook-Smith and Sister Teresa.
150. Register of Electors, 1997, plus others by survey.
151. *Ibid*.
152. This computation is based on the 1997 Register of Electors, plus a house-by-house survey to establish the number of adult non-electors, such as foreign nationals, of which there are some, and the children under eighteen. The newly converted houses at Pyle Gate, for example, were not occupied in the early autumn of 1997 so their inhabitants are not included. There have been some deaths and removals, so if we say that the population of Mark Beech is 300 give or take five, we will probably be as accurate as we can get.

Appendix A:

1. For a general description of older houses in the area see *inter alia*: R.T. Mason, *Framed Buildings of the Weald*; K. Gravett, *Timber and Brick Building in Kent*; J. Warren (ed.), *Wealden Buildings*; A. Quiney, *Kent Houses*; S. Pearson, *The Medieval Houses of Kent: an Historical Analysis*; S. Pearson, P.S. Barnwell and A.T. Adams, *A Gazetteer of Medieval Houses in Kent*; R.J. Brown, *Old Houses and Cottages in Kent*.

Bibliography

A Primary Sources:
(i) Manuscripts

British Museum, Manuscript Department:
Gladstone-J.C. Talbot Correspondence, Add MS 44363
Gladstone-J.G. Talbot Correspondence, Add MSS 44376-44514
Gladstone-E.S. Talbot Correspondence, Add MSS 44000-44525
Gladstone-Lyttelton Correspondence, Add MSS 44238-40
Extent of the Priory of Lewisham, 1370, Add Ms 6164, f. 416
Cartulary of Shene Priory, B.M. Cott. MS. Otho B, xiv, f. 70

Centre for Kent Studies, Maidstone:
Meade-Waldo Papers, U1512 and U2193
Streatfield Papers, U908
Talbot Papers, U1612
Woodgate Papers, U1050
Tithe Maps and Awards, 1841 (Cowden & Hever), CTR/99A & B
Land Tax Records, 1780-1832 (Cowden & Hever), Q/RPL/89ff.
Hearth Tax Returns of 1664, Somerden South, 129/702/21-22
Collection of Old Maps of Kent, Maps/17/1ff .
Mark Beech Riot Papers, QSD/W4/5 & 6
Civil Defence Logs, 1939-45, C/Ad/1/1-12
Belgian Refugees, 1914-15, C/A2/10/42 & 46
Kent Relief Committees, 1914-19, C/A2/6/28 & 10/43
Kent County Year Book, 1898-1951.

Centre for Kent Studies, Sevenoaks:
Gordon Ward Notebooks (Chiddingstone, Cowden & Hever)
Census Returns, 1841, 1851, 1861, 1871, 1881, 1891 (Cowden & Hever) (Microfilm) [another copy at Maidstone]
Manor of Lewisham: Cowden (Knocker Collection) U1000/7/M5-11
Manor of Westerham: Cowden (Knocker Collection) U1000/7/M28/T15-17
Manor of Otford: Cowden Pound (Knocker Collection) U1000/9/M18
Manor of Penshurst Halimote (Knocker Collection) U1000/9/M19-41
Sevenoaks Union Papers:
Pauper Index, W1z
Register of Deaths, 1866-99, W1d
Baptisms, 1846-1932, W1b
Letter Books, 1836-39, ACb.1
Letter Books, 1852-59, ACb.2
Register of Births, 1866-96, W1b.1
Register of Births, 1897-1913, W1b.2
Register of Births, 1914-31, W1b.3
Admission & Discharge Book, 1912- , G/Se W1a1
Ordnance Survey Maps, 1 inch and 6 inch

Cowden Parish Council:
Minutes of Council, 1894-1998

Falconhurst, Mark Beech:
Visitors' Book, 1873-1998

Hever Parish Council:
Minutes of Council, 1894-1998

Holy Trinity, Mark Beech:
Burial Register, 1852-1998
Baptism and Marriage Registers, 1945-98
Vestry Minutes, 1915-1998

Kingston Museum:
Downman, E.A., Plan of Dry Hill, 1903, S(913) No. 3666(9)

Lewisham Local Studies and Archives:
L.L. Duncan's Transcripts of Lewisham Manor Court Rolls, 181/45ff
Documents concerning the Priory and Manor of Lewisham in East Flanders State Archive, Ghent (microfilm)

Mark Beech Village Hall:
Trust Deed, Minute Books, Accounts, Correspondence, etc. (in custody of author)

Mark Beech Women's Institute:
Minute Books, 1950-65, transcripts by Mr. Michael Holland
Minute Books, 1971-98, the Secretary, Mrs. S. Eadie

Public Record Office, Kew:
Extents, writs and inquisitions relating to possessions of Alien Priories, including Greenwich, PRO/E106/101/1
Petitions relating to possessions of Alien Priories, including Greenwich PRO/E106/11/16
Receipts from Alien Priories, including Greenwich, PRO/E106/11/32
Special Collections, Court Rolls, PRO/SC2
Ministers' and Receiver's Accounts, PRO/SC6
Tithe Files: Chiddingstone, PRO/IR18/3565
Cowden, PRO/IR18/3579
Hever, PRO/IR18/3641
British Transport Historical Records: Surrey and Sussex Junction Railway/London, Brighton and South Coast Railway, PRO/BTHR/
    SSX/4/3-5; LBS/1/74

Queen Mary and Westfield College, University of London:
Sir Neville Lyttelton Papers, Fam/NGL/96

St Andrew's, Eden Hall:
Archives of the Community

Sheffield City Archives:
Wharncliffe Muniments, Papers of the 1st Earl and Countess of Wharncliffe: Letters to and from Mr. and Mrs. J.C. Talbot, Wh.M.563,
    605, 618, 629

Tunbridge Wells Museum:
Accession Nos. 85/324 (1-98); 85/325 (1-8)

Documents in Private Hands:
Deeds and other documents relating to High Buckhurst (courtesy Mr. and Mrs. Michael Roberts)
Land Registry Documents relating to Horseshoe Cottage (courtesy Mr. Peter Rayner)
Memorandum relating to Deeds, etc. of Rickwoods, 1891-1994 (courtesy Mr. James Calvocoressi)
Land Registry Documents relating to 2 Horseshoe Green Cottage (courtesy Mr. Jeremy Speakman)
Land Registry Documents relating to Fairholme Farm (courtesy Mr. Peter Jamieson)
Documents relating to Jessups (courtesy Hon. Robin Denison-Pender)
Deeds, Land Registry and other documents relating to High Buckhurst, including Ashtrees (courtesy Mr. Michael Holland)
Tenancy Agreements relating to Wilderness Farm, 1918-35 (courtesy Mrs. Walter Leppard)
Sale Catalogue and other documents relating to Victoria House and Horseshoe Green Garage (courtesy Mr. Donald Hepworth)

Brooksbank, D.H., née Baggallay, 'Sliding Down the Bannisters of Life', 1941, unpublished typescript in possession of Mr. Anthony Mauduit of Canterbury

Stephenson, A.W., *Some Memories of Falconhurst Cricket*, 1985, unpublished typescript in the author's possession

Stephenson, Sir John, *My Life: a Memoir for My Children*, unpublished typescript (courtesy Mr. A.W. Stephenson)

(ii) Printed Sources:

Bassett, A.T. (ed.), *Gladstone to His Wife*, London, 1936

Bede, *A History of the English Church and People* (trans. Sherley-Price, L.), London, 1955

Birch, W de G. (ed.), *Cartularium Saxonicum*, 3 vols., London, 1885-93

Boase, C.W. (ed.), *Registrum Collegii Exoniensis*, II, Oxford, 1894

Bryant, A., *The Turn of the Tide, 1939-43: a Study based on the Diaries and Autobiographical Notes of Field Marshal Viscount Alanbrooke*, London, 1959

Caesar, Julius, *The Conquest of Gaul* (trans. Handford, S.A., rev. Gardner, J.F.), London, 1982.

Calendar of Charter Rolls

Calendar of Close Rolls

Calendar of Inquisitions Post-Mortem

Calendar of Patent Rolls

Calendar of State Papers, Spain III, Henry VIII, 1527-29, London, 1877

Cavendish, Lady F., *The Diary of Lady Frederick Cavendish* (ed. Bailey, J.), 2 vols., London, 1927

The Church Magazine, being the magazine of the Rural Deanery of Tonbridge, 1919-39

Churchill, I.J., Griffin, R. and Hardman, F.W. (eds.), *Calendar of the Kent Feet of Fines*, Ashford, 1956

Cockburn, J.S. (ed.), *Calendar of Assize Records: Kent Indictments, Charles I*, London, 1995

Davis, H.W.C. (ed.), *Regestra Regum Anglo-Normannorum, 1066-1154, I, Regestra Willelmi Conquestoris et Willelmi Rufi, 1066-1100*, Oxford, 1913

Department of the Environment: List of Buildings of Special Architectural or Historic Interest: District of Sevenoaks, Rural Area

Dictionary of National Biography

Diodorus Siculus, *History* (ed. Oldfather, C.H.), London, 1939

Douglas, D.C. and Greenaway, G.W. (eds.), *English Historical Documents, II, 1066-1154*, 2nd edn., London, 1981

Du Boulay, F.R.H. (ed.), *Documents Illustrative of Medieval Kentish Society*, Ashford, 1964

Dugdale, Sir William, *Monasticon Anglicanum*, vol. VI, Parts I & II, London, 1830

Fayen, A. (ed.), *Liber Traditionum: Sancti Petri Blandiniensis*, Gent, 1906

Gladstone, W.E., *Diaries: III-IV, 1840-54* (ed. Foot, M.R.D. and Matthew, H.C.G.), Oxford, 1974; *V-IX, 1855-80*, (ed. Matthew, H.C.G.), Oxford, 1978-86

Haddan, A.W. and Stubbs, W. (eds.), *Councils and Ecclesiastical Documents relating to Great Britain and Ireland*, III, London, 1871

Hardwick, C. (ed.), *Historia Monasterii S. Augustini Cantuariensis*, London, 1858

Hardy, T.D. (ed.), *Rotuli Chartarum*, vol. I, Part 1, London, 1837

Hearn, T. (ed.), *Textus Roffensis*, Oxford, 1720

HMSO: Census Report 1991, Kent, I, London, 1993

Illingworth, W. (ed.), *Rotuli Hundredorum*, I, London, 1812

Inquisitions Post-Mortem: Kent, *Arch. Cant.*, II (1859), pp.281-336; III (1860), pp.243-76; IV (1863), pp.292-304; VI (1866), pp.237-50

Institute of Historical Research, University of London: Poll Books: Kent, 1754, 1790, 1802; West Kent, 1835, 1847, 1852, 1857, 1859, 1865, 1867

Johnson, C. (ed.), *Registrum Hamonis Hethe: Diocesis Roffensis*, Oxford, 1948

Johnson, C., Cronne, H.A. and Davis, H.W.C. (eds.), *Regestra Henrici Primi, 1100-35*, Oxford, 1956

Johnson, C. and Cronne, H.A. (eds.), *Regestra Regis Stephani ac Mathildis Imperatricis ac Ganfridi et Henrici, Ducum Normannorum*, Oxford, 1968

Johnson, N.E. (ed.), *The Diary of Gathorne Hardy, later Lord Cranbrook, 1866-92*, Oxford, 1981

Kemble, J.M. (ed.), *Codex Diplomaticus Aevi Saxonici*, 6 vols., London, 1839-48

Kent Feet of Fines, *Arch. Cant.*, I (1858), pp.217-88; II (1859), pp.239-78; III (1860), pp.209-40; IV (1863), pp.257-90; VI (1866), pp.223-34; XIII (1880), pp.289-320; XV (1883), pp.273- 310; XVIII (1889), pp.337-52

Lodge, E.C. and Thornton, G.A. (eds.), *English Constitutional Documents, 1307-1485*, Cambridge, 1936

Lokeren, A. van (ed.), *Chartes et Documents de l'Abbaye de Saint Pierre au Mont Blandin à Gand*, 2 vols., Gand, 1868-72

Macleod, R. and Kelly, D., *The Ironside Diaries, 1937-40*, London, 1962

Mandy, W.H., 'Notes from the Kent Assize Rolls', *Transactions of the Greenwich Antiquarian Society*, I (1905-14), pp.133-54, 202-22, 282-312, 442-73

Masterman, L. (ed.), *Mary Gladstone (Mrs. Drew): Her Diaries and Letters*, London, 1930

Morgan, P. (ed.), *Domesday Book: Kent*, Chichester, 1983

Nicolson, N. (ed.), *The Diaries and Letters of Harold Nicolson, 1939-1945*, London, 1967

Roake, M. (ed.), *Religious Worship in Kent: The Census of 1851*. (Kent Archaeological Society: Kent Record Series, XXVII), Maidstone, 1999

Round, J.H. (ed.), *Calendar of Documents preserved in France illustrative of the History of Great Britain and Ireland*, I, 918-1206, London, 1899

Royal Commission on Ancient Monuments in England and Wales, Swindon: Unique Identifier 407284, 12 February 1997

Rotuli Parliamentorum, III & IV

Salzman, L.F. (ed.), *An Abstract of The Feet of Fines relating to the County of Sussex*, 3 vols., Sussex Record Society, Lewes, 1902-16

Shewell-Cooper, W.E., *Land Girl: a Handbook for the Women's Land Army*, with introduction by Dame Meriel Talbot, London, n.d. but 1940

Strabo, *Geography* (ed. Aujac, G.), Paris, 1969

Tremlow, J.A. (ed.), *Calendar of Entries in the Papal Registers relating to Great Britain and Ireland: Papal Letters*, vol. X, 1447-55, London, 1915

Valor Ecclesiasticus, 2 vols., London, 1810-16

Whitelock, D. (ed.), *English Historical Documents*, I, *c.500-1042*, 2nd edn., London, 1979

Williams, R. Harcourt (ed.), *The Salisbury-Balfour Correspondence, 1869-92*, Hertford, 1988

Williamson, P. (ed.), *The Modernisation of Conservative Politics: the Diaries and Letters of William Bridgeman, 1904-35*, London, 1988

Zell, M.L. (ed.), *Kent Feet of Fines: Henry VIII*, Kent Records, New Series, II, Ashford, 1995

(iii) Pre-1852 Monographs and Articles:

Bagshaw, S., *A History, Gazetteer and Directory of the County of Kent*, 2 vols., Sheffield, 1848

Banister, J., *A Synopsis of Husbandry, being Cursory Observations in the Several Branches of Rural Economy*, London, 1799

Boys, J., *A General View of the Agriculture of the County of Kent*, London, 1796; 2nd edn., 1805

Brayley, E.W., *The Beauties of England, Wales and Scotland*, vols. VIII, XVII and XVIII: Kent, London, 1808

Brayley, E.W., *A Topographical History of Surrey*, IV, London, 1850

Buckland, G., 'On the Farming of Kent', *Journal of the Royal Agricultural Society*, VI (1845), pp.251-302

Bysshe, Sir Edward, 'A Visitation of the County of Kent, 1663-68' (ed. Sir George J. Armytage), *Publications of the Harleian Society*, LIV, 1906

Caird, J., *English Agriculture in 1851-52*, London, 1852

Camden, W., *Britannia: Kent*, London, 1586

Cobbett, W., *Rural Rides*, 2 vols., London, 1830

Dearn, T.D.W., *An Historical, Topographical and Descriptive Account of the Weald of Kent*, London, 1814

Defoe, D., *A Tour thro' the Whole Island of Great Britain, 1724-26* (ed. Cole, G.D.H.), London, 1927

Fiennes, C., *The Journeys of Celia Fiennes (c.1685-1703)* (ed. Morris, C.), London, 1947

Greenwood, C., *The County of Kent*, London, 1838

Harris, J., *The History of Kent*, London, 1719

Hasted, E., *The History and Topographical Survey of Kent*, 2nd edn., 12 vols., London, 1797-1801

Ireland, W.H., *A New and Complete History of the County of Kent*, 4 vols., London, 1829

Kilburne, R., *A Topography or Survey of the County of Kent*, London, 1659

Lambarde, W., *A Perambulation of Kent*, London, 1570

Markham, G., *The Inrichment of the Weald of Kent*, London, 1625

Marshall, W., *The Rural Economy of the Southern Counties comprising Kent, Surrey, Sussex and the Isle of Wight*, London, 1799

Nichols, J., *Some Account of the Alien Priories and of Such Lands as they are known to have possessed in England and Wales*, 2 vols., 2nd edn., London, 1779

Philipot, J., 'The Visitation of Kent taken in the Years 1619-21' (ed. Hovenden, R.), *Publications of the Harleian Society*, XLII, 1898

Philipott, T., *Vilare Cantianum; or Kent Surveyed and Illustrated*, 2nd edn., London, 1776 (1st edn., 1659)

Tanner, T., *Notitia Monastica: or an Account of all the Abbies, Priories and Houses of Friers heretofore in England and Wales*, London, 1744

Young, A., *A Six Weeks Tour of the Southern Counties of England*, 3rd edn., London, 1772

Young, A., 'A Fortnight's Tour in Kent and Essex', *Annals of Agriculture*, II (1784), pp.33-104

(iv) Reference Books:

Anon, *A Bibliography of Kent and Supplement*, 2 vols., Maidstone, 1977-81

Arrowsmith, R.L. (ed.), *Charterhouse Register, 1769-1872*, Chichester, 1974

Baillie, G.H., Ilbert, C. and Clutton, C. (eds.), *Britten's Old Clocks and Watches and Their Makers*, 9th edn., London, 1982

Boase, F. (ed.), *Modern English Biography*, III, London, 1901

Bosworth, J. and Noller, T.N., *An Anglo-Saxon Dictionary*, Oxford, 1898

Buckland, W.E., *The Parish Registers and Records of the Diocese of Rochester*, Maidstone, 1912

Burke's Peerage and Baronetage

Butler, D. and G., *British Political Facts, 1900-94*, 7th edn., London, 1995

Cook, C. and Keith, B., *British Historical Facts, 1830-1900*, London, 1975

Cook, C. and Stevenson, J., *The Longman Handbook of Modern British History, 1714-1987*, 2nd edn., London, 1988

Cook, C. and Stevenson, J., *The Longman Handbook of Modern European History, 1763-1991*, 2nd edn., London, 1992.

Crockford's Clerical Directory, 1896

Felstead, A., Franklin, J. and Pinfield, L., *Directory of British Architects, 1834-1900*, London, 1993

Foster, J. (ed.), *Alumni Oxonienses, 1769-1872*, IV, Oxford, 1898

Fryde, E.B., Greenway, D.E., Porter, S. and Roy, I. (eds.), *Handbook of British Chronology*, 3rd edn., London, 1986

Kain, R.J.P. with Fry, R.E.J. and Holt, M.E., *An Atlas and Index of the Tithe Files of Mid- Nineteenth Century England and Wales*, Cambridge, 1986

Kelly's Directory of Kent, 1855, 1859, 1867, 1878, 1882, 1887, 1891, 1895, 1899, 1905, 1911, 1913, 1915, 1918, 1922, 1924, 1927, 1930, 1934, 1938.

Marechal, G., *Inventaris van de rekingen van de Pieterssabjii te Gent*, Brussels, 1984

Mills, A.H., *A Dictionary of English Places-Names*, Oxford, 1991

Pearson, S., Barnwell, P.S. and Adams, A.T. (eds.), *A Gazetteer of Medieval Houses in Kent*, London, 1994

Sawyer, P.H., *Anglo-Saxon Charters: an Annotated List and Bibliography*, London, 1968

Venn, J. (ed.), *Biographical History of Gonville and Caius College, 1348-1897*, II, Cambridge, 1898

Vincent, J.R. and Stenton, M. (eds.), *McCalmont's Parliamentary Poll Book: British Election Results, 1832-1918*, 8th edn., Brighton, 1971

Whitaker's Almanac

Who Was Who

(v) Journals and Newspapers:

The Builder

Edenbridge Courier (now *The Kent and Sussex Courier*, Edenbridge edition)

Sevenoaks Express and District Advertiser

Sussex Advertiser

The Times

Tunbridge Wells Journal

Tunbridge Wells Standard

(vi) Interviews with residents and former residents of Mark Beech:

Mr. Stephen Bagnold, 25 November 1997

Mr. Richard Ballard, 12 September 1997 and 2 April 1998

Mr. and Mrs. Peter Bellamy, 4 September and 10 December 1997

Mr. and Mrs. Henry Bluff, 7 September 1997

Mrs. Joan Cole, 25 November 1997 (letter)

Mrs. Margaret Dale, 4 January 1997

Mr. Ken Dann, 29 August 1997

Hon. Robin Denison-Pender, 10 April 1997

Mrs. Sybil Eadie, 14 September 1997

The late Mr. Bert Everest, 21 May 1973

Mrs. Pamela Furno, 5 May 1997

Mr. Chris Gillett, 15 March 1998

Mrs. Jane Gladstone, 5 January 1997

Mrs. Betty Goddard, 17 December 1997 and 24 January 1998 (telephone)

Mr. Stephen Gower, 10 January 1998 and 1 April 1998 (telephone)

Miss Doreen Graves, 10 January 1998

Mr. John Green, 4 January 1997

Mr. Donald Hepworth, 8 March 1997

Mr. Michael Holland, 31 March 1998

Miss Pat Humphreys, 7 December 1997 (telephone)

Mr. Peter Jamieson, 25 May 1997

The late Mr. Robert H. King, 24 April 1994

Mrs. John Leppard, 9 December 1997

Mrs. Walter Leppard, 8 January 1998

Mr. Ian Lewis, 7 January 1998

Mrs. Jill Linden, 18 May 1997

Miss Elsie Maynard, 20 December 1997

Dr. Brian Milner, 16 June 1997

Mrs. Gwen Mott, 12 and 19 January 1998 (letters)

Mr. Cecil Paynter, 2 January 1997

Mrs. Margery Peters, 25 November 1997 (telephone)

Mr. Alan Raeburn, 11 February 1997

Mr. Peter Rayner, 6 June 1997

Mrs. Anne Roberts, 5 June 1997
The late Mr. Jack Seymour, 4 June 1978
Dr. John Shaw, 5 January and 27 February 1998 (telephone)
Mr. John Skinner, 12 March 1997 (telephone)
Mr. Alan Smith, 12 October 1997
Mrs. Joanna Smith, 18 April 1997
Mrs. Gladys Smoult, 1 April 1998
Mr. A.W. Stephenson, 7 January 1997
Mr. Charles J. Talbot, 24 February 1997
Sister Teresa, 19 December 1997
Mr. Alf Voyce, 31 March 1998
The late Mr. Billy White, 23 November 1969

B. Secondary Sources:
(i) Monographs:
Abell, H.F., *Kent and the Great Civil War*, Ashford 1901
Armstrong, A. (ed.), *The Economy of Kent, 1640-1914*, Woodbridge, 1995
Arnold, C.J., *An Archaeology of the Early Anglo-Saxon Kingdoms*, 2nd edn., London, 1997
Askwith, B., *The Lytteltons: a Family Chronicle of the Nineteenth Century*, London, 1975
Baker, A.R.H. and Butlin, R.A., *Studies of the Field Systems in the British Isles*, Cambridge, 1973
Barlow, F., *Edward the Confessor*, London, 1970
Barlow, F., *The English Church, 1000-1066*, 2nd edn., London, 1979
Barlow, F., *The English Church, 1066-1154*, London, 1979
Bates, H.E., *Flying Bombs over England* (ed. Ogley, R.), Westerham, 1994
Battiscombe, G., *Mrs. Gladstone: the Portrait of a Marriage*, London, 1956
Bebbington, D.W., *William Ewart Gladstone: Faith and Politics in Victorian Britain*, Grand Rapids, USA, 1993
Beckett, A., *The Wonderful Weald*, London, 1921
Bellamy, J.G., *Crime and Public Order in England in the Later Middle Ages*, London, 1973
Beresford, M., *The Lost Villages of England*, 5th imp. rev., London, 1965
Beresford, M. and Hurst, J.G. (eds.), *Deserted Medieval Villages*, London, 1971
Bignell, A., *Kent Villages*, London, 1975
Bignell, A., *The Kent Village Book*, Newbury, 1986
Blair, J. (ed.), *Minsters and Parish Churches: The Local Church in Transition, 950-1200*, Oxford, 1988
Blair, P.H., *An Introduction to Anglo-Saxon England*, 2nd edn., Cambridge, 1977
Bolton, J.L., *The Medieval English Economy, 1150-1500*, London, 1980
Boorman, H.R.P. and Torr, V.J., *Kent Churches, 1954*, Maidstone, 1954
Boyle, J., *In Quest of Hasted*, Chichester, 1984
Brandon, P. and Short, B., *The South East from AD 1000*, London, 1990
Brooks, R.J., *Kent Airfields Remembered*, Newbury, 1990
Brown, R.A., *The Normans and the Norman Conquest*, 2nd edn., Woodbridge, 1985
Brown, R.J., *Old Houses and Cottages in Kent*, London, 1994
Brundage, A., *The Making of the New Poor Law*, London, 1984
Bushell, T.A., *Kent*, Chesham, 1976
Butler, J.R.M., *The History of the Second World: Grand Strategy, II, September 1939-June 1941*, London, 1957
Butler, P., *Gladstone: Church, State and Tractarianism*, Oxford, 1982
Cameron, K., *English Place-Names*, London, 1961
Cave-Brown, J., *Knights of the Shire of Kent, 1275-1831*, London, 1894
Chalklin, C.W., *Seventeenth Century Kent*, London, 1965
Chambers, J.D. and Mingay, G.E. (eds.), *The Agricultural Revolution, 1750-1880*, London, 1966
Checkland, S.G., *The Gladstones: a Family Biography, 1764-1851*, Cambridge, 1971
Church, R., *Kent*, London, 1948
Churchill, Sir Winston S., *The Second World War: II, Their Finest Hour*, London, 1949
Clapham, Sir John, *An Economic History of Britain: Free Trade and Steel, 1850-86*, Cambridge, 1932
Clark, P., *English Provincial Society from the Reformation to the Revolution: Religion, Politics and Society in Kent, 1500-1640*, Brighton, 1977
Clarke, B.F.L., *Church Buildings of the Nineteenth Century: a Study of the Gothic Revival in England*, London, 1938
Clarke, D. and Stoyel, A., *Otford in Kent: a History*, Otford, 1975
Cleere, H. and Crossley, D., *The Iron Industry of the Weald* (ed. Hodgkinson, J.), 2nd edn., Cardiff, 1995
Cling, G., *Kent*, London, 1903
Coleman, D.C., *The Economy of England, 1450-1750*, Oxford, 1977

Coleman, T., *The Navvies*, London, 1966

Collyer, D.G., *Buzz Bomb Diary*, Deal, 1994

Colvin, H. (ed.), *History of the King's Works* vol. IV, 1485-1660 (Part II), London, 1982

Copley, G.J., *An Archaeology of South-East England*, London, 1958

Copley, G.J., *English Place-Names and Their Origins*, London, 1968

Cowen, P., *A Guide to Stained Glass in Britain*, London, 1985

Cox, B., *English Inn and Tavern Names*, Nottingham, 1994

Cox, J.C., *Kent*, 2nd edn., London, 1915; 3rd edn., 1920; 4th edn., 1923; 5th edn. (rev. Johnston, P.M.), 1927; 6th edn. (rev. Johnston, P.M.), 1935; 7th edn. (rev. Jessup, F.W.), 1950

Cox, J.C., *Rambles in Kent*, London, 1913

Crosby, T.L., *The Two Mr. Gladstones*, New Haven, USA, 1997

Crouch, M., *Kent*, London, 1966

Cunliffe, B., *The Ancient Celts*, Oxford, 1997

Cunliffe, B., *Iron Age Communities in Britain: an Account of England, Scotland and Wales from the Seventh Century B.C. until the Roman Conquest*, London, 1974

Darby, H.C., *Domesday England*, Cambridge, 1977

Darby, H.C. and Campbell, E.M.J., *The Domesday Geography of South-East England*, Cambridge, 1962

Darby, R., *Journey through the Weald*, London, 1986

Deanesley, M., *The Pre-Conquest Church in England*, London, 1961

Delany, M.C., *The Historical Geography of the Wealden Iron Industry*, London, 1921

Detsicas, A., *The Cantiaci*, Gloucester, 1983

Donald, A., *The Posts of Sevenoaks in Kent: Biggin Hill to Edenbridge, Westerham to Wrotham, AD 1085-1985/86*, Tenterden, 1992

Drewett, P., Rudling, D. and Gardiner, M., *The South East to A.D. 1000*, London, 1988

Du Boulay, F.R.H., *The Lordship of Canterbury*, London, 1966

Duncan, L.L., *A History of the Borough of Lewisham*, London, 1908, republished with supplement, 1963

Duncan, L.L., *The Parish Churches of West Kent*, London, 1895

Dunlop, Sir John, *The Pleasant Town of Sevenoaks: a History*, Sevenoaks, 1964

Eales, R., *An Introduction to the Kent Domesday*, London, 1992

Eastman, J., *Historic Hever: the Church*, Hever, 1905

Ekwall, E., *The Concise Oxford Dictionary of English Place-Names*, 4th edn., Oxford, 1960

Ellis, H., *The London, Brighton and South Coast Railway*, London, 1960

Ellis, L.F., *History of the Second World War, United Kingdom Military Series: the War in France and Flanders, 1939-40*, London, 1953

Elton, C.I., *The Tenures of Kent*, London, 1867

Everitt, A.M., *The Community of Kent and the Great Rebellion, 1640-60*, Leicester, 1966

Everitt, A.M., *Continuity and Colonization: the Evolution of Kentish Settlement*, Leicester, 1986

Everitt, A.M., *The County Committee of Kent in the Civil War*, Leicester, 1957

Everitt, A.M., *Landscape and Community in England*, London, 1985

Evison, V.I., *The Fifth Century Invasions South of the Thames*, London, 1965

Ewing, G., *Cowden: the Records of a Wealden Parish*, Tunbridge Wells, 1926

Fawcett, J. (ed.), *Seven Victorian Architects*, London, 1976

Fielding, C.H., *The Records of Rochester*, Dartford, 1910

Finberg, H.P.R. and Thirsk, J. (eds.), *The Agrarian History of England and Wales: Vol. Ii, Prehistory* (ed. Piggott, S.), Cambridge, 1981; *Vol. Iii, 43-1042* (ed. Finberg, H.P.R.), Cambridge, 1972; *Vol. II, 1042-1350* (ed. Hallam, H.E.), Cambridge, 1988; *Vol. III, 1348-1500* (ed. Miller, E.), Cambridge, 1991; *Vol. IV, 1500-1640* (ed. Thirsk, J.), Cambridge, 1967; *Vol. V, 1640-1750* (ed. Thirsk, J., 2 parts), Cambridge, 1984-85; *Vol. VI, 1750-1850* (ed. Mingay, G.E.), Cambridge, 1989; *Vol. VIII, 1914-39* (ed. Whetham, E.M., Cambridge, 1978

Fisher, D.J.V., *The Anglo-Saxon Age, c.400-1042*, London, 1973

Fisher, T., *Prostitution and the Victorians*, Gloucester, 1997

Fletcher, S., *Victorian Girls: Lord Lyttelton's Daughters*, London, 1997

Floud, R. and McCloskey, D. (ed.), *The Economic History of Britain since 1700*, 2nd edn., 3 vols., Cambridge, 1994

Forde-Johnstone, J., *Hillforts of the Iron Age in England and Wales*, Liverpool, 1976

Forsberg, F., *A Contribution to a Dictionary of Old English Place-Names*, Uppsala, 1950

Frere, S.S., *Britannia: a History of Roman Britain*, London, 1967

Furley, R., *A History of the Weald of Kent*, 2 vols., London, 1871

Gardiner, S.R., *History of the Great Civil War, 1642-49*, 4 vols., London, 1886-94

Garrard, G.H., *A Survey of the Agriculture of Kent*, London, 1954

Gasquet, F.A., *The Black Death*, London, 1908

Gelling, M., *Signposts to the Past: Place-Names and the History of England*, 2nd edn., Chichester, 1988

Gilbert, M., *Churchill: A Life*, London, 1991

Girouard, M., *The Victorian Country House*, 2nd edn., New Haven, USA, 1979

Glover, J., *The Place Names of Kent*, London, 1976

Glynne, Sir Stephen, *Notes on the Churches of Kent*, London, 1877

Godfrey, C.J., *The Church in Anglo-Saxon England*, Cambridge, 1962

Goodsall, R.H., *The Medway and Its Tributaries*, London, 1955

Grant, I. and Maddren, N., *The Countryside at War*, London, 1975

Graves, C., *The Home Guard of Britain*, London, 1943

Gravett, K., *Timber and Brick Building in Kent*, London, 1971

Grayling, F., *County Churches: Kent*, 2 vols., London, 1913

Green, J.A., *The Aristocracy of Norman England*, Cambridge, 1997

Griffiths, R.A., *The Reign of Henry VI: the Exercise of Royal Authority, 1422-61*, London, 1981

Grosvenor, C. and Lord Stuart of Wortley, *The First Lady Wharncliffe and Her Family*, London, 1927

Guest, I., *Napoleon III in England*, London, 1952

Gulvin, K.R., *Kent Home Guard: a History*, Rochester, 1980

Hammond, J.L. and B., *The Village Labourer, 1760-1832*, 4th edn., London, 1927

Hammond, R.J., *History of the Second World War: Food*, 3 vols., London, 1951-62

Harmer, F.E., *Anglo-Saxon Writs*, Manchester 1952

Harrison, M., *Victorian Stained Glass*, London, 1980

Harvey, I.M.W., *Jack Cade's Rebellion of 1450*, Oxford, 1991

Harwood, B., *The High Weald in Old Photographs*, Stroud, 1990

Harwood, B., *The High Weald in Old Photographs: a Second Selection*, Stroud, 1993

Higham, N., *Rome, Britain and the Anglo-Saxons*, London, 1992

Hill, B.W., *British Parliamentary Parties, 1742-1832*, London, 1985

Hinton, D.A., *Archaeology, Economics and Society: England from the fifth to the fifteenth century*, London, 1990

Hobsbawm, E.J. and Rudé, G., *Captain Swing*, rev. edn., London, 1973

Hodgkin, R.H., *A History of the Anglo-Saxons*, 2nd edn., Oxford, 1939

Homan, R., *The Victorian Churches of Kent*, Chichester, 1984

Horrox, R. (ed.), *The Black Death*, Manchester, 1994

Horsley, J.W., *Place-Names in Kent*, Maidstone, 1921

Hutchinson, H.G., *The Life of Sir John Lubbock, Lord Avebury*, 2 vols., London, 1914

Hull, A.D. and Russell, E.J., *A Report on the Agriculture and Soils of Kent, Surrey and Sussex*, London, 1911

Irwin, J., *Place-Names of Edenbridge*, Edenbridge, 1964

Ives, E.W., *Anne Boleyn*, Oxford, 1986

Jacob, E.F., *The Fifteenth Century, 1399-1485*, Oxford, 1961

Jacoby, N.M., *A Journey Through Medicine*, London, 1991

Jagger, P.J., *Gladstone: the Making of a Christian Politician*, Allison Park, USA, 1991

Jenkins, R., *Gladstone*, London, 1995

Jessup, F.W., *The Archaeology of Kent*, London, 1930

Jessup, F.W., *A History of Kent*, London, 1977

Jessup, F.W., *Kent History Illustrated*, Maidstone, 1966

Jessup, R.F., *South-East England*, London, 1970

Johnston, J.B., *The Place-Names of England and Wales*, London, 1915

Jolliffe, J.E.A., *Pre-Feudal England: the Jutes*, London, 1933

Jones A., *The Politics of Reform, 1884*, Cambridge, 1972

Jones, E.L., *The Development of English Agriculture, 1815-73*, London, 1968

Jones, P. and Pennick, N., *A History of Pagan Europe*, London, 1995

Jones, T. Barington, *Kent: At the Opening of the Twentieth Century, with Contemporary Biographies by W.T. Pike*, Brighton, 1904

Kain, R.J.P. and Oliver, R., *The Tithe Maps of England and Wales*, Cambridge, 1995

Kain, R.J.P. and Prince, H.C., *The Tithe Surveys of England and Wales*, Cambridge, 1985

Karlstrom, S., *Old English Compound Place-Names in ING*, Uppsala, 1927

Kaye-Smith, S., *The Weald of Kent and Sussex*, London, 1953

Keith-Lucas, B., *Parish Affairs: the Government of Kent under George III*, Maidstone, 1986

Kellet, J.R., *The Impact of the Railways on Victorian Cities*, London, 1969

Kemble, J.M., *The Saxons of England*, 2 vols. (rev. edn., Birch, W. de G.), London, 1876

Kerridge, E., *The Agricultural Revolution*, London, 1967

Kidner, R.J., *The Oxted Line*, Limpsfield, 1972

Knowles, D., *The Monastic Order in England: a History of Its Development from the Times of St Dunstan to the Fourth Lateran Council, 940-1216*, 2nd edn., Cambridge, 1963

Knowles, D., *The Religious Houses of Medieval England*, London, 1940

Knowles, D. and Hadcock, R.N., *Medieval Religious Houses: England and Wales*, London, 1953

Lebey, A., *Les trois coup d'états de Louis-Napoléon Bonaparte*, Paris, 1906

Leach, P.E. (ed.), *Archaeology in Kent to A.D. 1500*, London, 1982

Loomes, B., *Watchmakers and Clockmakers of the World*, 2nd edn., London, 1947

Longmate, N., *King Cholera: the Biography of a Disease*, London, 1966

Loyd, L.C., *The Origins of Some Anglo-Norman Families* (eds. Clay, C.T. and Douglas, D.C.), Leeds, 1951 (Harleian Society Publications, vol. CIII)

Loyn, H.R., *The Making of the English Nation: From the Anglo-Saxons to Edward I*, London, 1991

Lyttelton, E., *Alfred Lyttelton: an Account of His Life*, London, 1917

Lyttelton, Sir Neville, *Eighty Years: Soldiering, Politics, Games*, London, 1929

McClure, E., *British Place-Names*, London, 1972

McKisack, M., *The Fourteenth Century, 1307-99*, Oxford, 1969

Mansfield, A., *Edward Stuart Talbot and Charles Gore*, London, 1935

Margary, I.D., *Roman Roads in Britain*, 3rd edn., London, 1973

Margary, I.D., *Roman Ways in the Weald*, 3rd rev. edn., London, 1965

Marshall, C.F.D., *A History of the Southern Railway*, 2nd edn. (rev. Kidner, R.W.), London, 1963

Mason, R.T., *Framed Buildings of the Weald*, 2nd edn., Horsham, 1969

Matthew, H.C.G., *Gladstone, 1809-1898*, 2 vols., London, 1986-95

Mathias, P., *The First Industrial Nation: an Economic History of Britain, 1700-1914*, 2nd edn., London, 1983

Mawer, A. and Stenton, Sir F.M., *Introduction to the Survey of English Place-Names*, Part I, Cambridge, 1925

Maynard, D.C., *Old Inns of Kent*, London, 1925

Mayr-Harting, H., *The Coming of Christianity to Anglo-Saxon England*, London, 1972

Millett, M., *The Romanisation of Britain*, Cambridge, 1990

Mitchell, V. and Smith, K., *Branch Lines to Tunbridge Wells*, Midhurst, 1986

Myres, J.N.L., *The English Settlements*, Oxford, 1986

Namier, Sir Lewis and Brooke, J., *The History of Parliament: the House of Commons, 1754-90, I, Introductory Survey, Constituencies, Appendices*, London, 1964

Newman, J., *West Kent and the Weald*, 'Buildings of England' (ed. Sir Nikolaus Pevsner), 2nd edn., London, 1976

Newton, J., *Chiddingstone: an Historical Exploration*, Rainham, 1985

O'Brien, T.H., *The Official History of the Second World War: Civil Defence*, London, 1955

Ogley, R., *Doodlebugs and Rockets: the Battle of the Flying Bomb*, Westerham, 1992

Ogley, R., *In the Wake of the Hurricane*, Westerham, 1987

Ogley, R., *Kent: a Chronicle of the Century*, 3 vols. to date, Westerham, 1996-98

Ogley, R., *Kent at War: the Unconquered County, 1939-1945*, Westerham, 1994

Oleson, T.J., *The Witenagemot in the Reign of Edward the Confessor: a Study in the Constitutional History of Eleventh Century England*, Toronto, 1955

Oppermann, O. von, *Die alteren Urkunden des Klosters Blandinium und die Anfarge des Stadt Gent*, 2 vols., Utrecht, 1928

Oswald, A., *Country Houses of Kent*, London, 1933

Owen, G.R., *Rites and Religions of the Anglo-Saxons*, London, 1981

Pearson, S., *The Medieval Houses of Kent: an Historical Analysis*, London, 1994

Pelling, H., *Social Geography of British Elections, 1885-1910*, London, 1967

Phillips, C.J., *A History of the Sackville Family*, 2 vols., London, 1929

Platt, C., *The Great Rebuilding of Tudor and Stuart England*, London, 1994

Pollard, S., *The Development of the British Economy, 1914-90*, 4th edn., London, 1992

Poole, A.L., *From Domesday to Magna Carta, 1087-1216* (2nd edn.), Oxford, 1955

Popplewell, L., *Bournemouth Railway History: an Exposure of Victorian Engineering Fraud*, Sherborne, 1973

Powicke, Sir M., *The Thirteenth Century, 1216-1307*, 2nd edn., Oxford, 1962

Quiney, A., *Kent Houses*, London, 1993

Rayner, C., *Sevenoaks Past with the Villages of Holmesdale*, Chichester, 1997

Reaney, P.H., *The Origins of English Place-Names*, London, 1960

Rivet, A.L.F. and Smith, C., *The Place-Names of Roman Britain*, Princeton, USA, 1979

Roake, M. and Whyman, J. (eds.), *Essays in Kentish History*, London, 1973

Robbins, K., *The Eclipse of a Great Power: Modern Britain, 1870-1992*, 2nd edn., London, 1994

Rootes, A., *Front Line County: Kent at War, 1939-45*, London, 1980

Rose, M.E., *The Relief of Poverty, 1834-1914*, London, 1972

Roskell, J.R., *The Commons and Their Speakers in English Parliaments, 1376-1523*, Manchester, 1965

Sackville-West, V., *The Women's Land Army*, London, 1944

Salway, P., *Roman and Anglo-Saxon Britain*, Oxford, 1981

Salzman, L.F., *The History of the Parish of Hailsham, the Abbey of Otham and the Priory of Michelham*, Lewes, 1901

Saul, N.E., *Scenes from Provincial Life: Knightly Families in Sussex, 1280-1400*, Oxford, 1986

Sawyer, P.H., *From Roman Britain to Norman England*, London, 1978

Schubert, H.G., *History of the British Iron and Steel Industry, c.450 B.C.-A.D. 1775*, London, 1957

Searle, E., *Lordship and Community: Battle Abbey and Its Bainlieu*, 1066-1538, Toronto, 1974

Smith, A.H. (ed.), *English Place-Name Elements*, 2 vols., Cambridge, 1956

Smith, A.P., *King Alfred the Great*, Oxford, 1995

Smith, C.R., *Collectanea Antiqua: Notices of Ancient Remains*, vol. VII, London, 1890

Smith, R.A.L., *Canterbury Cathedral Priory*, Cambridge, 1943

Somers-Cocks, H.L. and Boyson, V.F., *Edenbridge*, Edenbridge, 1912

Stacey, C.P., *The Official History of the Canadian Army in the Second World War*, 3 vols., Ottawa, 1955-66

Stenton, Sir Frank M., *Anglo-Saxon England*, 3rd edn., Oxford, 1971

Stephenson, Lady Gwendolen, *Edward Stuart Talbot, 1844-1934*, London, 1936

Stevenson, J., *British Society, 1914-45*, London, 1984

Straker, E., *Wealden Iron*, London, 1931

Sutton, R.H., *Historical Notes on Wythyham, Hartfield and Ashdown Forest*, Tunbridge Wells, 1902

Syms, J.A., *Kent County Churches*, Sittingbourne, 1985

Syms, J.A., *Kent County Churches Continued*, Sittingbourne, 1987

Syms, J.A., *Kent County Churches Concluded*, Sittingbourne, 1989

Talbot, E.S., *Memories of Early Life*, London, 1924

Taylor, C., *Village and Farmstead: a History of Rural Settlement In England*, London, 1983

Thirsk, J., *Agricultural Regions and Agrarian History in England, 1500-1750*, London, 1987

Thomas, C., *Christianity in Roman Britain to A.D. 500*, London, 1981

Thompson, E.M., *The Carthusian Order in England*, London, 1930

Thompson, F.M.L., *English Landed Society in the Nineteenth Century*, London, 1963

Thorne, R.G., *The History of Parliament: the House of Commons, 1790-1820, I and II*, London, 1986

Topley, W., *The Geology of the Weald*, London, 1876

Varenbergh, E., *Histoire des relations diplomatiques entre le Comté de Flandre et l'Angleterre au moyen age*, Bruxelles, 1874

Vigar, J.E., *Exploring Kent Churches*, Stroud, 1992

Vincent, J.R., *Pollbooks: How the Victorians Voted*, Cambridge, 1967

Wallenberg, J.K., *Kentish Place-Names*, Uppsala, 1931

Wallenberg, J.K., *The Place-Names of Kent*, Uppsala, 1934

Ward, G., *Sevenoaks Essays*, London, 1931

Ward, S., *War in the Countryside, 1939-45*, London, 1988

Warnicke, R.M., *The Rise and Fall of Anne Boleyn*, Cambridge, 1989

Warren, J. (ed.), *Wealden Buildings*, Horsham, 1990

Wheatley, R., *Operation Sea Lion: German Plans for the Invasion of England, 1939-42*, Oxford, 1962

White, H.P., *The Forgotten Railways of the South East of England*, Newton Abbot, 1967

White, H.P., *A Regional History of the Railways of Great Britain: II, Southern England*, London, 1961

White, J.T., *A Country Diary: Kent*, Sheerness, 1974

White, J.T., *The South-East Down and Weald: Kent, Surrey and Sussex*, London, 1977

Whitehead, Sir Charles, *A Sketch of the Agriculture of Kent*, London, 1899

Wilson, D., *Anglo-Saxon Paganism*, London, 1992

Wilson, T., *The Myriad Faces of War: Britain and the Great War, 1914-1918*, Oxford, 1986

Witney, K.P., *The Jutish Forest: a Study of the Weald of Kent from 450 to 1380 A.D.*, London, 1976

Witney, K.P., *The Kingdom of Kent*, Chichester, 1982

Wooldridge, S.W. and Goldring, F., *The Weald*, London, 1953

Yarwood, D., *The Architecture of England*, 2nd edn., London, 1967

Yates, N., *Kent and the Oxford Movement*, Maidstone, 1983

Yates, N., Hume, R. and Hastings, P. (eds.), *Religion and Society in Kent, 1640-1914*, Woodbridge, 1994

Victoria County History: Kent, vols. I-III, London, 1908-32; *Surrey*, vols. I-IV, London, 1902-12; *Sussex*, vols. I-III, London, 1905-35; *Northamptonshire*, vols. II-III, London, 1906-30

Winstanley, M.J., *Kent at the Turn of the Century*, Folkestone, 1978

Ziegler, P., *The Black Death*, London, 1969

(ii) Articles and Pamphlets:

Addleshaw, G.W.O., 'The Beginnings of the Parochial System', St Anthony's Hall Publications, No. 3, York, 1953

Addleshaw, G.W.O., 'The Development of the Parochial System from Charlemagne (768-814) to Urban II (1088-89),' St Anthony's Hall Publications, No. 6, York, 1954

Anon, 'Charters of Cumbwell Priory, Part I', *Arch. Cant.*, V (1863), pp.194-222

Anon, *Cowden in the Great War*, Tunbridge Wells, 1928

Anon, *Hever Castle*, Hever, 1979

Anon, *Simple Guide to Hever Church*, Hever, 1951

Arnold, R., 'The Revolt of the Fields' in Kent, 1872-79', *Past and Present*, 64 (1974), pp.71-95

Baker, A.R.H., 'Field Systems in the Vale of Holmesdale', *Agricultural History Review*, XIV (1966), pp.1-24

Baker, A.R.H., 'Open Fields and Partible Inheritance on a Kent Manor', *Economic History Review*, 2nd Ser., XVII (1964-65), pp.1-23

Baker, A.R.H., 'Some Early Kentish Estate Maps and a Note on their Portrayal of Field Boundaries', *Arch. Cant.*, LXXVII (1962), pp.177-84

Baker, A.R.H., 'Some Fields and Farms in Medieval Kent', *Arch. Cant.*, LXXX (1965), pp.152-74

Baring, F., 'The Conqueror's Footsteps in Domesday', *EHR*, XIII (1898), pp.17-25

Barlow, F., 'Edward the Confessor's Early Life, Character and Attitudes', *EHR*, LXXX (1965), pp.225-51

Bird, D.G., 'Dry Hill Camp, Lingfield', *Surrey Archaeological Society Bulletin*, No. 209 (1986), p.4

Blencowe, R.W., 'Cowden and Its Neighbours', *Arch. Cant.*, I (1858), pp.111-23

Boyle, J., 'Hasted in Perspective', *Arch. Cant.*, C (1984), pp.295-304

Boyle, T., *Holy Trinity, Mark Beech*, Mark Beech, 1997

Boyle, T., 'The Mark Beech Riots, 1866', SAC, CXVI (1978), pp.11-18

Boyle, T., '1866 and All That', *Aspects of Edenbridge*, No. 5 (1983), pp.56-57

Bridbury, A.R., 'Before the Black Death', *EHR*, 2nd Ser., XXX (1977), pp.393-410

Bridbury, A.R., 'The Black Death', *EHR*, 2nd Ser., XXVI (1973), pp.577-92

Brooks, N.P., 'The Career of St Dunstan', in Ramsay, N., Sparks, M. and Tatton-Brown, T. (eds.), *St Dunstan: His Life, Times and Cult*, Woodbridge, 1992, pp.1-23

Brooks, N.P., 'The Creation and Early Structure of the Kingdom of Kent', in Bassett, S. (ed.), *The Origins of the Anglo-Saxon Kingdoms*, Leicester, 1989, pp.55-74

Brooks, N.P., 'The Organization and Achievement of the Peasants of Kent and Essex in 1381', in Mayr-Harting, H. and Moore, R.I. (eds.), *Studies in Medieval History presented to R.H.C. Davis*, London, 1985, pp.247-70

Buckatzsch, E.J., 'The Geographical Distribution of Wealth in England, 1086-1843', *EHR*, 2nd Ser., III (1950-51), pp.180-202

Cato, J., 'Religious Change under Henry V', in Harris, G.L. (ed.), *Henry V: the Practice of Kingship*, Oxford, 1985, pp.97-116

Chalklin, C.W., 'The Rural Economy of a Kentish Wealden Parish', *Agricultural History Review*, X (1962), pp.29-45

Chaplais, P., 'The Original Charters of Herbert and Gervase, Abbots of Westminster, 1121-57', in Barnes, P.M. and Slade, C.F. (eds.), *A Medieval Miscellany for Doris Mary Stenton*, Pipe Rolls Society, LXXIV, London, 1962, pp.89-110

Cleere, H., 'The Roman Iron Industry in the Weald and Its Connexion with the Classis Britannica', *Arch. Cant.*, CXXXI (1974), pp.171-99

Cooper, G.M., 'Some Account of Michelham Priory in Aldington', SAC, VI (1853), pp.129-63

Cooper, W.D., 'Jack Cade's Followers in Kent', *Arch. Cant.*, VII (1868), pp.233-71

Cooper, W.D., 'The Participation of Sussex in Cade's Rising', SAC, XVIII (1866), pp.17-56

Cooper, W.D., 'Proofs of Age of Sussex Families: Edward II-Edward IV', SAC, XII (1860), pp.23-44

Cox, E.A. and Dittmer, B.R., 'The Tithe Files of the Mid-Nineteenth Century', *Agricultural History Review*, XIII (1965), pp.1-16

Dewey, P.E., 'Food Policy and Production in the United Kingdom, 1914-18', TRHS, 5th Ser., XXX (1980), pp.71-89

Dhondt, J., 'La donation d'Elftrude à Saint-Pierre de Gand', *Académie royale de Belgique: Bulletin de la Commission royale d'histoire*, CV (1940), pp.117-64

Dodgson, J.M., 'Place-names from *ham*, distinguished from *hamm* Names, in relation to the settlement of Kent, Surrey and Sussex', *Anglo-Saxon England*, 2 (1973), pp.1-50

Dodgson, J.M., 'The Significance of the Distribution of the English Place-Name in *ingas/inga* in South East England', in Cameron, K. (ed.), *Place-Name Evidence for the Anglo-Saxon and Scandinavian Settlements*, London, 1975, pp.27-50

Du Boulay, F.R.H., 'Denns, Droving and Dangers', *Arch. Cant.*, LXXVI (1961), pp.75-90

Dumbreck, W.V., 'The Lowy of Tonbridge', *Arch. Cant.*, LXXII (1958), pp.138-42

Duncan, L.L., 'The Rectory of Cowden', *Arch. Cant.*, XXI (1896), pp.87-94

Duncan, L.L., 'The Renunciation of the Papal Authority by the Clergy of West Kent, 1534', *Arch. Cant.*, XXII (1897), pp.293-307

Everitt, A.M., 'The Making of the Landscape of Kent', *Arch. Cant.*, XCII (1977), pp.1-32

Field, D. and Nicolaysen, P., 'Surrey Earthworks', *Surrey Archaeological Society Bulletin*, No. 169 (1980), pp.5-6

Flaherty, W.E., 'The Great Rebellion in Kent of 1381, illustrated from Public Records', *Arch. Cant.*, III (1864), pp.65-78

Frere, S.S., 'An Iron Age Site at West Clandon, Surrey and some aspects of Iron Age and Romano-British Culture in the Wealden Area', *Archaeological Journal*, CI (1944), pp.50-67

Galbraith, V.H., 'Monastic Foundation Charters of the Eleventh and Twelfth Centuries', *Cambridge Historical Journal*, IV (1932-34), pp.296-7

George, R.H., 'The Contribution of Flanders to the Conquest of England 1066-86', *Revue Belge de Philologie et d'Histoire*, V (1926), pp.81-99

Glasscock, R.E., 'The Distribution of Lay Wealth in Kent, Surrey and Sussex in the early Fourteenth Century', *Arch. Cant.*, LXXX (1965), pp.61-8

Gray, P.J., 'Dry Hill and Its Origins', *Aspects of Edenbridge*, No. 2 (1974), pp.53-5

Gray, P.J., 'Hever Brocas', *Aspects of Edenbridge*, No. 7 (1987), pp.46-8

Greenstreet, J., 'Assessment of the Parish of Cowden, A.D. 1599', *Arch. Cant.*, XXI (1897), pp.392-3

Grierson, P., 'The Relations between England and Flanders before the Norman Conquest', TRHS, 4th Ser., XXIII (1941), pp.71-112

Griffiths, W., 'Edenbridge During the First Five Months of the Great War', *Aspects of Edenbridge*, No. 9 (1991), pp.34-43

Harvey, D.W., 'Fruit Growing in Kent in the Nineteenth Century', *Arch. Cant.*, LXXIX (1964), pp.95-108

Harvey, D.W., 'Locational Change in the Kentish Hop Industry and the Analysis of Land Use Patterns', *Transactions of the Institute of British Geographers*, No. 33 (1963), pp.123-44

Hawkes, C.F.C., 'The Jutes of Kent', in Harden, D.B. (ed.), *Dark-Age Britain: Studies presented to E.T. Leeds*, London, 1956, pp.91-111

Herbert, B.K., 'The London to Lewes Roman Road', *Wealden Iron*, 2nd Ser., No. 12 (1992), pp.4-8; No. 13 (1993), pp.5-12; No. 14 (1994), pp.4-8

Hewlett, G., 'Reconstructing an Historical Landscape from Field and Documentary Evidence: Otford in Kent', *Agricultural History Review*, XXI (1973), pp.94-110

Higgs, D.G., 'The Manor of Hever Brocas and the Brocas Family', *Aspects of Edenbridge*, No. 7 (1987), pp.42-5

Hoskins, W.G., 'The Great Rebuilding', *History Today*, V (1955), pp.104-11

Hoskins, W.G., 'The Rebuilding of Rural England, 1570-1640', *Past and Present*, 4 (1953), pp.44-59

Hoyt, R.S., 'A Pre-Domesday Kentish Assessment List', in Barnes, P.M. and Slade, C.F. (eds.), *A Medieval Miscellany for Doris Mary Stenton*, Pipe Roll Society, LXXIV, London, 1962, pp.189-202

Jacob, W.M., 'The Diffusion of Tractarianism: Wells Theological College, 1840-49', *Southern History*, V (1983), pp.189-220

Jalland, P., 'Mr. Gladstone's Daughters', in Kinzler, B.E. (ed.), *The Gladstonian Turn of Mind*, Toronto, 1985, pp.97-122

James, A., 'What's in a Name: a Note on Heathen Street, Stick Hill', *Aspects of Edenbridge*, No.9 (1991), pp.44-8

Jenkins, R., 'A Romano-Gaulish Statuette from Cowden, Kent', *Arch. Cant.*, LXXXVI (1971), pp.203-5

Johnson, C., review of Oppermann: *Die alteren Urkunden des Klosters Blandinium*, *EHR*, XLIII (1928), pp.615-7

Jones, G.R.J., 'Multiple Estates and Early Settlement', in Sawyer, P.H. (ed.), *English Medieval Settlement*, London, 1979, pp.20-9

Jones, G.R.J., 'Settlement Patterns in Anglo-Saxon England', *Antiquity*, XXXV (1961), pp.221-32

Kain, R.J.P., 'The Tithe Commutation Surveys', *Arch. Cant.*, LXXXIX (1974), pp.101-18

Keith-Lucas, B., 'Kentish Turnpikes', *Arch. Cant.*, C (1984), pp.345-69

Knocker, H.W., 'The Valley of Holmesdale: Its Evolution and Development', *Arch. Cant.*, XXXI (1915), pp. 155-77

Knocker, H.W., 'The Evolution of Holmesdale, 2: the Village Communities', *Arch. Cant.*, XL (1928), pp.159-63

Knocker, H.W., 'The Evolution of Holmesdale, 3: the Manor of Sundrish', *Arch. Cant.*, XLIV (1932), pp, 189-210

Laslett, P., 'The Gentry of Kent in 1640', *Cambridge Historical Journal*, IX (1948), pp.148-77

Leveson-Gower, Sir George, 'Notices of the Family of Uvedale of Titsey, Surrey and Wickham, Hampshire', *SuAC*, III (1865), pp.63-192

Loyn, H.R., 'The Hundred in England in the Tenth and Early Eleventh Centuries', in Hearder, H. and Loyn, H.R. (eds.), *British Government and Administration*, Cardiff, 1974, pp.1-15

Lynch, M.J. 'Was Gladstone a Tractarian? W.E. Gladstone and the Oxford Movement, 1833-45', *Journal of Religious History*, VIII, (1975), pp.364-89

MacMichael, N.H., 'Filston in Shoreham: a Note on the Place-Name', *Arch. Cant.*, LXXVII (1962), pp.133-41

Malden, H.E., 'Domesday Survey of Surrey', in Dove, P.E. (ed.), *Domesday Studies*, II, London, 1891, pp.450-74

Margary, I.D., 'The Early Development of Tracks in and near East Grinstead', *Sussex Notes and Queries*, XI (1946-47), pp.77-81

Margary, I.D., 'An Early Trans-Wealden Trackway', *Sussex Notes and Queries*, XI (1946-47), pp.62-4

Margary, I.D., 'A New Roman Road to the Coast: I, The Road from Edenbridge to Maresfield through Ashdown Forest', *SAC*, LXXIII (1932), pp.33-82

Margary, I.D., 'Notes on Dry Hill Camp, Lingfield', *SuAC*, LXI (1964), p.100

Margary, I.D., 'Roman Communications between Kent and the East Sussex Ironworks', *SAC*, LXXXVI (1949), pp.22-41

Margary, I.D., 'Roman Roads in West Kent', *Arch. Cant.*, LIX (1946), pp.29-63

Martin, A.R., 'The Alien Priory of Lewisham', *Transactions of the Greenwich and Lewisham Antiquarian Society*, III (1924-34), pp.103-27

Mate, M. 'The Agrarian Economy after the Black Death: the Manors of Canterbury Cathedral Priory, 1348-91', *EHR*, 2nd Ser., XXXVII (1984), pp.341-54

Money, J.H., 'Excavations at High Rocks, Tunbridge Wells, 1954-56, Appendix F: Sandstone Outcrops in the Weald', *SAC*, XCVIII (1960), pp.218-21

Money, J.H., 'Excavations in the Iron Age Hill-Fort at High Rocks near Tunbridge Wells, 1957-61', *SAC*, CVI (1968), pp.158-205

Montmorency, J.E.G. de, 'Early and Medieval Records of Greenwich', *Transactions of the Greenwich Antiquarian Society*, I (1905-14), pp.13-33

More, B.R. 'The Parish of Hever', *Aspects of Edenbridge*, No. 2 (1981), pp.20-42

Morgan, M.M., 'The Suppression of the Alien Priories', *History*, XXVI (1941-42), pp.206-12

Mortimer, R., 'The Beginnings of the Honour of Clare', in Brown, R.A. (ed.), *Proceedings of the Battle Conference on Anglo-Norman Studies*, III (1980), Woodbridge, 1981, pp.119-41

Mortimer, R., 'Land and Service: the Tenants of the Honour of Clare', in Brown, R.A. (ed.), *Proceedings of the Battle Conference on Anglo-Norman Studies*, VIII (1985), Woodbridge, 1986, pp.177-98

Page, W., 'Some Remarks on the Churches of the Domesday Survey', *Archaeologia*, LXVI (1915), pp.61-102

Payne, G., 'Report on Finds in Kent', *Proceedings of the Society of Antiquaries of London*, 2nd Ser. XIV (1891-93), pp.33-4

Philp, B.J., 'Romano-British West Kent, A.D. 43-100', *Arch. Cant.*, LXXVIII (1963), pp.74-82

Pollins, H., 'Railway Contractors and the Finance of Railway Development in Britain', *Journal of Transport History*, I (1957), pp.40-63

Reaney, P.H., 'Place Names and Early Settlement in Kent', *Arch. Cant.*, LXXVI (1961), pp.58-74

Reaney, P.H., 'A Survey of Kent Place-Names', *Arch. Cant.*, LXXIII, (1959), pp.62-74.

Richmond, C.F., 'Fauconberg's Kentish Rising of May, 1471', *EHR*, LXXV (1970), pp.671-92

Saint-Genois, J. de, 'Précis analytique: Des documents historiques concernant les relations de l'ancien comté de Flandre avec l'Angleterre, conservés aux archives de la Flandre Orientale', *Messages des Sciences Historiques de Belgique* (1842), pp.238-61

Saint-Genois, J. de, 'Note sur le sejour du roi Edouarde-le-Confesseur à l'Abbaye Saint-Pierre à Gand, en 1006, et sur les biens possédés par cette abbaye en Angleterre', *Bulletin de l'Acadèmie Royale des Sciences et Belles-Lettres de Bruxelles*, IX (1842), pp.253-67, 625-8

Salzman, L.F., 'Some Sussex Domesday Tenants', SAC, LVII (1915), pp.162-79

Salzman, L.F., 'Some Sussex Domesday Tenants: II, the Family of Dene', SAC, LVIII (1916), pp.170-89

Scott, J.O., 'Cowden Church, Kent', *Arch. Cant.*, XXI (1895) pp.87-94

Sisam, K., 'Anglo-Saxon Royal Genealogies', *Proceedings of the British Academy*, XXXIX (1953), pp.287-348

Smith, A., 'Regional Differences in Crop Production in Medieval Kent., *Arch. Cant.*, LXXVIII, (1963), pp.145-60

Stevenson, W.H., 'Trinoda Necessitas', *EHR*, XXIX (1914), pp.689-703

Straker, E. and Margary, I.D., 'Ironworks and Communications in the Weald in Roman Times', *The Geographical Journal*, XCII (1938), pp.35-60

Talbot, J.G., *Markbeech, 1852-1902*, London, 1903

Tanner, H.J., 'The Expansion of the Power and Influence of the Counts of Boulogne under Eustace II', Chibnall, M. (ed.), *Proceedings of the Battle Conference on Anglo-Norman Studies*, XIV (1992), Woodbridge, 1993, pp. 251-86.

Tatton-Brown, T., 'The Towns of Kent', in Haslam, J. (ed.), *Anglo-Saxon Towns in Southern England*, Chichester, 1984, pp.1-36

Tebbutt, C.F., 'Notes on Dry Hill Camp, Lingfield', SuAC, LXVI (1970), pp.119-20

Thirsk, J., 'Hasted as Historian', *Arch. Cant.*, CXI (1993), pp.1-15

Tomkinson, A., 'Retainers at the Tournament of Dunstable, 1309', *EHR*, LXXIV (1959), pp.70-89

Turner, E., 'Ancient Parochial Account Book of Cowden', SAC, XX (1868), pp.91-119

Vamplew, V., 'Tithes and Agriculture: Some Comments on Commutation', *EHR*, 2nd Ser., XXXIV (1981), pp.115-19

Vanden-Haute, C., 'Notes sur quelques chartes de l'Abbaye de Saint-Pierre à Gand', *Bulletin de la Commission Royale d'Histoire*, LXXI (1902), pp.401-11

Wallenberg, J.K., 'Studies in Old Kentish Charters', *Studia Neophilologica*, I (1928), pp.34-44

Walne, P., 'The Records of the Tithe Redemption Commission', *Journal of the Society of Archivists*, I (1955-59)

Ward, G., 'Hengest', *Arch. Cant.*, LXI (1948), pp.77-97

Ward, G., 'The List of Saxon Churches in the *Domesday Monachron* and the *White Book of St Augustine's*', *Arch. Cant.*, XLV (1933), pp.60-89

Ward, G., 'The List of Saxon Churches in the *Textus Roffensis*', *Arch. Cant.*, XLIV (1932), pp.39-59

Ward, G., 'The Manor of Lewisham and Its Wealden "Dens" ', *Transactions of the Greenwich and Lewisham Antiquarian Society*, IV (1939), pp.112-7

Ward, G., 'Note on the Yokes of Otford', *Arch. Cant.*, LXII (1950), pp.147-56

Ward, J.C., 'Fashions in Monastic Endowments: the Foundations of the Clare Family, 1066-1314', *Journal of Ecclesiastical History*, XXXII (1981), pp.427-51

Ward, J.C., 'The Lowy of Tonbridge and the Lands of the Clare Family, 1066-1217', *Arch. Cant.*, XCVI (1980), pp.119-32

Ward, J.C., 'Royal Services and Reward: the Clare Family and the Crown, 1066-1154', in Brown, R.A. (ed.), *Proceedings of the Battle Conference on Anglo-Norman Studies*, XI (1988), Woodbridge, 1989, pp. 261-78

Willsmer, R.J., 'Edenbridge Manors', *Aspects of Edenbridge*, No. 8 (1989), pp.27-34

Willsmer, R.J., 'A Fresh Look at Some Local Place Names', *Aspects of Edenbridge*, No. 7 (1987), pp.25-30

Winbolt, S.E. and Margary, I.D., 'Dry Hill Camp, Lingfield', SuAC, XLI (1933), pp.79-92

Witney, K.P., 'The Economic Position of Husbandmen at the Time of Domesday Book: a Kentish Perspective', *EHR*, 2nd Ser., XXXVII (1984), pp.23-34

Witney, K.P., 'The Woodland Economy of Kent, 1066-1348', *Agricultural History Review*, XXXVIII (1990), pp.20-39

Wormald, 'Sir Geoffrey Elton's *English*: A View from the Early Middle Ages', TRHS, 6th Ser., VII (1997)

Yates, N., 'Bells and Smells: London, Brighton and South Coast Religion Reconsidered', *Southern History*, V (1983), pp.122-53

Yates, N., *The Oxford Movement and Anglican Ritualism*, London, 1983

Zell, M., 'Population and Family Structure in the Sixteenth-Century Weald', *Arch. Cant.*, C (1984), pp.231-57

(iii) Theses:

Acum, T.E.A., 'A Study of the Place-Names of the Pre-Conquest Kentish Charters', University of London M.A. Thesis, 1923

Baker, A.R.H., 'The Field Systems of Kent', University of London Ph.D. Thesis, 1963

Coleman, D.C., 'The Economy of Kent under the Later Stuarts', University of London Ph.D. Thesis, 1951

Dutt, M., 'The Agricultural Labourers' Revolt of 1830 in Kent, Surrey and Sussex', University of London Ph.D Thesis, 1967

Gulley, J.L.M., 'The Wealden Landscape in the early 17th Century and its Antecedents', University of London Ph.D. Thesis, 1960

Harvey, D.W., 'Aspects of Agricultural and Rural Change in Kent, 1800-1900', University of Cambridge Ph.D. Thesis, 1961

Kain, R.J.P., 'The Land of Kent in the Middle of the Nineteenth Century', University of London Ph.D. Thesis, 1973

Miller, J., 'The Priory at Lewisham', University of London Thesis for Diploma in Local History, 1986

Short, B.M., 'Agriculture in the High Weald of Kent and Sussex, 1850-1953', University of London Ph.D Thesis, 1973

Smith, W.H.C., 'Anglo-Portuguese Relations, 1851-61', University of London Ph.D. Thesis, 1965

Index

i) Persons

ii) Places, Institutions, Events